PETER
BROADBENT
A BIOGRAPHY

Before Theo Walcott, was a little-known seventeen-year-old ever transferred to one of England's top sides for a big fee? Did anyone ever pass the ball with the accuracy of David Beckham? Was there a player with the trickery of Joe Cole? Did any midfielder score as many goals as Frank Lampard?

If you are a Wolverhampton Wanderers fan of a certain vintage, your answer to each of those questions would be – yes, Peter Broadbent.

For those were the qualities which emerged as the unassuming youngster made the long journey from the Kent coalfields to the football hotbed that was the Black Country in the 1950s. There he went from being the young apprentice in the team who made Wolves champions of England for the first time to assuming the mantle of schemer in chief as Stan Cullis's side dominated domestic football.

Only Broadbent played in the four great floodlit friendlies which captured the nation's imagination, Spartak, Honved, Dynamo and Real Madrid, three championship-winning sides and the FA Cup-winning side of 1960.

He is still revered by older Wolves fans who remember his sublime football skills with great affection and their contribution to making his club the best in the land.

Sadly, Broadbent now has Alzheimer's and the joy and memories he gave to many are lost to him. Here, with the help of his wife Shirley, former teammates and fans, I'll attempt to tell the story of the man who will always be Peter the Great.

Steve Gordos was born in Bilston. He was the son of a Wolves fan and brought up as a Wolves fan, his first memory of watching the team being in 1954. Educated at Tettenhall College, he began his journalistic career with the *Wellington Journal* and *Shrewsbury News* but spent the rest of his working life with the *Express & Star*.

Having been lucky enough to be a regular at Molineux during Wolves' greatest era, the Fabulous Fifties, he has first-hand memories of the many great players who made Stan Cullis's team the greatest in the land.

During his many years on the sports desk of the *Express & Star*, the Black Country's evening newspaper, Steve acquired a deep knowledge of Wolves' history. Before he retired in 2003, he had been Sports Editor for eight years.

PETER
BROADBENT
A BIOGRAPHY

STEVE GORDOS

breedon **books**
PUBLISHING

First published in Great Britain in 2007 by
The Breedon Books Publishing Company Limited
Breedon House, 3 The Parker Centre, Derby, DE21 4SZ.

ISBN   978-1-85983-558-6

Printed and bound by MPG Books, Bodmin, Cornwall.

CONTENTS

For Peter and Shirley

Foreword

At the *Express & Star*, where I worked for 40 years, it was traditional to send off retiring members of staff with a framed spoof front page. This would be a chance to use a few embarrassing pictures and generally take the mickey out of the departing colleague. When I left the Wolverhampton paper in 2003 I duly got my front page and one of the items on it was 'Steve Gordos's All-time World XI'. It read 'Broadbent; Broadbent, Broadbent; Broadbent, Broadbent, Broadbent; Broadbent, Broadbent, Broadbent, Broadbent, Broadbent. Subs: Maradona, Di Stefano, Puskas, Pelé.'

From this you can deduce that once or twice – or maybe more often – I had occasion to mention that Peter Broadbent was, in my opinion, the greatest player ever to tread a football pitch. Obviously fellow workers on the *Express & Star* sports desk had got the message. Maybe I had exaggerated somewhat, but to those of us fortunate enough to have seen the Wolves man in his heyday, Broadbent was something special.

Wolverhampton Wanderers, for a few short years, were the most successful club in England and Broadbent was one of their brightest stars. By talking to others fortunate enough to have seen Broadbent in his prime, I realise distance has not lent enchantment to my memory. In my conversations with fans and fellow players, there were two recurring themes: firstly, that Broadbent was special; and secondly, he was a genuinely modest and likeable man.

I have tried to trace the path of a career which, after a few games for Dover, took Broadbent to Brentford and then to the mighty Wolves just a few months later. The rest, as they say, is history, as Broadbent carved his name into Molineux's hall of fame with sublime skills that ought to have brought him more than the seven caps he won for England.

In trying to document how Broadbent secured his unique place in the hearts of a generation of Wolves fans, I am most grateful for the help and encouragement of Peter's wife Shirley, brother Jack and families, Peter Creed, honorary secretary of the Wolves Former Players Association, John Hendley at Wolves, and many playing contemporaries of Broadbent.

I would have dearly loved for this to have been an autobiography, but Peter has Alzheimer's now. He is well looked after at a home near Wolverhampton but one doubts whether he has any recall of the football pleasure he gave to so many. Hopefully, these pages will revive treasured memories for his legion of admirers.

Dover and Out

Some people can tell you the first time they saw their favourite football team in action. I envy them, because I cannot remember the first time I saw Wolverhampton Wanderers. I was, some time early in the 1950s, taken by an enthusiastic Wolves-supporting father to watch his team, my dad no doubt hoping to start the process of passing on his enthusiasm to the next generation. Just as I now see kids of five or six taken to Molineux and watching everything except what is happening down on the pitch, I must likewise have lost interest a few minutes after kick-off and made my dad regret he had ever taken me as I repeatedly asked 'When are we going home?'

I know I went, but when that first reluctant visit to Molineux was I have no idea – although I do remember the first time I saw Peter Broadbent. Saturday 21 August 1954 was the date. My father had a couple of season tickets in the old Waterloo Road Stand but it was not he who took me back to Molineux that day. For once putting business before pleasure, Dad had decided he had to be on his stall at Wolverhampton Market and had lent the tickets to my uncle 'Brock' – his name was Albert Edward Brockhurst – with the downside for him being that he had to take me. By then I was nine and my father's Wolves fanaticism had rubbed off on me as week by week he told me of their successes and setbacks during the historic 1953–54 season, when they beat off the challenge of local rivals West Bromwich Albion to become champions of England for the first time.

It had been a long wait for fans like my dad. He could remember the FA Cup being paraded around Wolverhampton after Wolves' shock 3–1 win over hot favourites Newcastle in 1908. He had seen Wolves relegated to the Third Division, he had been on futile Cup Final trips in 1921 to Stamford Bridge and in 1939 to Wembley. He had seen Wolves win the Cup in 1949 and seen them go close to the First Division title four times either side of World War Two. Now, at last, they were officially the best team in the country, so Dad was a happy football fan and his enthusiasm persuaded me to give Molineux another try.

It was a happy nine-year-old who tagged along with his uncle to see Wolves open the new season. This was a special day for the club. As newly-crowned champions, they had decided to shake off their old image. Gone were the drab shirts of old gold and in their place new brighter ones. That was the day the official club colours became gold and black, though even now many ill-informed commentators often refer wrongly to the shirts as 'old gold'.

Sheffield Wednesday were the opposition and Wolves beat them 4–2. I have no precise memory of the goals. The one thing I do remember is seeing Peter Broadbent for the first time. He had a certain way of beating players, with almost a shrug of the shoulders and a way of passing the ball, caressing it almost. There was just something about him. He was the one who took my eye yet he was in a team of stars. Goalkeeper Bert Williams, left-half Billy Wright, wingers Johnny Hancocks and Jimmy Mullen, and inside-left Dennis Wilshaw had all played for England. Bill Slater would soon be able to claim that same distinction. Bill Shorthouse was an uncompromising centre-half who had been very close to winning a cap, Roy Swinbourne was a marauding yet stylish centre-forward. At full-back Eddie Stuart was tall and athletic, Roy Pritchard quick and neat. An array of talent, yet Broadbent was the one who stuck in my memory.

Had I got it wrong? To check I consulted the record books of former *Express & Star* sportswriter Phil Morgan. His pocket-size books provide a fascinating story of Wolves' glory days. His cuttings would be on the left-hand page while on the right he would list the teams, scorers, referee, attendance, which end Wolves defended in the first half and note any other events of significance, including the weather. The entry of 21 August 1954 includes the brief note 'Wolves wore new strip for first time.' He also reports that as well as the new brighter gold shirts there was a golden flag too, fluttering from a flagpole by the Molineux Street Stand. On it was 'WWFC – First Division champions 1953–4.'

There is only a brief mention of Broadbent. It reads 'Broadbent, without scoring, was as effective as any forward on the field.' That is good enough for me. My memory, though hazy, was not wide of the mark. Studying the teams I can see that Morgan's to-the-point summing-up of Broadbent is still quite a compliment. As well as Wolves' international trio of forwards, Wednesday could boast two England inside-forwards in Albert Quixall and Jackie Sewell. The latter was at the time a record buy, at £34,000. Quixall would set a new record at £45,000 when he joined Manchester United in 1958. So Broadbent was in top class company, yet he had been as effective as any forward. Phil Morgan said so.

Broadbent had been the one who had attracted my attention. I went home happy, hooked on football, hooked on Wolves, hooked on Broadbent. It is funny how a player can show a brief piece of skill and it sticks with you forever. So it was with Broadbent and that slick way he slid past his opponent.

Those of us who saw him reach his peak in the late 1950s treasure the memory. He was definitely a bit special, I knew that, but it is reassuring if other opinions reinforce your own. As opinions go they do not come much more valid than those of Sir Tom Finney and Sir Bobby Charlton, both contemporaries of Broadbent who respectively won 76 and 106 caps for England. 'He was the complete player,' Finney, the flying Preston winger, told me. 'He was quality,' endorsed World Cup winner Charlton, who added 'He had great ball control, could change direction and was a cute passer of the ball. He was recognised as one of the outstanding players of his day.' A final few words from Finney complete a top-notch evaluation of my hero, 'Peter was a good ball player, had great distribution and could score goals. He was playing in a very good side, of course, but he still stood out. A lot of rubbish is talked about today's players being quicker and such but if you are outstanding in your own era you'd be outstanding in any era. Peter, with his ability, would have adapted to today's game, I've no doubt of that.'

For a more local view let me turn to Peter Knowles, the gifted midfielder who decided he should leave football at the age of 24 after becoming a Jehovah's Witness. Knowles pinpointed a certain quality of Broadbent's that only a special few players possess – the ability to excite a crowd. Knowles says 'I will always remember the first game it happened. Peter got the ball for the first time and suddenly the crowd came alive. The only other time I've heard that special noise from a crowd was with George Best.' Knowles happily admits he modelled his style of play on Broadbent, adding 'His skill and talent were something I could only scratch the surface of.'

Stylish wing-half John Holsgrove, who gave Wolves sterling service in the late 1960s, was a fan of the club when he was a young lad in London, watching them whenever he could, and his views on Broadbent are similar to those of Knowles. Says Holsgrove, 'He was a lovely player and when he opened his body to do that body swerve... I had never seen anything like that. It was unique to Peter, like the Cruyff turn was to Cruyff, and something other players later tried to copy. When you do something which other players want to copy, then you know you're something special.'

Perhaps a voice from the terraces should also testify, early on in this story, to Broadbent's brilliance. Leon Hickman grew up as a Wolves fan before becoming one of the most respected sports journalists in the country during his years at the *Birmingham Evening Mail*. Says Hickman, 'At first he was quite frail and there was feeling that he was a home player only but, by golly, you suddenly began to see things. He was the first player I ever saw stick his foot about 4ft in the air and bring the ball down no matter how hard it was hit. Then there was that famous body swerve when he dipped his shoulder so low it nearly hit the ground. It was so exaggerated, so clever. It was unique. George Best had that same balance. I would have said of Broadbent that today he would be a £30million footballer.'

So there you have it – the unassuming man from the Kent village of Elvington is held in great esteem by the very best of those who played with him, against him and who watched him. There were many great players at Molineux to make Wolves the most feared team in the country during the 1950s, with only Matt Busby's Manchester United to rival them. Yet Broadbent retains a unique place in the affections of those who followed the Molineux side during the greatest period in their history. Driven by their demanding, almost fanatical, manager Stanley Cullis, Wolves relied on powerful half-backs and a simple direct football that made for fast action and lots of goalmouth incidents. If one man was allowed to deviate from the long-ball master plan it was

Broadbent. He was truly a player of all the talents, possessing silky skills and a way of beating an opponent with a mere turn of the shoulders or a swivel of the hips that remain his trademarks. From the junior apprentice in the team he would blossom into their orchestrator.

To trace the roots of Broadbent's genius we need to go back to Elvington, where Peter Frank Broadbent was born on 15 May 1933 at the family home in Adelaide Road, the second son of John and Elizabeth Broadbent – known to family and friends as 'Jack' and 'Lily'. Broadbent's older brother John, also known as 'Jack', confirmed that both boys loved their sport and were good at it. 'That's what you did as youngsters in those days – football in the winter and cricket in the summer. We'd use the dustbin as the wickets when we played cricket at home. Many years later when Peter came to see us with his wife Shirley we would jokingly get a bat and ball and go out to the bin for a game.

'We often wondered where Peter's talent came from because Dad was no good at sport, not at all. We've even checked on grandparents and there is no evidence of sporting talent there either. It was just one of those things. Peter was a natural at all sports. I was not bad but I could never beat him, whether it was tennis, table tennis or snooker.'

Probably the first to spot the younger Broadbent's football talent was another Elvington resident Bill Parfitt. He worked at the local Tilmanstone Colliery and took a big interest in football, particularly the village youth club who went three years undefeated with the Broadbent boys in the team. Jack Broadbent said the first attempt by Parfitt to give the younger Broadbent's football career a lift was quickly rebuffed. 'Bill introduced him to Folkestone Town manager Wilf Armoury but he said perhaps he should come back when he was a bit bigger. So he eventually joined Dover. A few years later I joined Folkestone and Wilf said something like "I'm not going to miss another Broadbent opportunity" when he signed me.'

It was not surprising that the younger Broadbent was on the frail side. He had been seriously ill when he was about 10 years old. 'He had double pneumonia,' said Jack, 'and it was touch and go if he'd recover. The doctor was very worried about him. He was ill for several weeks and at one stage was not expected to live. At the height of his illness the doctor said the next 24 hours would be crucial and when Peter came through that my father cried with relief. That's the only time I saw my dad cry.'

During his illness Peter was treated with the drug sulphonamides. 'They called them M and B tablets,' said Jack. 'He did not go into hospital, the doctor put him on these tablets and he pulled through.'

So Broadbent survived and as his strength built up he was able to renew his schooling first at the village school in Elvington and then Deal. There was no suggestion of evacuating the Broadbent lads when war broke out, even though Dover, as a port, was a prime German target. The boys probably did not worry about the dangers of bombing raids. Said Jack, 'We lads used to chase after crashed aircrafts and collect souvenirs, shrapnel and the like. We did not think about the dangers. There was no suggestion of evacuating us. Dad wanted the family to stay together.'

Broadbent played for his school team Deal County Modern, later with the Deal and Sandwich representative side and then on up the ladder to Kent Boys. Before the match between Kent and Essex at Northfleet, Broadbent, a mere slip of a lad at 14, was introduced to Tottenham and future England goalkeeper Ted Ditchburn. Just a few years later Broadbent would be playing against him in the First Division. A typical report of a Deal County Modern game, now just a faded cutting in one of the scrapbooks lovingly compiled by his father, says 'The mainspring of the Deal attack was Broadbent, who was to be found wherever the ball was.'

A report on a Deal Boys' win over Dover says 'Broadbent, playing at outside-right, time after time gave the inside-forwards opportunities which they failed to use.' Another cutting is equally complimentary, 'Broadbent, the Deal schoolboy forward, played a brilliant game for Kent, who drew 1–1 with Middlesex at Dover. Playing on the right-wing, Broadbent, the smallest of the Kent forwards, gave a dazzling display of speed and footwork.'

Broadbent played in an English Schools FA trial at Portsmouth in 1948. He was in the B team and one N.V. Deeley of South Staffs was in the A team. Many years later Broadbent and the same Norman Deeley would pair up to form one of the best wing partnerships in English football. Broadbent often recalled that trial match. His wife Shirley told me 'Peter always said Norman was brilliant that day. He could have played them on his own.' Not surprisingly, Deeley went on to win his England schoolboy cap that year, playing against Wales. Broadbent did not get the selectors' call, however.

After leaving school, Peter and Jack, 16 months his senior, worked at Tilmanstone Colliery. Peter was a haulage boy, below ground, responsible for looking after the tubs that carried coal to the surface. 'It was hard work and poorly paid,' confirmed Jack 'The haulage boys were responsible for the tubs getting through, putting the ropes or chains on them.'

Tilmanstone Colliery had been opened in 1913 and closed in 1986, the shafts being permanently sealed in 1987. Nothing remains of the pit – only some concrete slabs covering the shafts and a small monument. The area is now occupied by the Pike Road Industrial Estate.

For a young lad in Elvington the most likely future was a job in the coal industry but Broadbent junior was determined to be a footballer, though his cricket talent was also obvious. He once took 4–16 playing for Kent Boys against London at Walthamstow.

Jack Broadbent is the first to admit he did not have the same sporting talent as his brother, but he was still good enough a goalkeeper to have six seasons as a semi-professional with Dover and have trials at Wolves and Charlton. He later left the mines for a career in the police force.

Another part of Peter's football education when he was in his early teens was to take the occasional trip to London to watch top games. He did not attach himself to a particular club, preferring to watch wherever his favourite players were in action – men like Blackpool's 'wizard of the dribble' Stanley Matthews, Middlesbrough inside-forward Wilf Mannion or Preston's aforementioned Tom Finney.

After his rejection by Folkestone, Broadbent eventually signed for Dover and came under the influence of their player-manager George Poyser, who was destined to play a key role in his career. Poyser did not achieve great heights as a player. He was on Wolves' books as a full-back in the late 1920s and then moved to non-League Stourbridge, before giving useful service to Port Vale and Brentford. As a coach and manager he had far greater impact.

Poyser, as manager of the Kent League club, signed Broadbent as an amateur and the youngster began to blossom. His Dover displays earned him a game in Brentford's A team. He soon gained an outing in Brentford's reserve team and received a glowing report when he helped them beat Brighton in the Football Combination Cup. It said the crowd remained behind at the final whistle so they could give an ovation to the youngest player on the field. Tall, fair-haired and only 16 years of age, Peter Broadbent had played at inside-right, said the report, and was every bit as good as manager Jackie Gibbons promised that he would be in his programme notes.

Dover would soon lose the services of Poyser to the Griffin Park outfit – he was appointed coach – and a farewell 'gift' to the departing manager came in the shape of a 4–0 triumph over Kent League champions Ramsgate in the final of the Kent Senior Shield at Margate in front of a crowd of over 6,000. A match report said special mention had to be made of 'brilliant young Peter Broadbent, who mesmerised Ramsgate's left flank most of the time and paved the way for two of the goals.'

There was some concern among Dover followers that their club received nothing when Broadbent duly signed for Brentford. It was the subject of some correspondence in the *Dover Express*. The point was made that Broadbent had received valuable playing experience and coaching while at Dover. However, Broadbent was an amateur and, though some may have seen Poyser's influence at work, the player himself was adamant in rejecting Dover's overtures to turn professional with them. He wanted to start his pro career with a Football League club.

Poyser was moved to put the record straight in a letter to the *Dover Express*, saying that only when Broadbent made it clear he wanted to turn pro with a League club did he then alert Brentford. Poyser's letter added 'At this stage the directors of Dover were kept fully informed of the position, some of them even journeying to Brentford to see Peter play in Brentford's A team and Combination side.' It was left to Broadbent's father, Jack, to finish the matter when he, too, wrote to the local paper. 'I should like to substantiate all Mr Poyser most correctly reported,' he wrote. 'Peter took part in a number of matches playing for Dover as an amateur. He did not, however, agree to sign any professional forms for the club. Speaking on Peter's behalf, I would like to add that he appreciates the fact that while playing for Dover he had the opportunity to display his ability, which eventually led to him being taken up by a League club. This, I am sure, he will not forget.'

So impressed with Broadbent were Brentford that they were determined not to miss out on his signature when he reached 17 and was old enough to sign professional forms. The club ensured that on the eve of his birthday they had a car waiting to take him up to London. He and his father Jack were accommodated in a hotel so that young Broadbent could sign the forms on 15 May 1950.

When he first saw the young Broadbent in action, Poyser knew he was a bit special. He said 'I have never been more confident that any player will reach the top grade of soccer. He's the quickest thinking pupil I have ever trained.' Broadbent admitted some years later that he had turned to football to get away from the Kent coalfield where he had begun his working life as other members of his family had done before him. 'The others are still there,' he said, speaking in 1955, 'but they encouraged me when I wanted to get out. They seemed to sense what I already knew – that football had been in my blood since I was a youngster.'

Broadbent's stay at Brentford would be a brief one but he would find himself among some of the game's best brains, as the Bees included on their playing staff Ron Greenwood, destined to manage both West Ham and England, and Jimmy Hill, who would do so much to get the players' maximum wage abolished in 1961. It was Hill who later took Coventry into the top flight and showed clubs the way they could make best use of their commercial potential. So there would be no shortage of advice for young Broadbent as he took the big step from non-League football into the Football League Second Division.

Brentford were then, as they are now, one of London's least fashionable clubs, but they did have a much higher profile in those days. They had surprised a lot of people by gaining promotion to the First Division in 1935. They made a good fist of life in the higher grade too, finishing in the top six for three seasons before slipping to 18th in the final campaign before World War Two. When League football resumed in 1946–47 Brentford's flirtation with the high life came quickly to an end when they were relegated. The Bees soon assumed a mid-table role in the Second Division but still retained ambitions to return to the top flight under manager Jackie Gibbons. An amateur with Tottenham before the war, Albert Henry Gibbons, to give him his full name, had turned professional with Brentford after the war, proving a useful centre-forward. He had taken over the managerial reins at Griffin Park from long-serving Harry Curtis, the man who had steered the club from the Third Division South into the First Division. So it was Gibbons who Poyser briefed on the subject of this young lad he had found at Dover with star quality written all over him. When he moved up to London, Broadbent was a welcome lodger with Poyser and his family who lived at Ealing.

Broadbent made his Brentford debut against Manchester City on 14 October 1950 at Maine Road. Also making his bow for Brentford was another 17-year-old – left-half George Bristow, who would go on to make 244 League appearances for the Bees. It was an unhappy day for the newcomers as City won 4–0, two of the goals coming from one-time Wolves hero Dennis Westcott. Broadbent would make only 16 starts for Brentford and score just one goal – in a 7–2 defeat at Grimsby on 11 November 1950. Word about Broadbent and, indeed, Jimmy Hill – who was five years older – soon had other clubs showing interest. When Brentford beat Hull 2–1 in January 1951 scouts from 10 clubs were reported to have been at the game.

It was here that Broadbent's mentor George Poyser stepped in once more. By then he was a coach with Wolves and doubtless urged manager Stan Cullis to take a look at his former Dover protégée, who was making a big impression at Griffin Park. Broadbent would later say in an interview that Poyser was the foremost influence on his career, outside his family. 'He gave me my first chance and my second! For when I moved to Brentford, there, too, was George, as coach – as he was again by the time I had moved on to Wolves.' With the nagging of Poyser, Wolves must have been among those represented at the Hull game and quickly made their move to beat off the opposition for his signature.

Wolves did not make a habit of buying players during the early part of the Cullis era. Broadbent was one of the exceptions and a good-sized fee was paid for him, said at the time to be a record for a 17-year-old. Most sources have the transfer fee as £10,000, some list it as £7,000, while others put it as high as £13,000. Whatever the cost, the move paved the way for a career that carved out for Broadbent a special niche in Molineux history.

A fee of about £10,000 may seem like pocket money by 21st-century standards, but the British record was at the time only £29,500 – paid by Sunderland for Villa's Welsh centre-forward Trevor Ford in October 1950. Broadbent's departure from Brentford did not go down well with the Londoners' fans. They still nursed hopes of a return to the top flight and selling talented young players did not tie in with that ambition. Such was the criticism that manager Jackie Gibbons took up nearly a whole page in the club programme to defend the decision to sell Broadbent, listing one of the reasons as the player's proximity to doing two years' National Service, which was still the duty of all young men in those days. It was an excuse that did not hold much water. The fans realised Brentford's loss was Wolves' gain.

Another man who played for Brentford before becoming a true Wolves legend was Bill Slater. 'I was still an amateur in those days and playing when I could,' he told me. 'Brentford was a lovely club, very friendly. I joined them just after Peter had left and all the talk was of him. The fans were sad to see him go. Ron Greenwood and Jimmy Hill were still there when I played and I am sure they would have helped Peter in the same way they helped me.'

The Wolves side Broadbent joined were still trying to build on the success of winning a major trophy for the first time in 41 years – the FA Cup in 1949. That triumph went some way to atoning for a succession of near misses in the League, either side of World War Two. The last two seasons before the outbreak of hostilities had seen Wolves, under the managership of the legendary Major Frank Buckley, finish runners-up in the First Division on each occasion. In 1939 also, despite being hot favourites, they were beaten 4–1 by Portsmouth in the Cup Final at Wembley. Cullis's final playing season, 1946–47, would see Wolves needing only to win their final match, against Liverpool, to be, at last, crowned champions. They lost it 2–1 and eventually finished third behind winners Liverpool and Manchester United.

Cullis, in due course, ousted Ted Vizard as manager and, at 32, became the youngest ever boss of a Cup-winning side. Many fancied Wolves to build on that success by at last bringing the League Championship to Molineux and 1949–50 saw them get the closest yet, being beaten to the title by Portsmouth only on goal average. It was a memorable season in other ways for the Wolverhampton club as their home gates averaged over 45,000, a figure they have never bettered.

Optimism must have been high among Wolves fans for the start of the 1950–51 season but, while Broadbent was impressing a lot of people around Brentford way, Wolves were stumbling along in mid-table as the famous Tottenham side, featuring the likes of Ramsey, Nicholson, Burgess and Baily, took the First Division by storm. Compensation for Molineux regulars came in the shape of another FA Cup run and so the arrival of young Broadbent could have been overshadowed when he signed for Wolves on Thursday 22 February 1951, two days before the sixth-round Cup trip to Sunderland. Nevertheless, his picture was on the back page of the final edition of the *Express & Star* with a prominent headline proclaiming 'Brentford inside-forward signs for Molineux'. This is how the back page report read:

'In Brentford's Second Division side although not yet 18, Peter Broadbent was today transferred to Wolves at a substantial four-figure fee. He will play in Wolves' Central League side against Stoke City on Saturday.

'Broadbent, who stands 5ft 9in and weighs about 11st, is a native of Dover where he began his football career with his school team. He played for Dover boys and Kent boys, and was selected for the south international trial at Fratton Park, Portsmouth.

'Although playing at inside-left for his school team he was invariably chosen for the right-wing for representative matches.

'Leaving school he went to play for Dover in the Kent League and there, playing either at inside-right or on the right-wing, attracted the attention of George Poyser (once on Wolves' books) who began to take his coaching in hand.

'At the beginning of this season he moved to Brentford and, after playing in the Football Combination team, was chosen for the first XI. Apart from occasional absence through injury he has played in the first team at inside-forward ever since. He did not play for Brentford in the Cup.

'Wolves began to take an interest in him some time ago. Mr Stanley Cullis regards the investment on the youngster as a long-term one and is convinced he will develop into a first-class player.

'Negotiations between the clubs completed, it remained only for Broadbent to make up his mind whether to leave Griffin Park. After he had been to see his family in Dover he decided on the move.

'Soon after his arrival in Wolverhampton today he signed the necessary forms and was in time to join the players at their lunch in one of the local restaurants. This afternoon he began his training as a Wolves player.

'Broadbent, who has yet to carry out his National Service, is shortly going into the RAF.

'Mr A.H. Gibbons, Brentford manager, said tonight, "We were reluctant to part with Broadbent but we did not want to stand in his way".'

These paragraphs, few though they are, still tell us what a big step it must have been for Broadbent in an age when 17 still seemed very young to become a professional player. To check with mum and dad first, before deciding to travel even further away from his home town and then signing in time to have lunch with the many famous names then at Molineux. It must have been a whirlwind sequence of events.

Having chatted often with the players of that era, I know they had a special camaraderie then and it is evident still in their get-togethers 50 years later. So I can well imagine how welcome they would have made young Broadbent. There may have been a bit of good-natured ribbing, but I suspect there would have been no shortage of new teammates ready to make the youngster feel at home. Over lunch the players may well have discussed the fact that Fred Davis was 37–23 up in the World Snooker Final against Walter Donaldson in Blackpool. They played 97 frames in the Final in those days. Or they could have noted that all-rounder Trevor Bailey was fit after injury to face the Australians in the fifth and final Test in Melbourne. England were already 4–0 down by then.

It's also interesting to note that there was no allowing Broadbent time to get his bearings. After lunch, probably at Reynolds Restaurant, or Lyons, in the centre of Wolverhampton, it was straight down to Molineux for training.

Jimmy Dunn, that splendid inside-forward who had played a big part in Wolves' 1949 FA Cup triumph, confirmed that young Broadbent would have been made to feel at home. 'They were a good crowd. The team spirit was tremendous. There would be plenty of banter but anybody coming in was made welcome.'

Dunn added that for a player to be fully accepted by his teammates and manager Stan Cullis, he would have to show he conformed to the Molineux ethos – hard work. 'That was Stan's motto. If you'd given all you could then you could not do any more, but he expected that from everyone all the time. I respected Stan for that. I had a lot of time for him. Apart from Stan, there was the good example set by Billy Wright. He did not drink, did not smoke and loved training.'

Broadbent would probably never before have encountered a man quite like Cullis, almost fanatical in his devotion to his club and to football, a man whose word was law. Dunn, always quick-witted, recalled that Cullis once told a gathering of the old players he had had a pacemaker fitted to his heart and Dunn quipped 'I never knew you had a heart.' Dunn recalls 'We all laughed but looking back I wish I'd never said it, even though he took it in good part, because I did respect him. I got on well with him.'

There was no doubt that Cullis would not tolerate any easing up, as evidenced by a Dunn anecdote from Wolves' Ireland tour after their successful 1949 Cup run. 'We thought it was a holiday and we were there to enjoy ourselves,' Dunn remembers, 'but Stan wanted to win every match. In one, we were 2–1 down at half-time and when we went into the dressing room Stan made straight for me. If he did that you knew you were in trouble. He said "You're letting that wing-half walk all over you. If you don't get your finger out you'll be on the next boat home." So I really got wound up and the first time in the second half I challenged this wing-half, a big fella, we went up for a header and I went in so hard I cut his eye open. We were in Cork and they gave us a banquet afterwards at the town hall and you might know I'd be sitting next to this fella with a great bandage on his eye. He was all right about it – but we'd won the game 3–2 and I didn't have to go home. That was the effect Stan had on you.'

Another of the inside-forwards on Wolves' books at the time was Scotsman Johnny Walker. He was enjoying the best time of his Molineux career. Walker recalled 'I'd joined Wolves after completing National Service in 1947. I had been in the Royal Army Service Corps where Jimmy Hill, who was an amateur with Reading at the time, was one of my instructors. It took me a couple of years to get into the Wolves team but I was so proud to have played for them. There were so many good inside-forwards there then and you could see Peter would be yet another. I remember him arriving. He was a very quiet lad, not at all big-headed and he was willing to listen. He came on really well and really quickly.'

One long-time Wolves fan who remembered the signing was Peter Wollam from Darlaston. He told me 'I'd bought an early edition of the paper and remember seeing something in the Stop Press – they still had a Stop Press in newspapers in those days – and it said Wolves had signed Peter Broadbent. I thought I'd take a look at this fella and went to watch him play in the reserves against Stoke reserves on the Saturday. I'll never forget one little incident. He got the ball almost on his own goalline and he went on a run beating player after player, almost the full length of the field. I thought "We've signed someone a bit special here."'

Many years later Broadbent would recall that he jumped at the chance to join Wolves, 'I wanted to better myself in the game, and I knew the competition of trying to get into the first team when there were players like Jesse Pye, Jimmy Dunn and Sammy Smyth was sure to be good for me. I aimed high to get high.'

When he first joined Wolves, Broadbent lodged temporarily with George Poyser and his family. They had a house in Waterloo Road near to Molineux. Like so many Wolves players, Broadbent was eventually found digs of his own in a reputable home. In his case it was with Mrs Long in Chester Street in the Whitmore Reans area of Wolverhampton. It was literally a five-minute walk from Molineux. That was a good job, as 17-year-old footballers did not usually have cars in those days. Even the great Billy Wright would still be living at the home of his landlady, Mrs Colley, when he was captain of England and famous the world over.

In August 1951 another teenager was billeted with Mrs Long – Ron Flowers. He had been sent down from Wolves' Wath Wanderers nursery club in Yorkshire, run by former player Mark Crook. Flowers recalls Broadbent's reassuring words about Mrs Long, 'She'll look after you like a mother.' Flowers also came to appreciate the value of George Poyser, the man who had shaped Broadbent's early football years. Poyser, as he had done with Broadbent, took Flowers under his wing. Says Flowers, 'He treated me as if I were his son, gave me the full value of his own great experience and made me understand that you have to be prepared to put a great deal into football before you can expect to take anything out of it.'

What was he like, this man Poyser who played such a big part in Broadbent's development and that of Flowers and others? 'He was a very laid-back fella,' said Flowers. 'Joe Gardiner, the trainer, was much the same. They were quiet men, in contrast to Stan Cullis, and they would always offer you advice and in practice games would encourage you quietly and tell us things we needed to look at in our game. They were both very good.'

Broadbent's wife Shirley said that Peter and Ron Flowers had to share a bed at Mrs Long's – 'Ron still jokes about it today. He always says he slept with Peter before I did.'

Flowers confirmed 'There were only two bedrooms at the Longs' and Peter and I shared this big double bed. Two 17-year-old kids sharing a bed was nothing unusual in those days. We stayed at Chester Street until we both joined the RAF. She was very strict, Fanny Long. She had a husband Bert who worked at Courtaulds factory just down the road, but she ruled the roost. She was a Mrs Mopp type and she was very strict. There was a pal of mine Roy Mason – he was at Lester's, the men's outfitters in Market Street, for many years – and he started to give me driving lessons. Afterwards we'd go back to his house and have a cup of tea and a chat. Once I did not get back until after 10 o'clock and Mrs Long gave me a real ticking-off. It was a case of "What would Mr Cullis say?" She was a stickler.'

Not that there was much night life to distract two young men in Wolverhampton in the early 1950s. 'We were too young to go to pubs,' said

Flowers 'but if we had been old enough Stan Cullis would not have liked us to do that anyway. We'd go to the pictures two or three times a week. I don't know if Wolves gave the cinemas tickets for Molineux but the cashiers always let us in. So when I started courting it was very welcome, being able to get in the pictures for nothing.'

Centre-forward Roy Swinbourne was also in digs in Whitmore Reans. 'I lived in Evans Street. I think most of us were in digs in those days and we'd walk up to the ground among the fans. We used to use a passageway past the old British Restaurant. That's the way it was. I think Billy Wright was first to have car, one of the old Ford Prefects with the flying duck on the bonnet. I remember Peter signing, it was big news, a 17-year-old and for a big fee. He fitted in well. He had a nice sense of humour, too. Put it this way, he sometimes said things which he did not think were funny – but we did. He was a very nice lad.'

Flowers and Broadbent would be lucky to have around them men like Wright, Bert Williams and Jimmy Mullen. All three had started their careers before the war and despite their fame had kept their feet on the ground, still relishing training as much as playing. Flowers says Wright was always full of enthusiasm and it made the youngsters so much more eager to train and practise. If it was good enough for the captain of England, it was good enough for them.

General opinion was that Cullis saw Broadbent as one for the future, as Molineux already had its fair share of inside-forwards in Cup Final heroes Dunn, Jesse Pye and Sammy Smyth, Johnny Walker and the gifted Dennis Wilshaw, who could also play centre-forward or left-wing. However, a series of injuries to those established forwards, plus the team's poor League form, meant the youngster would soon be given his chance.

Wolves were struggling in the League. In the FA Cup it was a different story as they fought their way past Plymouth, Villa and Huddersfield. So, while Broadbent, just a few days after signing, was playing for the reserves against Stoke reserves on Saturday 24 February 1951 and impressing a few thousand people at Molineux, Wolves' senior side were performing in front of more than 60,000 at Roker Park and battling to earn a 1–1 draw in the sixth round of the Cup. Wolves reserves had a four-point lead at the top of the Central League and

Broadbent helped them maintain their position with a 6–1 win, despite going a goal down on 15 minutes. Ken Whitfield (3), Leslie Smith (2) and Sammy Smyth got the goals. Broadbent made several sparkling runs and nearly made it a scoring debut but his header to Dennis Wilshaw's left-wing corner hit the angle of upright and bar.

Broadbent was able to watch his new club win the replay with Sunderland 3–1 four days later. The semi-final draw saw Wolves pitted against Newcastle United, who were about to make themselves kings of FA Cup football in the early 1950s. Wolves and the Geordies fought out a 0–0 draw at Hillsborough, Sheffield, but the replay at Leeds Road, Huddersfield, four days later saw Newcastle triumph 2–1, scoring two goals in the space of a minute after Walker had given Wolves an early lead. Manager Cullis would probably have given the beaten side a vote of confidence by naming them to meet Portsmouth in the First Division three days after the replay. An injury to Jimmy Dunn prevented Cullis from doing so – cue young Broadbent.

On Saturday 17 March 1951 Broadbent was handed his First Division debut for the visit to Molineux of champions Portsmouth.

Broadbent was named at inside-right, Walker switching to the left, and the lad could hardly have picked a worse day to make his bow. The match was played in a constant drizzle with the Bushbury end of the ground a sea of mud. Broadbent found the going heavy, according to Phil Morgan in the *Express & Star*, but did enough to impress the watching 32,142. He faced a tough opponent for his debut – England half-back Jimmy Dickinson. Wolves lost the game 3–2, the limelight being stolen by Albert Mundy, playing only his second game for Pompey. He hit the winner three minutes from time, his second goal of a game that had begun with a second-minute goal from Walker for Wolves. The *Express & Star* verdict was still encouraging for Broadbent 'He could not have chosen an unhappier day for a first appearance. The heavy ground was all against him but there was sufficient in what he was able to do to show promise of better things in more amenable conditions.'

Many years later Broadbent would recall his debut, 'It was on a day when the mud came over your boot tops. But I'm not likely to forget it for another reason. I had to face one of England's key men at the time, Jimmy Dickinson, and he wasn't having a young stripling taking his reputation to town.' The teams that day were:

Wolves: Williams; Short, Pritchard; Wright, Shorthouse, Russell; Hancocks, Broadbent, Swinbourne, Walker, Mullen. Goals: Walker (2), Swinbourne (29).

Portsmouth: Butler; Stephen, Ferrier; Scoular, Froggatt, Dickinson; Harris, Reid, Mundy, Phillips, Gaillard. Goals: Reid (16), Mundy (36, 87).

Still only 17 years old, Broadbent had not filled out and if he thought he might have it easier when he quickly got another first-team chance, he was wrong. A week after the Portsmouth game Wolves visited Arsenal and Broadbent, instead of making a swift return to reserve team football, was called on to deputise for Johnny Hancocks, who had a throat infection. This meant a game on the right-wing against lanky Gunners full-back Lionel Smith, capped by England for the first time earlier in the season. The return to London saw Broadbent play before his biggest audience yet – 54,213. Arsenal, who were giving a debut to future Welsh skipper Dave Bowen at left-half, won the game 2–1, their goals coming from bustling centre-forward Cliff Holton – the first a penalty. The pitch was again heavy but Broadbent did not let the conditions get the better of him and seems to have impressed Maurice Smith, leading sportswriter at the time with *The People* newspaper.

In the paper's *Soccer Parade* annual for 1951–52, Smith has a section called 'Golden Boys of Tomorrow' and Broadbent was one of those featured. Smith wrote of Broadbent, 'In one of his earliest matches in the old gold and black I saw him lead Arsenal's defenders a fox-trot – which is no way for a wolf cub to treat the masters. At Highbury, too! Young Broadbent already has the coolness that usually only experience can bring and the touch of artistry guaranteed to put noughts into any man's transfer cheque.' Brentford boss Jackie Gibbons had asked Smith early in the 1950–51 season what he thought of young Broadbent and so had that doyen among football writers Charles Buchan, the former Arsenal and England forward. Wrote Smith, 'I told them both that in my view young Broadbent would one day be a great player – a natural. Ability was written all over him.'

Smith noted that Buchan rated him the best young player he had seen since Cliff Bastin, the Arsenal legend, who won Championship and Cup medals and an England cap while still in his teens.

If Broadbent did not sink without trace in London, the same could not be said of the Oxford University rowing eight. In the annual Varsity boat race the same day, the choppy Thames water proved too much and their boat sank. Cambridge won the re-run a couple of days later.

After his outing at Highbury, Broadbent was left out for the 3–2 home defeat by Aston Villa two days later, Easter Monday, but was given a quick recall for the return fixture at Villa Park the following day. He was named in his third different position in three games, inside-left, and, as in the previous two, he was up against an international player – Northern Ireland's Danny Blanchflower, who a decade later would skipper Tottenham to the first League and Cup double of the 20th century. An even bigger crowd than the Arsenal game, 60,000, saw Wolves beaten 1–0. Again Broadbent had to perform on a heavy pitch but received some credit in the report of the match. Wrote Phil Morgan, 'Broadbent was the one inside-forward who tried to take the ball to the slightly drier ground in order to use it.'

Broadbent kept his place for the visit of Burnley when Wolves were beaten 1–0 again. It was back to the reserves after that, as Wolves reverted to experienced Jesse Pye and Jimmy Dunn as the inside men alongside Roy Swinbourne.

Wolves' fortunes improved only slightly and a 3–2 home defeat by Stoke saw both inside-forwards dropped and Broadbent and Johnny Walker recalled to first-team action for the visit to old rivals West Bromwich Albion, on Saturday 21 April 1951. That proved another landmark date for Broadbent as he registered his first Wolves goal at first-team level. Dennis Wilshaw, playing on the left-wing, made it for him. He beat Albion's Irish international centre-half Jack Vernon on the left and centred behind the backs so that Broadbent could run in and drive the ball home. It was not a happy ending, as Albion surged into a 3–1 lead, two goals coming from their versatile half-back Ray Barlow, playing at centre-forward. Wolves managed only one in reply, though it, too, was historic. Johnny Hancocks fired home a 78th-minute penalty for his 19th League goal of the season. That bettered the record for a Wolves winger set by Sammy Brooks just before World War One. Phil Morgan noted in the *Express & Star* that Broadbent looked much happier on a drier ground and was one of few successes in the visitors' attack, always trying hard to prompt the others.

Broadbent kept his place in the midweek game that followed against Chelsea at Stamford Bridge, but despite an improved display Wolves were beaten 2–1. Broadbent was clearly beginning to feel his feet and was described as 'the worker of the line'. After that, outings at outside-right at Bolton and inside-right at home to Newcastle saw Broadbent on the losing side each time.

However, the match against Newcastle on Wednesday 2 May 1951, four days after the Geordies had beaten Blackpool at Wembley to win the FA Cup, really saw Broadbent's potential revealed. Regular *Express & Star* Wolves man Phil Morgan had a touch of lumbago – yes, it is recorded in Phil's cuttings book – so the match was covered by the sports editor George Gillott. Usually a desk-bound journalist who therefore got little chance to see the area's various teams in action, Gillott was mightily impressed by the teenage Wanderer, even though Wolves were beaten 1–0. Indeed, the headline on his match report proclaimed 'Boy Broadbent starred in a Wolves defeat'.

Gillott said the home fans, who had watched the Cup paraded around the pitch at half-time, did not take defeat too hard. Gillott wrote 'For one thing, they had seen a rousing match with Wolves forcing practically all the play in the second half and Newcastle defending grimly. For another, they saw the splendid promise of 17-year-old Broadbent, the Wolves inside-right.' He continued 'How the boy worked! One of the best things of the match was when in the second half, after he had shot just outside, following a grand dribble, Cowell, Newcastle's right-back, gave him a pat on the back, expressing both hard luck on this particular occasion and congratulations on his untiring efforts in general.

'Broadbent's display was by no means faultless, but the times when he tied up two, three and even four opponents by body swerve and intricate footwork stamped him as a fine player in the making. No greater compliment can be paid than to say he compared favourably with the Newcastle inside-right, wee Taylor. Here is a player who has fulfilled every promise. He, too, has body swerve, ball control and a quick-thinking brain.' The sports editor said it was when Broadbent started laying on passes to Hancocks in the second half that Wolves really asserted themselves. Newcastle, who were without their two-goal Wembley hero Jackie Milburn, scored the only goal of the game against the run of play through George Robledo 19 minutes from time.

George Gillott's look at Broadbent was probably his first and, like me a few years later, he had been taken by his style and the way he did things. Even at an early age, Broadbent had the various attributes that add up to one thing – class.

Broadbent could bask in his individual glory but he had not helped Wolves out of their dismal run of form. He had played eight first-team games and had tasted defeat each time. He got rid of that taste in the final match of the season, a trip to Sunderland, which brought a goalless draw. He also took up where he had left off in the game against Newcastle, the match report declaring 'Broadbent was again the best forward.'

So Broadbent's entry into the top flight of English football was complete. His new team had not exactly set the League season alight but he had done enough to attract attention and to suggest that here was a decent player in the making. His move from Brentford to high profile Wolves had been quite an adventure, but an even bigger adventure was about to start. Wolves were off on a close season tour of South Africa.

Out of Africa

The trip to South Africa was a rare experience, even for players like Billy Wright and Jimmy Mullen who had been on overseas jaunts with England teams – including the 1950 World Cup Finals in Brazil – but for young Broadbent it meant foreign travel for the first time in his life. Leaving Dover for London had been a big step, now he was off on a journey to a place he had only read about.

That Billy Wright would be going was an unexpected bonus to the Wolves party. For the only time in his career the England captain was out of the international side – first through injury and then because he had lost form. He would miss three internationals, the only England games in which he did not take part in 13 consecutive seasons after World War Two. However, England's loss was the gain of Wolves in general and Broadbent in particular. Wright had a great ability to look after young players and nurse them along on the field of play. He would always retain that common touch in later life, which is why he was so respected by fellow pros and fans alike. Both he and Broadbent had points to prove on that tour. Wright needed to recapture his form away from the glare of publicity that inevitably followed England matches, while Broadbent aimed to build on his unexpectedly early introduction into the Wolves first team. Both would be successful on a trip that saw Wolves sweep all before them.

Getting to South Africa was a long trek in those days – over 30 hours of flying. Wolves made the trip in two parties, Broadbent being in the first group who flew out via Tripoli, Kano and Brazzeville, taking the western route to Johannesburg. The other party went via Rome and Lydda and the eastern route to the city. Broadbent did not play in the opening game, a 4–1 win over Southern Transvaal, but was among those on the touchline watching remarkable scenes before the match in Johannesburg. Segregation still applied at sporting events there in those days and about 600 'non-Europeans' broke down one of the gates and poured into the ground when they found there was not enough room in their section of the stadium. Others gained entry by cutting a wire fence, so the official attendance of 35,000 may well have been some way below the true figure. Broadbent would recall that, significantly, virtually all the non-white fans were cheering on Wolves at every match.

There would soon be a chance for Broadbent to play in the outside-right position as he had done against Arsenal, for Johnny Hancocks, the little man who had made the number-seven shirt his own at Molineux, did not make the trip. He, like Arsenal's Dennis Bergkamp many years later, had a hatred of flying. He did go on an FA tour to Canada a year earlier but that party had travelled by boat. So the way was open for Broadbent to show his paces as a winger. Before he could think about that, Broadbent had another big event to get through – his 18th birthday, which was then not the landmark that it is now but still a significant date as it meant eligibility for National Service.

The birthday, 15 May 1951, happily coincided with a banquet in Wolves' honour in Johannesburg. Broadbent recalled in an article in *Football Monthly* that 'it became an occasion to remember'. He added 'There was a gift from the South African FA and somebody had the happy idea of having a cake specially made and decorated for the occasion. I was still boy enough to think that was something pretty good.'

Broadbent played in the next two games, the first a 4–0 win over Orange Free State in Bloemfontein. He was not mentioned in dispatches but must have done well, as a report of the game said all Wolves' forwards impressed. Broadbent was again on the right-wing when a Roy Swinbourne hat-trick saw Wolves beat Natal 3–1 in Durban. The home defence was given a gruelling time, particularly in the second half, and special mention was made of 'the speed and thrust of right-winger Broadbent'. Les Smith was given a game on the right-wing when Wolves met Transvaal at the end of May, with Broadbent his partner at inside-right. Wolves hit seven goals without reply, three of them to Jesse Pye. Broadbent scored the final one with a header 11 minutes from the end. He and the other forwards relished the new lightweight boots the team were trying out during their time in the Union. General verdict was that they were a must back home in good conditions, though no substitute for the traditional ones on heavy pitches.

Broadbent was rested for the 4–0 defeat of Western Province in Cape Town but came back to join in a goal spree at Mossel Bay when South West Districts were beaten 11–0. He hit three goals, as all the tourists' forwards found the net, but one name on the scoresheet would have raised a few eyebrows back home – Stanley Cullis. The Wolves boss decided to come out of retirement after four years and joined the goal rush with a long-range shot. It was the only goal he ever scored for the club. The boss was obviously pleased with himself and after Eastern Province had been beaten 5–1 at Port Elizabeth he decided he would play again, this time against Border at East London. Border, however, were one of the best teams in South Africa. Broadbent was on the right-wing again and though Wolves won 2–0 to chalk up their eighth victory in eight games, it was clear Cullis, playing at right-half, was struggling. Broadbent was one of those who had to work extra hard to cover for Cullis as the pace of the game began to tell on the boss. Cullis, being Cullis, would not come off and carried on until the final whistle, though clearly in difficulty. He never played again.

The final four matches brought four more wins – over Eastern Transvaal (13–0), Natal (2–1), South Africa in Durban (4–1) and South Africa again (1–0) in Johannesburg. Broadbent played in the Natal match at inside-right and on the left-wing in the two against South Africa. The chance to play in the number-11 shirt came because England winger Jimmy Mullen was allowed to return home early because of his wife's pregnancy. So Broadbent in his short time with Wolves had played in four of the five forward positions, which were then still the norm among English clubs. A few years later he would complete the feat of playing in every forward spot when he was given several games at centre-forward in the 1958–59 season.

One of the visits the Wolves party undertook in South Africa was to State Express, the cigarette manufacturers, where each player was presented with a pack of 500. Today, smoking is rightly frowned upon but in 1951 nothing wrong was seen in sportsmen taking a 'drag' on a regular basis. The Broadbent scrapbooks also contain an advert showing him, Johnny Walker, Jimmy Dunn and Norman Deeley holding cigarette lighters. The advert proclaims 'By any Test, say the Wolves, Ronson means World's Greatest Lighter!'

Peter was not the only Broadbent in Africa, as his wife Shirley explained to me. 'Nan Broadbent, Peter's paternal grandmother, had a son who lived in Southern Rhodesia, as it was then called. I don't think she'd ever been abroad but she decided to visit him, even though she was 80. The trip coincided with Wolves' tour, so they threw a party for her and Peter took Billy Wright along. She was so proud to have the captain of England there.'

Wolves had made a big impression in South Africa, winning all 12 matches with a goal tally of 60 against only five. Broadbent, with four goals in his eight games, had done his prospects no harm at all. It is difficult to understand some 50 years later the impact of Wolves' visit. They were the first Football League side to tour South Africa and when the first group of players made the long flight home, Broadbent told the waiting *Express & Star* reporter he was thrilled with the trip. The paper's headline echoed the view 'Wolves home again after a wonderful time'. He emphasised how much support the team had received from the non-European section of the crowds. The team had also got some unexpected support for the match against South Africa in Durban. Sailors from a British warship had marched on to the pitch before kick-off carrying a pro-Wolves banner.

So why did Wolves fly to South Africa in two parties? Johnny Walker explained that in May 1949 the plane carrying Italian club Torino back from a game against Benfica had crashed at Superga, killing the entire team, and it was felt unwise for a few years after that for an entire team to travel together. The decision provided Walker and a few others, who were in the second group, with an unexpected bonus. 'There was a problem with our plane and it wasn't like today where you'd quickly get another,' Walker recalled. 'We had to wait a few days while they found another plane. So, we'd played all our matches, the main party had gone home and we could just enjoy ourselves. I'll always remember that.' However, there was no bonus stay for Broadbent; he was in the first party who left for home on schedule.

Broadbent, in a short time, had tasted life in the mining industry and in the more glamorous world of football. Now he would have to do what all young men were required to do in those days – serve King and country for a couple of years. National Service loomed and a stint with the RAF. At least Broadbent would spend much of his time close to his footballing employers stationed at Bridgnorth, just 14 miles down the road from Wolverhampton. The old base at Stanmore on the edge of the Shropshire town closed down in 1962 but in 1951 it was still buzzing. It was, like all bases in the Armed Forces, a place where discipline was paramount. It was the sort of regime that would prepare Broadbent for life at Molineux under the strict rule of Stan Cullis. The RAF also offered a youngster with sporting ability plenty of chance to fulfil his potential and hone his skills. Broadbent, a natural sportsmen, would be of use all year round, as he was a fine cricketer as well as a talented footballer. He also served at RAF Padgate, near Warrington.

Early displays for his battalion saw Broadbent win selection for the RAF representative side and one of his first games was against an FA XI at Stamford Bridge in October 1951. That RAF team also included future Wolves goalkeeper Malcolm Finlayson and Charlton's Ted Croker, later to be secretary of the FA.

Service commitments, plus the fact that Jimmy Dunn and Jesse Pye were back to fitness and able to occupy the inside-forward positions, meant Broadbent had several reserve team outings but made no further first-team appearance until the very last game of 1951. After a promising start to the season Wolves had struggled, their form reaching rock bottom on Boxing Day when they lost at home to Aston Villa. It was time for changes and manager Cullis made no fewer than six for the game with Blackpool on a muddy Molineux pitch three days later. Broadbent was given his chance in the forward line alongside another youngster, Ken Whitfield. Making his home debut, Whitfield collected a hat-trick in a 3–1 win while Broadbent was said by Phil Morgan in his *Express & Star* report to have come through with flying colours – an apt verdict on an RAF lad.

Broadbent had done well enough to earn an extended run in the side and his first FA Cup tie for the club also brought his first goal in the competition, when they held Manchester City 2–2 at Maine Road. Broadbent struck after nine minutes and Whitfield made it 2–0 on 28, only for a second-half revival to force a replay. Broadbent would score many more goals for Wolves, but Whitfield's would prove to be his last. His early promise was never fulfilled, though he later switched to wing-half and made 175 League appearances for Brighton. Whitfield was unfortunate enough to miss the replay and, as Wolves had a long list of casualties, full-back Jack Short was the shock choice at centre-forward. He made the most of it as he scored two late goals in Wolves' 4–1 win.

Three days later Broadbent was on target in the First Division when Wolves were held 1–1 at home by Portsmouth. He scored when he finished off a bout of crisp passing with what Phil Morgan described as a 'first-rate left-foot drive'. There was no extended Cup run for Broadbent and Co. They went out 2–1 to Liverpool in the next round before a crowd of 61,905, which remains the record attendance for Anfield. Bob Paisley, then the team's left-half and later their most successful manager, gave Liverpool the lead after only five minutes and centre-forward Cyril Done made it two four minutes later. Wolves never recovered.

There was an extensive run in the League, however, for young Broadbent. Cullis had faith in him, and, though his form sometimes dipped, he kept his place in a stuttering Wolves team. Broadbent made 16 League appearances in the 1951–52 season and 16 was also the team's placing in the First Division. They lost seven and drew two of their final nine League games, including defeats at the hands of local rivals Albion on Easter Monday and Tuesday. The Molineux match with the Baggies, lost 4–1, saw another defender tried at centre-forward – and South African Eddie Stuart marked the occasion by scoring what proved to be the only goal in a distinguished 10-year Molineux career. Broadbent's form may have been variable but skipper Billy Wright had played well enough for club and country to be named Footballer of the Year.

Four times Wolves had got close to becoming champions of England, which is what winning the First Division of the Football League meant in those days. For a time in 1952–53 Wolves looked as though they might at last win that elusive title, but a mid-season wobble proved costly and they eventually finished third behind Arsenal, the winners, and Preston.

That season had signalled the start of changes at Molineux. Of the stalwart inside-forwards, 1949 Cup-Final heroes Jesse Pye and Sammy Smyth had moved on, respectively, to Luton in July 1952 and Stoke in September 1951, but Dennis Wilshaw, Johnny Walker and another 1949 Wembley man Jimmy Dunn were still on the books. Broadbent had other rivals for the inside berths and, contrary to the myth that surrounds Wolves in the 1950s, not all were home-grown. Manager Cullis had signed Birmingham-born Ron Stockin from nearby Walsall and John Taylor from Luton.

On the opening day of the 1952–53 season Taylor and Dunn were named against newly-promoted Cardiff, and even though Wolves won 1–0 Broadbent took over from Dunn in the next match against Bolton, two days later, and received a rave notice from Phil Morgan in the *Express & Star* after a 3–1 win. Broadbent, who was still doing his National Service, had received a bit of criticism from Morgan the previous season. But now Morgan wrote, 'Peter Broadbent, young RAF player, with a newly-developed technique crowned by a rousing goal, threw back into my remaining teeth much of the criticism I levelled at him last season. My complaint used to be that he tended to hold up the attack. What a difference last night, with Broadbent thrusting towards the Bolton goal and doing so with a touch of dash which used to be so foreign to him. In the first couple of minutes he had figured in three such bursts but he capped everything when he took that side flick from Swinbourne eight minutes after the interval and went through the middle to beat Hanson all ends up with a scorching shot and score his first goal since last January.'

That display earned Broadbent an extended run in the first team and made Cullis realise he was the future. Dunn never regained his place and was transferred to Derby County in November 1952. He was just 29 and went on to make 57 League appearances for the Rams.

For eight games early in 1952–53 it would be Taylor and Broadbent at inside-forward alongside Roy Swinbourne. Taylor, however, did not make the most of his opportunity and was dropped. Broadbent was switched from inside-left to inside-right and in came Dennis Wilshaw to make the number-10 shirt his own.

Broadbent continued to weigh in with a goal or two, including one when Wolves sent a side to Rotterdam to play an unofficial Dutch XI, the game ending 2–2.

It all seemed to be going well for Broadbent until just after Christmas. Then, Wolves lost four successive games, three of them in the League including, vitally, a 5–3 reverse to title rivals Arsenal at Highbury. There was also a heavy defeat in the third round of the FA Cup, 5–2 against Preston at Deepdale, where centre-forward Charlie Wayman hit a hat-trick to complete a run of nine goals in four games. Someone had to go after this mayhem. Broadbent, still not 20, had obviously lost form and was dropped in favour of Bill Slater. However, Slater was, by then, primarily a half-back and Ron Stockin staked his claim to a League debut when he hit three goals as Wolves beat Bristol City 4–1 in a friendly to officially open the floodlights at Ashton Gate.

Stockin was duly given his chance and made the most of it. Wolves kept an unchanged forward line for the final 13 games of the season. Stockin, a couple of years older than Broadbent, got better with each appearance and ended the campaign by scoring six goals in five matches. There was no question of changing a successful forward line. Broadbent had to bide his time in the reserves, so when the 1953–54 season came around with hopes high that Wolves would, at last, bring the title to Molineux, he seemed unlikely to play a significant role.

For the new season Broadbent was offered the following terms – '£1 weekly throughout the season, £5 matchly, with an extra £1 per match in the reserve team, £2 per match in the first team.' The term 'matchly' meant per match and the letter from club secretary Jack Howley added, somewhat confusingly, that as Broadbent would be paid £1 throughout the season the £5 matchly fee would in fact be £4. All of which meant he would get £7 when in the first team and £6 in the reserves.

The start of the 1953–54 season was an unusual one. It had been decided the FA Cup should be the climax to the campaign and that there be no programme of League matches to detract from it. So the last day's League fixtures were switched to the beginning of the season, which thus started not on a Saturday but in midweek. This meant Wolves began with three successive away games.

They lost two of them and Stockin could not recapture his excellent form of the closing weeks of the previous campaign. He was guilty of some bad misses as Wolves lost 3–2 at Sunderland and so the time was ripe for Broadbent's return. His role as the forgotten man of Molineux had been a brief one.

Broadbent had not baulked at being asked to play in the reserves. When he joined Wolves he probably did not think he would have made such rapid progress, with first-team appearances coming his way so quickly, so he merely knuckled down to the task and helped the reserves become Central League champions for the third season running. He had busied himself with improving his game, knowing that his chance would come again. His patience was rewarded when he displaced Stockin for the club's first home game of the season, which saw them beat Cardiff 3–1. This was the day a great forward line was truly born – Hancocks, Broadbent, Swinbourne, Wilshaw and Mullen. Wolves fans of my vintage can reel it off without prompting. It may not have been the most successful, in terms of goals scored, but it remains the most famous in Wolves history. The five had appeared together only twice before, but that was during the run of defeats that had proved decisive in 1952–53. Now they would gel and become something very special.

The success against Cardiff started a run of 18 games unbeaten, which proved the backbone of Wolves' season. The sequence took Wolves briefly ahead in what developed into a two-horse race for the Championship, between them and Black Country rivals Albion. Early in that run came a 3–2 win over Arsenal at Highbury, where Wolves had not won for 21 years. Broadbent had done well on his first visit to the famous ground but it was a poor 1952–53 display there that had then seen him dropped. Now he was back on the Gunners' famous turf to turn in a sparkling display, encouraged by hitting the opening goal early in the game. The limelight, however, was stolen by Broadbent's diminutive right-wing partner Johnny Hancocks, who, two minutes from time, scored with a flying header that would have done Nat Lofthouse proud.

Two days after the win at Highbury, Broadbent showed his growing assuredness by hitting a dramatic winner against Liverpool at Molineux, which brings me to one of my favourite moans as I cement my status as a grumpy old man. I never cease to be amazed when people leave a football game before the final whistle. Obviously, it is not a new phenomenon and back in 1953 the game against Liverpool provided ample evidence of the stupidity of sloping off early. With Wolves leading through Roy Swinbourne's 44th-minute goal, a few home fans drifted away as the game went into its final three minutes. The trickle of fans through the exits became a steady flow when Liverpool winger Brian Jackson equalised, seemingly to rob Wolves of victory. But Broadbent had other ideas. Full-back Jack Short, playing up front as he had been badly injured early on, managed, straight from the restart, to push the ball through a gap in the Liverpool defence ahead of the on-rushing Broadbent and Swinbourne. Now Swinbourne may have had seniority and been an established goalscorer, but Broadbent brushed him out of the way with supreme confidence and fired home the winning goal. It had come just 30 seconds after Liverpool's equaliser. Those who stayed on had witnessed a finish they would talk about for years. Those who left early could not even see the goals on TV in the days when only one channel operated and that did not cover one League game, never mind all of them.

The unbeaten 18-match sequence included an 8–1 home win over Chelsea and a 2–1 defeat of Newcastle at St James' Park, a ground where Wolves had not won for 50 years. That was another occasion where the early leavers missed a dramatic finish. Having to play without Billy Wright, Dennis Wilshaw and Jimmy Mullen, who were on international duty, Wolves trailed until nine minutes from time. Then, reserve-winger Leslie Smith equalised and two minutes from time Roy Swinbourne won the game.

Four days after the goal glut against Chelsea, Molineux had staged its first floodlit friendly when the touring South Africa national side were beaten 3–1, Broadbent scoring the night's best goal with a cross shot from a narrow angle.

Evidence that Broadbent was now establishing himself as a key member of the team came in the 1–1 draw at Burnden Park against a Bolton side who were then on the fringe of the title race. Phil Morgan's *Express & Star* match report declared 'Best of the attack was undoubtedly Broadbent'. In a 3–3 draw at Middlesbrough, Broadbent picked up an injury that caused him to miss the title showdown with Albion at The Hawthorns. Wolves also had to make do without

Bill Slater, who was required to play for England in an amateur international. Stockin deputised for Broadbent in a game settled by Jimmy Mullen's fourth-minute goal, but there was no suggestion that Broadbent would not return to the side if fit.

So Broadbent quickly took up where he had left off, opening the scoring as Wolves won 2–0 at Charlton on 21 November 1953. That win kept Wolves just a point behind Albion, but within four days no one would be talking about the Black Country rivals' intense duel for the First Division crown. The attention switched dramatically from domestic football affairs to those of the national side, for football's old order was blown apart as Ferenc Puskas and the Magical Magyars came to Wembley and put on a devastating display. The scoreline, England 3 Hungary 6, is etched into sporting history. Any lingering thoughts that England might be the world's top footballing nation disappeared on that November afternoon in North London.

Wolves were soon in London themselves, to beat Tottenham 3–2 and once more go ahead of Albion in the title race. Broadbent yet again rose to the occasion in the capital. He headed in a Jimmy Mullen centre in the 54th minute, just as Dennis Wilshaw had done a minute earlier, but it was his all-round display that caught the eye. Over, once again, to Phil Morgan, 'In a Wolves team who played magnificently I give special marks to Short and Broadbent, who had no superior, even including Baily, when it came to controlling the sometimes difficult ball.' The 'Baily' referred to was Spurs inside-forward Eddie Baily; he had played nine times for England and was a mastermind of the celebrated Spurs 'push and run' team who won the Second Division and First Division in successive seasons at the start of the 1950s. A skilful player, who could score goals too, Baily was one of the most highly-rated midfield men in the game at that time. For Broadbent to outshine him said much about the Wolves man's blossoming talent.

Broadbent had every reason to be proud of his progress, but within a few weeks he began to lose form. There's no suggestion this was due to him getting too big for his boots or thinking he had truly arrived. It was more likely down to the fact that he was still only a youngster and it takes very little to knock a young player off his game. Just when he thought he could do no wrong, he lost his edge and, often, the harder he tried to regain it the more difficult it became. As Wolves faltered with successive defeats at the start of 1954, it was clear young Broadbent needed a rest. Significantly, it was not his former rival Ron Stockin who took over but half-back Ron Flowers who was tried in the number-eight shirt.

The Flowers experiment was not a big hit and Broadbent's exile lasted only two games. He returned to bring the Hancocks-Broadbent-Swinbourne-Wilshaw-Mullen forward line back together once more, and they revelled in the reunion by beating Sheffield United 6–1 at Molineux. Phil Morgan obviously liked the familiar line-up being back in harness, 'Almost as important as the goals was the way in which they were engineered. There was an ease of movement about the forwards that was more like a month or two ago, with Wilshaw and Broadbent getting through some splendid preparatory work.'

Just a week later, in a match that brought a February snowstorm to Molineux, Broadbent was again in scintillating form and again outshone an England inside-forward. This time it was Newcastle's Ivor Broadis, who had to play in Broadbent's shadow as the Wolves man began as he meant to go on – with a spectacular fourth-minute solo effort. 'Broadbent's run for more than half the length of the pitch to score the goal set him off on one of his best displays yet,' wrote Phil Morgan. To drive home my point about staying until the final whistle, this game brought three goals in the last 10 minutes. Wolves let slip a two-goal lead when Broadis and Jackie Milburn struck only for wing-half Bill Slater to pop up with the winner.

As the title race reached its climax Wolves suffered a setback when they were held 1–1 by Bolton in a midweek match at Molineux, but it did provide the opportunity for Broadbent to show that he had the confidence to try the occasional pot shot. He hit home a fierce 30-yard drive to cancel out Nat Lofthouse's early strike and, according to Phil Morgan, was the one home forward to find some semblance of method in a below-par display.

If Wolves were stumbling a little, nothing was going right for Albion. Hit by injuries they were faltering badly so that by the time the sides met in the second title showdown at The Hawthorns, a win for Wolves would have put them level on 50 points with Albion with just five games left. Even though England calls had robbed Albion of star-strike duo Ronnie Allen and Johnny Nicholls, and Wolves of Billy Wright and Jimmy Mullen, it was still a huge occasion with 55,000 packed into the ground. Big Wolves occasions would rarely bother Broadbent. The more important the game, the more the adrenaline would flow and he would show a determination to impress. This occasion was no exception as Phil Morgan would confirm in his match report. 'Apart from the two goalkeepers, who did their jobs well, there were five men who strove mightily to bring to the game the touch of class it deserved. They were the four wing-halves and Broadbent, and the greatest of these, I thought, was Broadbent.' Morgan went further, 'In the language of the terraces, he "stood out a mile". He was the fetcher and carrier, using, much as Mannion (Middlesbrough) had done at Molineux a week earlier, the big gap that constantly opened up between the Albion defence and attack.'

Albion's woes got worse in this of all matches, with an early injury to wing-half Ray Barlow playing at centre-forward. His opposite number Roy Swinbourne decided the match with its only goal on 58 minutes. Broadbent had a key role in it. He headed on a Leslie Smith corner to Swinbourne who was able to turn and volley the ball home.

The following week Wolves hammered Charlton 5–0 while Albion lost at Cardiff. So a two-point gap was established. Albion won only one of their final four games so Wolves eventually took the title by four points, a margin that had hardly seemed likely. The Championship was virtually certain by the time Wolves came to the final game of the season, against Spurs at Molineux. Wolves needed to lose heavily and Albion win heavily. Neither event happened, the Hawthorns outfit losing 3–0 at Cardiff and two Roy Swinbourne goals being enough to see off Tottenham 2–0 at Molineux – where the tension probably accounted for Wolves not being at their best. There was nothing below par with what followed the final whistle. Fans swarmed on to the pitch and refused to leave until Broadbent and the rest put in an appearance in the directors' box to acknowledge the cheers. Billy Wright said the main thank yous, but each player was handed the microphone to say a few words. Afterwards, Broadbent found himself inside the hallowed walls of the boardroom, probably for the first time, as, after getting changed, the team were invited to toast the success with champagne.

Not yet 21, Broadbent had come a long way in four years, both literally and metaphorically. Slugging it out for Dover in the Kent League must have seemed a distant memory as he savoured his new-found success.

There was no time to relax for Broadbent and the newly-crowned champions. Three days after beating Tottenham they began a three-match Scandinavian tour, beating an Aarhus XI – drawn from the AGD and AIA clubs – 5–0, Helsingborg 5–0 and drawing 2–2 with a Copenhagen XI. On the trip Broadbent was able to team up with right-winger Tommy McDonald, signed from Hibernian near the end of the season as cover for Johnny Hancocks.

Holidays still had to wait as on their return the players were feted at a civic banquet. Among the 500 guests at the Civic Hall in Wolverhampton were local dignitaries, representatives from other clubs, and, occupying pride of place, the Football League Championship trophy itself on a table bedecked with gold and black ribbons. Broadbent and the other players took their bow on the Civic Hall stage, with, according to the *Express & Star*, the band of the First Battalion, the South Staffordshire Regiment, 'striking the appropriate chord' before they then marched to the table of honour.

Floodlit Marvels

In one of many speeches made at the civic banquet, Wolves director Arthur Oakley, deputising for chairman James Baker, who was unwell, said he thought Wolves 'were on the crest of a very much bigger wave of success'. Most in the Civic Hall audience felt the same, but the remarkable thing about that 1953–54 Wolves team is that they did not go on to lift the title at least another couple of times. It is true that in those days the likely contenders were not restricted to four very rich clubs and the First Division of 1954 was a far more level playing field than the FA Premiership of 50 years later. However, Wolves were at the height of their powers with a splendid mix of youth and experience. Men like Bert Williams, Billy Wright, Bill Shorthouse, Johnny Hancocks and Jimmy Mullen provided the latter ingredient while Broadbent, Ron Flowers, Roy Swinbourne and Eddie Stuart were the younger men who were already more than useful players and would only get even better. In addition, men like Dennis Wilshaw and Bill Slater were at their peak.

Yet they failed to hold on to the title in 1954–55, despite setting the early pace and despite looking on paper to be the best team in the Football League. The points total of eventual champions Chelsea, 52, under the old system of two for a win, equalled the lowest ever recorded to win the title in a 42-game season. Wolves managed only 48 points, and there were any number of matches to which one could point as being key to their inability to defend their title successfully. Not least of these was the visit of Chelsea themselves to Molineux early in December. Wolves led 3–2 with four minutes to go only, for the Londoners to score twice and pinch victory.

Wolves had started as though they meant to hang on to their newly-won crown. Broadbent was in fine form in the new gold kit – what Phil Morgan called their 'merry marigold shirts' – and the *Express & Star* scribe was praising Broadbent early in the season when the inside man found himself in a new role. An injury to veteran centre-half Bill Shorthouse meant a reshuffle in the game against Portsmouth at Fratton Park. 'The performance of Broadbent was an eye-opener,' wrote Morgan. 'As a back-cum-half-back he had no superior on the field in those last 33 minutes. His tackling was swift and sure, his kicking strong and he cleared several delicate goalmouth situations.'

After the Portsmouth match Wolves reeled off four wins in a row, lost a couple of games and then had a run that brought only one defeat in 12 outings. Significantly, that defeat was the seven-goal thriller with Chelsea. A miserable festive period also cost Wolves dear. I well remember watching them play Everton on the last occasion Molineux staged a Christmas Day game. The Merseysiders won 3–1 with two goals from Dave Hickson, a fair-haired fleet-footed centre-forward who became a Goodison Park legend. Two days later Hickson scored again as Everton completed a double with a 3–2 success, with Broadbent's goal six minutes from time making the match seem a closer contest than it really was.

While losing key games was a tangible reason why Wolves did not retain their First Division title, there were other factors that could have helped take their eye off the ball. Not least of these was a succession of prestige floodlit matches, which had the whole country cheering for Wolves. Their success in those must also have increased the desire of opponents to lower their colours.

Even before the season began, Stan Cullis had taken his newly-crowned champions to Austria for a pre-season friendly against First Vienna. Wolves played well, despite being held to a 2–2 draw, and the Austrian club's World Cup goalkeeper Kurt Schmied declared 'Wolves are the best English team in Vienna since the war'.

With the advent of the Molineux floodlights, Wolves had commissioned a special set of satin shirts, which it was felt would be more visible in the artificial light. They took them to Vienna but ultimately did not wear them. The match marked First Vienna's 60th anniversary and on such an occasion the home club wanted to play in their traditional yellow shirts, which would have clashed with Wolves' new colour.

In mid-September, Broadbent showed a Scottish audience what he could do as Wolves braved the Glasgow rain to play a friendly against Celtic, whom they led 2–0 after 15 minutes only for the match to end 3–3. Broadbent scored the second goal in fine style, taking a return pass from Leslie Smith before racing between two defenders to slot the ball home. Nine days later came more midweek action when Wolves and Albion shared eight goals and the FA Charity Shield in a classic encounter before 40,800 fans at Molineux. Wolves led by two goals in this one too. They were 4–2 up only for Ronnie Allen to complete his hat-trick and level the scores. The match saw something new at Molineux, with substitutes brought on for the first time in a first-class match at the ground. Albion replaced George Lee and Jimmy Dudley in the second half with Ken Hodgkisson and Jimmy Dugdale, though only because of injuries.

Still the friendlies came thick and fast. The return with First Vienna ended in a goalless draw in stark contrast to the visit of Israeli champions Maccabi Tel Aviv, who conceded 10 goals without reply. Broadbent hit two goals in that one while Roy Swinbourne struck three times. All this was leading up to what must still rank as the two most famous games in Wolves' history – the visits of USSR champions Spartak and Hungarian champions Honved.

It is difficult to comprehend, over 50 years later, the importance of these games, but important they definitely were. With English football at a low ebb, there was added significance to these encounters at club level. As Phil Morgan wrote in his *Express & Star* match report of the Spartak game, Wolves 'were carrying all Britain's prestige on their golden clad shoulders'. The introduction to brief pictures of the match on Pathe News had the commentator declaring 'Here it is, the match of the year'.

Under the Communist regime in the USSR, increasing emphasis was put on sport in order to show the world the success their political system brought. Spartak had already beaten Arsenal 2–1 and Belgian side Anderlecht 7–0 before they came to Molineux on Tuesday 16 November 1954. Wolves took time to master the Soviet side and Dennis Wilshaw did not break the deadlock until the 63rd minute. The game remained on a knife-edge until five minutes from the end when Wolves scored three times through Johnny Hancocks (two) and Roy Swinbourne. Wolves had triumphed 4–0 before a crowd of 55,184 to win the acclaim of the national press.

Ian 'Sludge' Lees, that wonderful Black Country comedian and a big fan of Wolves, reminded me of a story that circulated after the win over Spartak.

Apparently, the Spartak manager was afterwards asking Stan Cullis, through an interpreter, about his players. He said how good he thought goalkeeper Bert Williams was and asked where he got him from. 'Walsall,' replied Cullis. Then the Russian wanted to know where Hancocks, the little winger with the big shot, came from. 'Walsall,' was again Cullis's answer. Finally he asked whence came Wilshaw, who had scored the first goal. Yet again Cullis's answer was 'Walsall'. After some thought the Russian said 'What a good job we didn't play Walsall!'

Walsall, had the Russian but known it, had just finished bottom of the Third Division North for three successive seasons.

If Broadbent and his teammates thought that win was special, even greater glory awaited them if they could beat top Hungarian club Honved, who, in the previous six seasons, had four times been their country's champions and twice runners-up. Hungary had not only beaten England 6–3 at Wembley a year earlier, they had then inflicted on them their heaviest ever defeat, 7–1, in the return game in Budapest. Six of the team who triumphed at Wembley were in the Honved side at Molineux – Bozsik, Lorant, Budai, Kocsis, Puskas and Czibor. It would have been seven had acrobatic goalkeeper Grosics been fit. His deputy was also an international.

Quite clearly Wolves were playing to try to restore England's battered pride. They did so memorably and dramatically on Monday 13 December 1954. They trailed 2–0 at half-time but hit back to win 3–2 thanks to a Johnny Hancocks penalty and two goals from centre-forward Roy Swinbourne. It was after this special win that manger Cullis hailed his team 'champions of the World' and prompted journalists at French sports paper *l'Equipe* to promote the idea of having a competition for all of Europe's top teams. It led to the founding of the European Cup, the forerunner of the Champions League. Phil Morgan would pinpoint the mastery of half-backs Bill Slater and Ron Flowers over the deadly duo of Ferenc Puskas and Sandor Kocsis as the key to Wolves' win, in which every man played his part. He also said Wolves' inside trio compared more than favourably with their Hungarian counterparts, adding 'I made Wilshaw the craftsman of the line, with Swinbourne the hardest forager and Broadbent the midfield collector and distributor.'

Wolves had the same line-up against both Spartak and Honved, namely: Williams; Stuart, Shorthouse; Slater, Wright, Flowers; Hancocks, Broadbent, Swinbourne, Wilshaw and Smith.

The whole town of Wolverhampton was on a high after this victory. The win had also captured the imagination of the country at large and many people had been able to see the second-half drama unfold as BBC TV broadcast it live. Did the glory of Honved affect Wolves on the domestic front? The players would probably say that it did not. Manager Stan Cullis would have tried to bring them down to earth but one can only wonder whether sub-consciously the team found it hard to get motivated when they returned to the bread-and-butter fare of League football. Results immediately after the Honved match were crucial in Wolves ultimately losing out in the title race.

First up were Sheffield Wednesday, who were destined to finish bottom of the table that season, yet they held Wolves 2–2 at Hillsborough with only a late goal from Dennis Wilshaw earning the champions a point. Still the talk was not of League football but of more prestige action, with Milan contacting Wolves to say they wished to try to succeed where Spartak and Honved failed. To his credit, Cullis said that while such a match would be welcome it would depend upon Wolves' League and Cup commitments. Certainly, attention needed to be paid to Wolves' League form as the draw at Sheffield was followed immediately by those two Christmas defeats at the hands of Everton. Into the new year and Wolves slipped again, held 2–2 at home by Portsmouth.

A Cup run was probably the last thing needed if the Championship was to stay at Molineux, but a Cup run was what Wolves next embarked upon. It began at Grimsby Town who were struggling near the foot of the Third Division North. The minnows rocked Wolves by going two up in 18 minutes and kept the lead until half-time. Manager Cullis was incensed by his side's first-half display and harangued them from the touchline. His inevitable verbal lashing during the break must have had some effect, as Wolves hit five goals without reply in the second half. Broadbent was one of those who lifted his game, laying on at least two of the goals. However, Cullis's touchline antics had incurred the wrath of the referee, whose report was received with some concern by the FA. In due course Cullis was fined £50 and banned from coaching his players from the touchline.

After the Grimsby game, Broadbent was soon wondering whether he had a chance of adding an FA Cup-winner's medal to his Championship one. Arsenal, who included veteran former-England centre-forward Tommy Lawton, were seen off 1–0 at Molineux thanks to a Roy Swinbourne header and then Charlton were beaten 4–1, also at Molineux, with Dennis Wilshaw ploughing through the snow to score a first-half hat-trick. Just as a Wembley trip loomed, it all went wrong against the expensively-assembled Sunderland side at Roker Park. Of all people, tough-as-iron full-back Bill Shorthouse suffered concussion when he collided with a Sunderland player after only four minutes. He was carried off and taken to hospital. Wolves' 10 men, with Ron Flowers outstanding, rose to the occasion but two second-half goals by rampaging centre-forward Ted Purdon saw Sunderland through.

If it could be argued that the Honved game affected Wolves' League form, the same could be said of the Cup campaign. For instance, after the win over Arsenal there came a result no one could have forecast. Wolves, pride of the nation, were humbled 6–1 at Bolton, fielding the same line-up who had conquered Spartak and Honved. It was Wolves' biggest defeat in 20 years.

There had been some talk of Wolves doing the double earlier in the season, but, like so many before them, they had failed. Maybe if the fabulous floodlit friendlies had come a little later in the season the twin aims might have been fulfilled. It's all conjecture, of course, and while the two domestic honours eluded the club the success against the Russians and Hungarians was a unique double that has a special place in English football folklore.

To be a part of that was something Broadbent would always treasure. It was fitting that his last appearance at Molineux should be for the fans to pay tribute to the survivors of the team who had beaten Honved. To mark the 50th anniversary of the great game, they were entertained to a celebration lunch at the *Express & Star* and then paraded before the crowd at the evening's Molineux

League game against Millwall. Broadbent, with Alzheimer's then beginning to take its toll, was well looked after by his old teammates. One never knows with such a condition, but one hopes Broadbent was able to appreciate the tribute paid to him and his famous colleagues that night in December 2004.

The wins over Spartak and Honved may have put Wolves on the world football map but there was no doubt they had missed a great chance to make it two successive title wins. They finished runners-up to Chelsea, and the right-wing duo of Johnny Hancocks and Broadbent contributed 31 goals between them. Hancocks's share was 26, the best seasonal total of his career. Broadbent's goalscoring may have taken a back seat but his creative work had helped Wolves finish joint top scorers in the First Division with 89 goals.

Wolves may have fallen short in their double bid but finishing runners-up netted Broadbent what in those days was called 'talent money'. It amounted to £36 3s 9d (£36.19). For reaching the FA Cup sixth round, he was given an extra £20. Of that total sum of £56 3s 9d, a letter from the club secretary Jack Howley informed Broadbent that HM Inspector of Taxes would require £20 14s (£20.70). Not exactly a rich man's game, football in 1955!

Wolves' new status as England's football ambassadors meant their focus was not on League football as the 1955–56 season approached. They had been given permission by the Government to visit the USSR for two pre-season friendlies, part of improving relations between two great powers during the 'Cold War'. After South Africa, Broadbent was about to embark on another adventure, courtesy of football.

Wolves had agreed to play the Soviet Union's top teams, Spartak and Dynamo. Unlike Wolves, Dynamo had been champions of their country for two seasons running, pipping Spartak to the title each time. In the two seasons before that, Spartak had taken the title. The football was important but the forging of friendships with the Communist heavyweights was of far greater significance. On that score, the trip was successful, though Wolves lost 3–0 to Spartak and then 3–2 to Dynamo.

Broadbent was in the first party of Wolves players who flew to Moscow via Helsinki. I tracked down some British Pathe News footage of the team departing and the clipped accent of the newsreel commentator takes one back to another era as he declares 'Leaving London Airport for Moscow to meet crack Russian teams Spartak and Dynamo, 11 members of the Wolverhampton Wanderers team look fighting fit and ready for anything the Russian footballers have up their sleeves.' The commentary then adds a supposedly funny note, 'If they don't have good luck it won't be the airline's fault. Chicken was served for lunch and Stan Cullis commented "It's the first time I've known a chicken have 11 wishbones."' As the plane is seen moving along the runway, the commentary concludes 'Handle them carefully, pilot, those 11 boys are insured for nearly a quarter of a million pounds.'

Broadbent and the other players were able to train on a pitch alongside the Olympic stadium during the stop in Helsinki. While in the Finnish capital, Broadbent and a few teammates had a scare in their hotel. He, Bert Williams, Bill Slater, Bill Shorthouse, Ron Flowers, Roy Swinbourne, Eddie Stuart and Billy Wright got stuck in a lift. Wright recalled it as one of his most frightening experiences abroad, 'The lift halted between floors and with our air supply rather limited we all felt an unusual sensation until someone unscrewed the door and out we marched feeling rather sorry for ourselves.'

Each match in Moscow saw 80,000 people packed into the massive Dynamo Stadium. Before both games Broadbent and his teammates received bouquets of flowers and stood sheepishly grinning after this gesture not usually associated with the macho world of football. That Wolves played without incident was what really mattered and the diplomatic nature of the visit was emphasised by the fact the team were accompanied by Wolverhampton's Mayor Alderman Frank Mansell and one of the town's MPs, John Baird. A lavish banquet was held after the second match and the Wolves senior director Jim Marshall urged that more sporting exchanges be arranged between the two nations. As for the football, Wolves clearly lacked match practice. Broadbent had Leslie Smith as his right-wing partner in the Spartak game and Scotsman Tommy McDonald started the Dynamo clash, being later replaced by Smith.

As for the match action, Pathe News showed only brief clips but one superbly illustrates Broadbent's skill. Tatushin, the Spartak right-winger, has the ball near the edge of Wolves' penalty area out on the right flank. Broadbent robs him but another Spartak player comes to help out Tatushin and it seems certain they will regain possession. However, Broadbent manages to put his foot on the ball and swivel round in one movement to completely wrong-foot the Soviet pair before clearing the ball upfield. It is just a brief moment but it captures perfectly Broadbent's natural ball control and body movement that made him so special.

The party stayed 12 days in Moscow, and Broadbent and Co were able to do plenty of sight-seeing. Roy Swinbourne recalled 'There were a couple of security men assigned to us. I remember us going to a university and Bill Slater took some photographs from the top of the building. They said to him that you can't take pictures of the city from that height, you'll have to destroy them. And they took the camera off him and took the film out. Apart from that, they made us very welcome, they could not do enough for us.' The party returned back home via Helsinki, no doubt making sure that if they could not read the warning notices inside lifts, then they would at least get a translation before piling in.

Despite the warmth of the welcome, Broadbent was not too impressed with the USSR. Wife Shirley makes no bones about it, 'He used to like going on the foreign trips, even though he said he missed home, but not Russia. He hated it. He said the people looked poor and he could not stand to see the women working on the roads, using drills. He thought it was all very drab and the people did not look happy. He did bring me some perfume back from Moscow and I've never smelled anything like it. It was awful.'

Only four days after returning home, Wolves began the 1955–56 season and were not quickly into their stride. However, by the time the first meeting of the season with Matt Busby's exciting young Manchester United arrived, they had picked up 11 points from their opening nine games with goals a-plenty, including a 7–2 home win over Manchester City and a sensational 9–1 success at Cardiff. The latter equalled the highest-ever away win in the top flight, set by Sunderland at Newcastle in 1908. Centre-forward Roy Swinbourne could not stop scoring and had collected 14 goals. United had two more points than

Wolves, but had played 11 games when the sides clashed at Old Trafford. Broadbent had missed a couple of games after sustaining a nasty cut to the eye against Blackpool at Bloomfield Road. He returned for what proved a pulsating match but not to face the huge talent of young Duncan Edwards. The Dudley-born England international was injured and so United gave a debut to an even younger player – Wilf McGuinness, still a few days short of his 18th birthday.

In time, McGuinness would play alongside Broadbent in the England team and would take over from Matt Busby as manager at Old Trafford. On this day his task was to stop Broadbent. Now a very successful after-dinner speaker, McGuinness tells a lovely yarn about his debut and how United assistant manager Jimmy Murphy wound him up in the dressing room. The McGuinness story goes that Murphy had asked him if he knew much about his opponent and an innocent McGuinness had replied that it was Broadbent, a good player and a sportsman. Murphy promptly painted a very different picture; Broadbent knew he was up against a youngster, he would be out to make him look stupid and if he did that, McGuinness might never make it in football and would have to find some other way to earn a living. Not to put too fine a point on it, Broadbent would be out to pinch his wages from his pocket. So McGuinness strode out, fired up and bristling, and Broadbent, gentleman that he was, offered to shake hands as he said 'Good luck, son,' to which McGuinness retorted 'F… off you thieving bastard'.

In the days before all-seat stadiums and a guaranteed place, fans used to get to grounds early, so United, on this occasion, decided to provide something for the waiting crowd rather than the usual music blaring from the PA system. They had a marching band as well as a fitness display by young women from the Butlin's holiday camp organisation. Yet the real entertainment came from the football. United and Wolves put on a cracker before 48,638 fans. David Pegg gave United the lead three minutes before the break, but on the hour Bill Slater headed Wolves level. Seven minutes later Broadbent put a cross in the path of Roy Swinbourne, who swept the ball home. United levelled through Swinbourne's opposite number Tommy Taylor, only for Swinbourne to restore the lead two minutes later. Four goals had come in 14 minutes but Wolves must have thought they would hang on for a memorable win when the game entered its final five minutes. They were left reeling, however, when John Doherty made it 3–3 and then Taylor gave United victory three minutes from time.

It had been a game to savour with Phil Morgan writing 'This was the sort of soccer with the lid off which, if it could be guaranteed every week, would bring back those missing millions – with or without the bonny beauties and the band as curtain raisers.' That game must have done wonders for the morale of the young United side, who roared on to take the title by a massive 11 points from runners-up Blackpool.

After the Old Trafford epic, a month down the line would be another challenging floodlit friendly – the visit of Dynamo, who had just got the better of Wolves in Moscow during the summer. Before Broadbent did battle once more with the men from the USSR, a funny thing happened to him. He became, briefly, a half-back. He had done well in that position when switched there during that game at Portsmouth through injury to defender Bill Shorthouse, but he had never started a game at half-back. Now, with Ron Flowers out with a knee injury, manager Stan Cullis decided to play Broadbent at left-half against newly-promoted Luton Town, while giving a League debut at inside-right to Bobby Mason.

If the match at Old Trafford was memorable, then so was the match at Kenilworth Road, but for the wrong reasons. Those were still the days well before substitutes in League matches, so an early injury to Roy Swinbourne hampered Wolves' experiment. With the First Division football a new experience for Luton, nearly 28,000 packed into their compact ground to see the visit of the mighty Molineux men and several youngsters were seated almost on the pitch. It was in trying to avoid some of them that Swinbourne 'braked' sharply and pulled a muscle. Little did Wolves fans know it, but the injury was the beginning of the end for the wonderful centre-forward, whose goalscoring had put him on the brink of England selection. Wolves were hammered 5–1, even though Hancocks had equalised Bob Morton's early strike for Luton. Phil Morgan wrote 'This was a most unfortunate day for experiments with Broadbent at left-half and Mason at inside-right. With the team at full strength both might have worked out, but against the handicap it was asking a little too much.'

What a preparation for the match against Dynamo four days later! Flowers was still not fit to resume but there was no suggestion of continuing with Broadbent at left-half. In came Eddie Clamp and Broadbent was restored to the forward line in place of 19-year-old Mason. There was no chance Swinbourne would recover for the big game so Jimmy Murray was given his debut, just a month past his 20th birthday and on the biggest night of Wolves' season.

Murray's inclusion meant the little Kent mining village of Elvington had two of its sons in this prestige match – and from the same street. For Murray, too, had grown up in Adelaide Road. 'Our house was the other side of the street to Peter's,' Murray recalled. 'He was two years older than me but I well remember us playing football together as kids. There was a piece of ground – it may have belonged to the pit – that we all used to play on. About 20-a-side sometimes. I did not become a miner like Peter, though. My dad was manager of the canteen at the pit but he said "You're not going down the pit". I played football for Canterbury City and then joined Wolves.'

His road to Molineux had some similarity to Broadbent's. 'George Poyser had heard about me when he was at Dover and when he joined Wolves I think he told their chief scout George Noakes about me. When I moved up to Wolverhampton I was in digs in a street near to the ground, though I can't recall the name. I got a job as well in case the football did not work out – as a mechanic with Don Everall, the coach company.' Murray need not have worried about his chances of making it as a footballer. One of the unsung heroes of the Wolves team that did so well in the latter half of the 1950s, he was not a robust centre-forward but a highly skilful one, who had the vital gift that no trainer nor manager can teach – the natural striker's instinct to be in the right place at the right time.

Murray was doing his National Service in the Army, based at Lichfield, when he learned that he would be facing the Soviet stars. 'I saw a headline in the paper saying "Unknown to lead Wolves" and when I read on it was me. When I got to the ground I found that the story was right.' So Murray took his place in the Wolves side on Wednesday 9 November 1955, knowing that playing was the only way he would have been able to see the Russians in action, for it's doubtful his regiment would have granted him a pass to go and watch the game. Murray could easily have been overawed by the occasion. That he was not was due, in no small way, to how the other players calmed any nerves. 'All the players made me feel at home straight away. Peter, Clampy, Ron Flowers, Billy Wright – they were all so friendly. Over the years we all got on and that team spirit played a big part in our success.'

The Russians arrived at Wolverhampton with no fewer than 17 players plus a team manager, assistant team manager, masseur, the USSR state coach, club doctor, a chief of the delegation (who was doubtless a leading Communist Party official), the Dynamo club's vice president, a radio commentator and, for some reason that escapes me, the president of the Bicycle Club of the USSR.

Wolves' 2–1 success provided them with another notable foreign scalp. Wolves took the lead after 14 minutes when a Jimmy Mullen shot from a Johnny Hancocks right-wing corner flew across the goal. The ball ricocheted off Bill Slater on to Murray, just in front of him, and came back to Slater, who hit a low shot past the legendary Lev Yashin in the Russian goal. Four minutes into the second half, Mullen, who had missed out on the other two famous wins, made it 2–0. He chased a Murray pass and held off the challenge of Rodionov to fire the ball past the advancing Yashin. Broadbent was desperately close to making it 3–0, when his header to a Hancocks corner beat Yashin but rebounded off the bar. Mullen and Billy Wright, the oldest men in the team, were Wolves' stars with Wright rallying his defence after Ilyin had pulled back a goal on 62 minutes. This is how they lined up:

Wolves: Williams; Stuart, Shorthouse; Slater, Wright, Clamp; Hancocks, Broadbent, Murray, Wilshaw, Mullen.

Dynamo: Yashin; Rodionov, Krizhevsky, B. Kuznetsov; Boykov, Sokolov; Sabrov, Feodosov, Y. Kuznetsov, Ilyin, Ryzhkin.

Referee: A.E. Ellis (Halifax). Attendance: 55,480.

Broadbent had figured in yet another historic Molineux match and was enjoying the plaudits, as the national press hailed another great blow for English football prestige. Returning to domestic football, Wolves hardly set the world on fire and at the start of December came a bad day for the club, as they lost 2–0 at Preston's quaint Deepdale home. Roy Swinbourne had returned to lead the attack but failed to inspire his colleagues. Dennis Wilshaw pulled a muscle after only 16 minutes but Wolves' handicapped attack still had Preston back-pedalling for much of the game.

Then came the body blow. Swinbourne wrenched his knee and was carried from the field on a stretcher. He remembers it well, 'I think my right leg was still weak from the injury at Luton a month earlier. I went for the ball with Tommy Docherty and took it on my chest, and then tried to turn. All the weight was on my right leg and it just gave way.'

Swinbourne had started the season wonderfully and was freely being tipped to win England honours, but now his career was in tatters. He made several attempts at a comeback but, despite three operations, his knee never recovered sufficiently to stand up to the rigours of First Division football.

While Wolves still had the veterans Hancocks and Mullen on the wings, Broadbent found himself with more responsibility after the Swinbourne and Wilshaw injuries. He had to get in tune with the relatively inexperienced duo Murray and Colin Booth, who were two very talented young players. The year ended with Wolves' only home defeat of 1955 – against Cardiff. I remember going along to the match and, with the naivety of youth, wondering that if Wolves had scored nine goals away to Cardiff earlier in the season, just how many would they score at Molineux. Logic and football do not go together, which I found out that day as Wolves scored nine goals fewer than they had at Ninian Park while Gerry Hitchens, who, like Broadbent, had once been a miner, struck twice to give the Welsh club an unlikely victory.

Manchester United were running away with the Championship so maybe the FA Cup could revive Wolves' season. That hope was knocked immediately on the head when Wolves met Albion at Molineux. A feature of the game was that three half-backs figured at centre-forward. Albion's Ray Barlow was no stranger to the position, but Stan Cullis had decided to try Ron Flowers at number nine against Sunderland a week earlier when Jimmy Murray was ill. Flowers had scored in a 1–1 draw at Roker Park and so was retained up front. He may have started as a centre-forward but did not finish as one. Cullis eventually ordered him and Bill Slater to change places, and it was Slater who grabbed a late goal to revive Wolves' hopes after first-half goals from Albion wingers Frank Griffin and George Lee. Broadbent was wide of the target with a couple of shots, but Phil Morgan reckoned in the *Express & Star* he was 'quite the most effective Wolves forward'.

At least the Cup exit left Wolves with a blank Saturday on fourth-round day so that they were able to accept a friendly with Argentinian side San Lorenzo. That game would spark off the best scoring run of Broadbent's career – seven goals in three games. This impressive sequence began on Saturday 28 January 1956. This was a rare chance for Wolves fans to see Latin American opposition and over 32,000 turned up at Molineux, only for the limelight to be stolen by Broadbent when he hit three goals in a 5–1 victory.

The heavy pitch clearly did not suit San Lorenzo but Broadbent positively revelled in it. The Argentinians used 15 players, which, in the days before substitutes were allowed in competitive football in England, must have been quite confusing for the fans, who were stunned into silence when the tourists went ahead in the second minute.

Then Broadbent found his shooting boots, for which Phil Morgan's *Express & Star* report was fulsome in praise, 'Then came the brilliance of Broadbent to put into shade anything the South Americans could provide. Before he retired injured in the 75th minute (Mullen deputised) he had scored a most welcome hat-trick.' That game also provided the unusual occurrence of Wolves' usually deadly penalty ace Johnny Hancocks twice having spot-kicks saved. He was lucky that referee Mervyn Griffiths ordered a re-take of the first and he was able to make amends. However, there was no reprieve after he had missed a second one, maybe his concentration being hampered by the delay caused when the angry Argentinians surrounded the official. Morgan noted that referee Griffiths 'disappeared beneath a wave of Argentinos'.

Broadbent's injury was nothing serious and a week later he had the chance to make the London pressmen take note when he faced champions Chelsea at Stamford Bridge. This was the ground where, a year earlier, Wolves had virtually surrendered their League crown to the Londoners, losing the showdown game 1–0. So revenge was Wolves' aim and Broadbent had special reason to want to do well as he was being watched by his family. He did not disappoint them. He scored twice in Wolves' 3–2 win, with Phil Morgan declaring 'Broadbent was again the best forward on view. His parents and brother from Dover saw him add to his San Lorenzo hat-trick a couple of neat goals, the first a perfectly-timed header and the second a shot on the volley.'

Clearly, Broadbent had found his goal touch and he hit two more a week later when Wolves beat Bolton 4–2. The Lancashire side fielded a 16-year-old goalkeeper, Joe Dean, who distinguished himself with some fine saves before going off to have stitches put in an eye injury. During his brief absence, England centre-forward Nat Lofthouse went between the posts and proved an able deputy. Dean had gifted Wolves the lead when he turned a Johnny Hancocks corner into his own net, but he was helpless when Broadbent made it 3–1 for Wolves with a waist-high left-foot volley, which Phil Morgan reckoned was a candidate for his 'Goals I Remember' notebook. After Bolton had reduced the deficit, Broadbent struck in the final minute with a crafty, rather than thunderbolt, shot this time.

Broadbent's scoring run came to an end when Wolves lost 2–0 at Molineux to Manchester United, then well on their way to becoming First Division champions. Broadbent had an impressive game despite the attention of the mighty Duncan Edwards.

By then Broadbent had his mind on other matters. He had been courting Shirley Nicholls for some four years and on Sunday 18 March 1956 they married at St Chad's Church, Owen Road, Wolverhampton. His brother Jack was best man and the reception was at the Molineux Hotel, the former private house whose vast gardens had become Wolves' ground in 1889. Shirley remembered 'It was in the season and so we could not go on honeymoon. I think Peter and Jack even went off to the races the next day. When we did go on a honeymoon, to Newquay in Cornwall in the summer, Norman Deeley and his wife Dorothy came with us.'

The Broadbents had met about four years earlier at a dance at Wolverhampton's Civic Hall. Shirley worked at the chemist's Timothy White and Taylor in Lea Road, in the Penn Fields area of the town. 'Peter came to live with us in Manlove Street eventually,' Shirley told me. 'There was no hanky-panky – separate bedrooms. I don't think Stan Cullis liked it, Peter living with us. I think the club doctor came round once when Peter had tonsillitis and he had a good nose around to see everything was above board. I think Stan thought Peter was too young to get married. He was 22. It was the same when Peter got a car, a Ford Prefect. Cullis did not like that. He did not think footballers should have cars. He thought Peter was getting above himself. He had him in the office about it and he wrote a letter to his father.'

The newly-weds were eventually allocated a house owned by Wolves in Wimborne Road, Fallings Park, at a rent of 35s (£1.75) a week. 'There was a verandah attached to it with a little bar,' remembers Shirley, 'but Cullis did not like that either. We thought it was great but Cullis ordered that it be taken out. I think they took it to Molineux and put it in the players' lounge. Cullis was very strict but I think Peter came to realise many years later that Cullis was only like it for the best reasons. He had the interest of the club at heart.'

Having taken one of life's more significant steps, Broadbent had quickly to turn his attention back to football once more as Wolves still had a chance to finish runners-up in the First Division. With Jimmy Murray at centre-forward and Dennis Wilshaw back at inside-left, a place still had to be found for young Colin Booth. So Broadbent was moved to outside-right in preference to veteran Johnny Hancocks, who was coming to the end of his magnificent Molineux career. Wolves had paid £25,000 for West Ham winger Harry Hooper as his successor, but he was not eligible to play until the new season. With Broadbent wearing the number-seven shirt, Wolves did well enough to come to their final game of the season needing a win against Sheffield United at Bramall Lane to pip Blackpool for the runners'-up spot. Wolves led 3–1 after 37 minutes, Booth scoring all three goals for the visitors, only for the Blades to strike twice before the break. The score stayed 3–3 after a further 45 minutes and so Wolves finished level on 49 points with Blackpool, who had the better goal average and so took second place.

While there had been first-half drama aplenty, there had been more even before the midweek game began. Because of his duties at Birmingham University, Bill Slater could not travel with the team so the plan was to fly him from Elmdon Airport, as Birmingham was then known, and land at Lodge Moor airfield, six miles from Sheffield, where a car would be waiting. The pilot, however, was misled by the small size of Lodge Moor, did not spot the car and so thought he was in the wrong place. When the car driver realised the plane was not going to land he waved frantically but in vain. The plane eventually landed at Worksop about 20 miles away from where, even if a car had been waiting, it would have been impossible to get Slater to the ground on time. So reserve George Showell was drafted in at centre-half with Billy Wright switching to right-half, where he looked far from happy.

By the time the 1956–57 season rolled around, the limelight had switched from Wolves to Manchester United. Matt Busby's young side had captured the imagination of the football public and the manager defied the home authorities to enter the European Cup, unlike Chelsea who had bowed to Football League concern about possible fixture congestion and did not take part. If the focus had switched from Molineux to Old Trafford, there was still plenty of interest in what was happening at Wolverhampton.

Johnny Hancocks had been put on the transfer list and all eyes were on Broadbent's new right-wing partner, Hooper. The season began well with a 5–1 defeat of Manchester City, Jimmy Murray scoring four times. Results were mixed in the opening weeks and that's how the season would continue, but Broadbent would play his part in one of the greatest League matches ever seen at Molineux. It came against Luton Town, but equally interesting was the prelude to that match. Clubs often met home and away early in the season in those days, and Luton and Wolves met first at Kenilworth Road where Luton won 1–0 to make it three successive League wins over Stan Cullis's side. Cullis felt the goal was offside and got involved in an altercation, which, if it had taken place nowadays, would probably have been treated like the Old Trafford pizza-throwing incident. Things were different then, however, and this is how the *Express & Star* dealt with the matter:

'Wolves manager, Mr Stanley Cullis, was concerned in an incident at Luton last night. Feeling, with Wolves defenders, that the winning goal was offside, he was not slow to say so. This got him into an argument with Mr Tom Hodgson, one of the Luton directors, and (writes 'Commentator'), I was told by a colleague who saw the incident that things became "heated".

'According to some accounts, Mr Hodgson called Cullis "a baby" and added that the Wolves manager behaved like a baby throughout the match. Cullis was also reported to have grabbed hold of Mr Hodgson's tie.

'There was, however, a happy ending, for Mr Cullis, in company with Wolves directors Mr John Ireland and Mr Jim Marshall, quickly offered an apology to the Luton club and, explaining the incident to me, he said "Mr Hodgson and I had a few words about what I considered to be an offside goal, but we had a cup of tea together afterwards and when we shook hands we considered the whole incident closed."

'This was also the attitude of the Luton chairman, Mr Percy Mitchell, who said afterwards "We have received an apology from Mr Cullis and so far as this club is concerned nothing has happened".'

One can only imagine what the tabloid press of the 21st century would have made of the business, involving, as it did, one of the highest profile managers of the day. As it was, the *Express & Star* contented themselves in headlining the story, which was given only single-column space, with 'An apology closed Luton soccer scene'.

All of this set the atmosphere for the return game a week later, 29 August 1956, when the sides staged one of the most pulsating first halves I have ever seen. Luton led 2–0 after only nine minutes but by 27 minutes Wolves were 3–2 up. The goal that put them ahead came from Broadbent, who raced through on to a Hooper pass to beat Bernard Streten in the visitors' goal. Gordon Turner then scored his second of the game for Luton to make it 3–3, only for Murray and Jimmy Mullen to put Wolves 5–3 up at the interval. The match ended 5–4, Turner completing his hat-trick in the 65th minute.

A spectator at the game was Malcolm Finlayson. The big Scotsman had been signed earlier in the day from Millwall. Finlayson, due to be groomed as the successor to England goalkeeper Bert Williams, could not quite believe what he saw at Molineux that night. 'There were nine goals but the goalkeepers were great. They were both internationals, they were both cats and they pulled off no end of fine saves. I've never seen a match quite like it.'

Young reserve Gerry Harris could have been an enthralled spectator too, but instead made his League debut. He had been told to turn up at the ground along with other Central League players, only to learn from trainer Joe Gardiner on his arrival at Molineux that left-back Bill Shorthouse was injured. Recalled Harris, 'Joe just came up to me and said "You're playing" and that was it. What a fabulous game for your debut!'

Not surprisingly, Phil Morgan waxed lyrical in his match report but there was a telling note of criticism. He wrote that Murray had his best game yet for Wolves and 'he received splendid support from the busy Bs, Booth and Broadbent, who, if they can use those left feet a little more often to send the running passes in front of Hooper, may make this a forward line to go down in Wolves' history.' He may not have said so in as many words, but the Hooper-Broadbent wing was not proving a hit.

They were still together when the awed Luton match spectator Finlayson made his debut at Molineux against newly-promoted Leeds, who had the wonderful John Charles playing at inside-right. Everyone, Broadbent included, was overshadowed, metaphorically and literally, by the big Welshman, who scored both goals in Leeds' 2–1 win and then moved into defence to keep Wolves at bay. It was in the late revival that Broadbent, who had earlier hit the bar, weaved his way through to grab a consolation goal two minutes from time. Broadbent almost did it again but there was to be no dramatic last-gasp equaliser.

Cullis had by then decided it was time for a change and moved Broadbent to inside-left to partner Jimmy Mullen. The switch lasted just three games. Broadbent had a poor match against Albion at The Hawthorns — watched by 17-year-old winger Des Horne, newly arrived from South Africa to join Wolves — and Cullis decided another change was needed. He dropped Broadbent. Murray switched to inside-left and his place at number nine went to the recalled Dennis Wilshaw. The new forward line proved an instant hit as Portsmouth were beaten 6–0 at Molineux.

It was not the first time Broadbent had been dropped and he would have to do what all Wolves players did in those days — get his head down in the reserves and hope to do well enough to earn a recall. It was not only the men in possession who were Broadbent's rivals for the inside-forward berths. Bobby Mason was making rapid progress and there was also Scottish youngster Bobby Thomson on the Molineux books. Broadbent did get some first-team action when Dennis Wilshaw was hurt after 28 minutes of the floodlit friendly against Rumania CCA. He came on as substitute and scored the third goal in a 5–0 win before a crowd of 47,284. However, he was still not first choice and Wolves' rejigged forward line clicked again against Arsenal with a 5–2 win at Molineux, Booth collecting four goals. An injury to Wilshaw led to a one-game recall when Wolves lost 3–0 at Burnley.

In all, Broadbent was omitted for six out of seven League games before injuries eventually let him back into the team, and, when he partnered young amateur Pat Neil as Wolves beat Manchester City 3–2 at Maine Road, it was clear, after his spell in the reserves, that he was determined to keep his place. Phil Morgan wrote in the *Express & Star* that the 'most heartening feature was the vast improvement in the attack, the brains and the driving power behind, which were provided by a re-energised Broadbent, playing with all the skill of his most promising early days, plus the wisdom of experience.

'He should be as much encouraged as the club followers themselves. It was he who inspired the others to play football, he who made the best use of the speed of wingers Neil and Hooper, and he who grafted in the spaces behind the line to collect and distribute the ball as it came through from the defence. Finally, it was he who showed the sort of thrust that gave him Wolves' second goal and, when he beat Trautmann to a back pass, was close to getting another.'

It was high praise indeed from Morgan, still writing in the paper under the nom de plume 'Commentator' in those days. Several years later, as a sports sub-editor at the *Express & Star*, I came to know Morgan well. Born in Southampton – he never lost his Hampshire burr despite years working in the West Midlands – Morgan would never go over the top in his criticism of players, nor in praise. So to write as he did in this instance says a great deal for Broadbent's display.

Four days before the game against City, Broadbent added another name to the list of famous players against whom he had played. Hungarian side Red

Banner (MTK) played a goalless draw before a crowd of 43,540 at Molineux and included in their line-up the great Nandor Hidegkuti. His three goals had helped the fabulous Hungary side win at Wembley three years earlier. That wonderful team had been torn apart by December 1956 – a casualty of the Hungarian uprising, which was ended when the USSR sent tanks into its Communist satellite neighbour. The purpose of Red Banner's visit to Wolverhampton was to raise money for the Hungarian Relief Fund and a cheque for £2,213 was sent to it.

Hidegkuti played only the first half of the game, while Wolves also introduced a substitute as famous locally as Hidegkuti was globally. Johnny Hancocks came on for an injured Jimmy Murray nine minutes from time and received the biggest cheer of the night. Broadbent's old right-wing partner only touched the ball a few times in what proved to be his last first-team outing for Wolves before joining Wellington Town, the Shropshire club who later became Telford United. Hancocks and Broadbent had formed Wolves' right-wing in exactly 100 League matches and eight FA Cup games.

At the turn of the year, Broadbent showed his scoring potential again after grabbing the consolation goal in a 3–1 defeat at Everton, striking twice as Wolves won 3–2 at Sunderland, being on target when Wolves beat Swansea 5–3 in the third round of the FA Cup and then hitting two more in a 3–0 home League win over Spurs. It was the first time he had scored in four successive games and his display at Sunderland, where young Joe Bonson made his debut, had Phil Morgan drooling. 'This was not only Broadbent the scorer and schemer but Broadbent the grafter, for there were countless times when he was back fighting for the ball, and getting it, in the very spot where it should have been commanded by Anderson, the Sunderland right-half. In this form he was able to make the best use of Mullen and do a lot towards bringing in Hooper.'

Just when it seemed the campaign might be picking up, Broadbent and his teammates would be victims of one of football's greatest shocks. Bournemouth of the Third Division South came to Molineux and knocked Wolves out of the Cup with a lone goal from former-Albion winger Reg Cutler. If the fourth-round result alone was not enough to cement the game into the memories of all Wolves fans, another unlikely occurrence made sure – Cutler collided with, and snapped, a goalpost at the Hotel End of the ground. It was scant consolation for Wolves that Spurs were also victims of the giantkillers in the next round, before Bournemouth were finally eliminated by double-chasing Manchester United.

A 7–3 home win over Charlton, in which Broadbent again scored twice, helped restore Wolves' wounded pride and they got welcome relief from the hard slog of an English football season in winter when, in March 1957, they visited Spain to play Valencia. It was a trip Broadbent enjoyed. It was fiesta time and Wolves were among thousands who watched a bull fight, which featured the matador Litzi, who was to bull fighting what Alfredo di Stefano was to football – a national hero. Broadbent liked the spectacle, if not the actual purpose of it all. He and the other players also enjoyed the lavish banquet to which they were treated and the impressive firework display later. The game ended 3–1 to the Spaniards and was marred by a home referee, who frequently penalised Wolves for tackles that would have been of no consequence in the Football League. Phil Morgan said in his report, telephoned back to the *Express & Star,* that it was 'a travesty of the English conception of the game', while manager Cullis dismissed the refereeing with one word – 'ridiculous'. Broadbent had made it 1–1 for Wolves just before half-time, when he stabbed the ball home after Eddie Clamp's cross had been headed on by Jimmy Murray. As well as the refereeing, the bumpy bone-dry pitch was not to Wolves' liking, Morgan writing 'Only Broadbent, the ball player, was near to being at home'.

As the season drew to a close, the floodlit friendlies were still a Molineux feature. Valencia were beaten 3–0, to avenge the defeat in Spain, and Borussia Dortmund lost 4–3. Broadbent scored after only two minutes against the Germans and then had a goalbound shot saved by the 'keeper Kwiatkowski. The Valencia game saw inside-right Bobby Thomson given his chance and he scored twice. Three days later he made his League debut against Newcastle and scored in a 2–0 win. Three goals in two games, yet Thomson never played another competitive game for the first team and was three years later transferred to Villa, whom he served with some distinction before joining Birmingham. Not that another serious contender for an inside-forward place would be a worry to Broadbent. His career was about to reach its peak.

Before Broadbent helped Wolves embark on the greatest seasons in the club's history, there was a trip to familiar territory – South Africa, where Broadbent had first really got to know his new teammates after his dramatic transfer from Brentford. On that trip in 1951 he had been the raw teenager, now he was reaching his football prime.

In South Africa Broadbent would help Wolves win every match, just as they had done six years earlier. They played only eight games this time, compared with 12 on the previous tour, and Broadbent figured in all of them, seven at inside-left and one on the wing. He also scored nine goals as if to emphasise his new-found scoring prowess. Goalkeeper Malcolm Finlayson recalls that manager Stan Cullis had made it clear to the players that this trip was not a holiday, it was serious business. 'I'm convinced that on this tour we laid the foundations for our success in the next three seasons,' says Finlayson.

Not only did Wolves return with added confidence, they also returned with a 17-year-old forward named Cliff Durandt. He hit two goals for the Southern Transvaal President's XI when they were beaten 7–3 by Wolves. At Molineux, Durandt would join another South African teenager Des Horne. In time, both would be Broadbent's wing partners. Broadbent hit three goals in a 5–1 win over Natal and another three in the toughest game of the tour against the South Africa national side, who were defeated 4–1 in Johannesburg.

Full-back Eddie Stuart skippered the team for most of the tour, as Billy Wright was with England and, as a South African, was feted in his home land. 'We were made very welcome and I was very honoured to be captaining Wolves in my own country,' Stuart told me. 'They even let me have a huge American car, and I always remember driving it through Jo-burg and stopping at some traffic lights and opposite us were Stan Cullis and Joe Gardiner, our trainer, in an old jalopy. When Stan saw it was me in this magnificent car, his face was a picture.' On a more serious note, Stuart confirms the Finlayson view, 'It was probably the most successful tour in the history of the club. We won all our games and played well. Players like Peter and Norman came into their own and it set us up for the success which followed.'

Before they set out for South Africa – the trip took 25 hours compared with 36 in 1951 – Wolves had said farewell to three retiring stalwarts, goalkeeper Bert Williams, defender Bill Shorthouse and centre-forward Roy Swinbourne, who were honoured with a special tribute dinner. Their departure marked another subtle increase in responsibility for Broadbent. He was now one of the old heads, no longer the new kid on the block.

However, time was running out for Harry Hooper. Things happened on that tour in far-off South Africa that caused manager Stan Cullis to discard the talented winger, who had won an England B cap against Scotland B in February 1957. Hooper's fall from grace in the eyes of the boss would open the door for Broadbent's old pal Norman Deeley. The little man grabbed his chance gloriously over the next three seasons by collecting two First Division Championship medals, an FA Cup-winners' medal and England caps. All that might have been Hooper's, but at the end of November 1957 he was transferred to Birmingham City. He later played for Sunderland but never gained the honours that would surely have been his at Molineux.

Soon after returning home, Broadbent received a letter from club secretary Jack Howley. It said 'The board wishes to congratulate and thank you for your part in the great success of the tour. The directors are particularly pleased with the splendid impression left behind in South Africa by your exemplary conduct both on and off the field throughout the whole tour.'

Championship Double

After they had lost their opening game of the 1957–58 season 1–0 to Everton at Goodison Park, Wolves found their goal touch in their opening home game, hammering Bolton 6–1. Broadbent was still partnering Jimmy Mullen on the left-wing and Phil Morgan reckoned in his match report that these two had an impressive night, with only a superb display from Ron Flowers edging them out for star of the game. Morgan said Mullen had given burly Bolton full-back Roy Hartle the runaround while Broadbent was the master of the neat touch, even if there were occasions when he was too quick for his colleagues. Broadbent was a scorer with a volleyed goal from a Deeley centre and the little winger himself struck twice.

After those first two games of the 1957–58 season Broadbent was switched from inside-left to inside-right to partner Deeley, and a great partnership began to develop. Deeley did not have the exceptional pace of Hooper, nor the rocket shot of Johnny Hancocks, but he had other qualities – neat control and that ability, which is given not taught, to turn up in the right place at the right time to score goals. Manager Cullis had long felt that Broadbent could have made an international winger had circumstances allowed him to play Broadbent there on a regular basis. Now, however, he encouraged Deeley to be a Wolverhampton wanderer and Broadbent to move out wide on to the right.

Broadbent and Deeley became a highly-effective partnership. One fan Ted Tudge, who now lives in Wordsley, near Stourbridge, told me he thought they had a telepathy. 'They always seemed to know what the other had in mind, always knew where each other was and knew when to switch positions. It was uncanny, really.'

It was a happy accident that the wing pair clicked so well, as Deeley explained 'We did not really work at it. It was just one of those things. We knew when to leave the ball to the other, when to move inside, when to swop places. We just worked well together. It was not something you could practise in training. It was just instinct.'

It was not only on the field that Broadbent and Deeley got on together, as Bobby Mason confirmed 'Peter had a dry sense of humour, especially with his good friend Norman. He used to dangle the bait and Norman would bite. Things would go on from there and we'd have a good laugh, and it usually ended with Peter saying "Don't look at me, Norman, nothing to do with me." Yet Peter had started it all. Once when we were staying at the Norbreck Hotel in Blackpool, the barman said the local snooker champion was in and did anybody want to challenge him. Well, Norman was a very good snooker player and said he would play this chap. Even then Peter had to get Norman going and asked how many blacks start this player would give him. Of course, that annoyed Norman, who said "I don't need a start, I'll play him off scratch." It was just Peter winding him up as usual. As it turned out, Norman beat the local champ two frames to one and won it on the final black. He was a good snooker player all right, Norman.'

Other off-field activities for the right-wing pair included enjoying a day's racing, though it was not something that met with the approval of manager Cullis. 'One day, when training finished early, we went to Warwick Races,' Deeley recalled, 'and someone told Stan they had seen us there. He had Peter in first and let him know he'd been seen at the races and thought it was not the best way to spend his spare time. Then he had me in and said "If we were playing a big match and Wolverhampton Races was on in the afternoon, would you go?" and I said "Yes, if I thought I could win five hundred pounds." That's when he told me to get out of his office – I think he just wanted to make his point about gambling and also let us know that whatever we did it would always get back to him. Stan was not that bad, really. As long as you did it on the pitch – that's what counted with him.'

Despite the goal rush against Bolton in that first home match of 1957–58, manager Cullis took the decisive step to switch inside-forwards Broadbent and Colin Booth. The theory was that Broadbent could play out on the right closer to Deeley, with whom he could interchange while still being able to swing long-raking passes out to left-winger Mullen who, unlike Deeley, was not encouraged to stray from the touchline. The theory quickly worked in practice as, three days after the Bolton game, Wolves beat Sunderland 5–1 under the Molineux lights.

The new right-wing survived only three games together and after the almost traditional defeat at Luton, Mason was given his chance in preference to Booth. As Mason was seen as principally an inside-right at that stage, Broadbent went back to the number-10 shirt. It was a brief interlude as Mason was injured after just a couple of appearances, which brought a recall for Dennis Wilshaw despite the former England man being a transfer target of Birmingham and Stoke. So Deeley and Broadbent were reunited on the right, and the combination would remain settled for the rest of the season and would blossom. Their reunion came in time for the visit of champions Manchester United on Saturday 28 September 1957.

Seeking a third consecutive title, Matt Busby's team had begun the season with three successive wins but had slipped a little so that both United and Wolves came to Molineux with a record of 13 points from nine games. The unlikely leaders of the First Division at that stage were newly-promoted Nottingham Forest. The showdown in Wolverhampton was spoiled a little, as the flu epidemic raging through Britain had robbed United of Roger Byrne, Eddie Colman, Liam Whelan and Dennis Viollet, while Wolves had Eddie Stuart on the sick list as well as manager Cullis. Yet such was United's strength that they could still field seven internationals compared with Wolves' four. The outcome was a 3–1 win for Wolves in front of 48,825 fans, with Broadbent and Deeley among those who flourished in a fine all-round team display. The home goals came in a seven-minute second-half spell from Deeley (two) and Wilshaw, John Doherty grabbing a last-minute consolation for United.

Despite United's sickness problems, this was a huge win for Wolves. It showed that in Deeley, Gerry Harris, Eddie Clamp and Jimmy Murray, Wolves had also produced young players to rival those of the much-vaunted Busby Babes. Bobby Mason would also emerge at inside-left as the season unfolded, while Broadbent would go from strength to strength. Evidence that he was now in his pomp came four days after the United match. Tottenham were the visitors as Wolves switched on their brand new set of bigger and better floodlights.

Not only did the Molineux lights shine more brightly, so did Broadbent. Against United he had been a match for England left-half Duncan Edwards and against Tottenham he had the better of the midfield action, despite the presence of Northern Ireland skipper Danny Blanchflower and diminutive box of tricks Tommy Harmer. In a 1990 interview for the Wolves programme, Broadbent had no hesitation in naming this game as his best for Wolves. Other fans have told me they remembered vividly how left-half Jim Iley, a more than useful player, and Blanchflower had failed in turn to curb Broadbent that night. Jimmy Murray swopped passes with Deeley to give Wolves an early lead and Ron Flowers made it two with a 30-yard shot, before Broadbent capped his special night with two second-half goals. The first saw him stride through the Spurs defence after Murray had flicked on a pass out of defence. His second was a header, or, as Phil Morgan's *Express & Star* match report put it, 'Broadbent studiously took a splendid Mullen cross on his forehead and directed the ball into the net in the wide space to Reynolds's right.' While it was a magical night for Broadbent it was also a significant one for Wolves in their quest to knock Manchester United off their title perch – the two points put them top of the table for the first time that season and they would hardly look back.

Evidence of Wolves' growing confidence came a couple of games later when they strolled to a 5–1 win over Birmingham City at St Andrew's. Phil Morgan wrote that Wolves' display was their best of the season so far, and a key ingredient was 'the crafty positioning and use of the ball by Broadbent'. This match was an ideal preparation for yet another high-profile floodlit friendly, Wolves' biggest test since Dynamo's visit. This time Real Madrid were the visitors, having been winners of the first two European Cups – a competition whose very existence owed much to the early deeds of Wolves against foreign opposition.

The European champions came to Molineux parading an array of Spanish internationals, as well as the sublimely skilful Frenchman Raymond Kopa. Broadbent was enjoying a purple patch and nearly always rose to these special occasions as, indeed, did all the Wolves men. It was a good job they did too, as they were without their inspirational leader Billy Wright, who was with the England squad preparing for the game against Wales and could only monitor the match from their training base in Porthcawl. As ever, George Showell proved a capable stand-in for Wright, while Eddie Stuart set a captain's example by curbing the menace of Francesco Gento on the left-wing. There were echoes of the Honved game, though not quite so dramatic. Wolves had to come from behind after trailing at half-time just as they had against the Hungarians, and the outcome was the same – a 3–2 win for Stan Cullis's side. Marsal had opened the score for Real on 14 minutes and it was Broadbent who brought Wolves level seven minutes after half-time, with a route-one goal. Goalkeeper Malcolm Finlayson collected the ball and noticed the Real defence had pushed upfield. His long kick was nodded on by Jimmy Murray and Broadbent coolly lobbed the ball over the Real 'keeper. Murray's header to Norman Deeley's corner gave Wolves the lead eight minutes later, only for Marsal to grab his second goal on 71 minutes. With nine minutes left, Dennis Wilshaw hooked a Jimmy Mullen pass into the net and Wolves had claimed another famous scalp. The teams on Thursday 17 October 1957 were:

Wolves: Finlayson; Stuart, Harris; Clamp, Showell, Flowers; Deeley, Broadbent, Murray, Wilshaw, Mullen. Goals: Broadbent (52), Murray (60), Wilshaw (80).

Real Madrid: Dominguez; Atienza (Marquiotos), Lesmes; Santisteban, Santamaria, Zarraga (Ruiz); Joseito, Kopa, Di Stefano, Marsal, Gento (Rial). Goals: Marsal (14, 71).

Referee: M. Guigue (France). Attendance: 55,169.

So to Spartak, Honved and Dynamo was added the name of the European champions. Four historic floodlit wins and Broadbent had figured in each one, a distinction he shared only with Stuart and Wilshaw. It's difficult to imagine in the 21st century the significance of these games, which were classed as friendlies but in their day were as important as any international. Yet there was no suggestion of the players gathering at a hotel before this special match. Malcolm Finlayson said the players had to make their own way to Molineux as usual, with Cullis's parting shot at the end of the previous day's light training session lingering in their minds – 'Catch the bus early won't you.' As rallying calls before epic contests go, it hardly ranks with 'Cry God for Harry, England and St George'.

After the heady atmosphere of the Real Madrid game, it was back to League fare for Broadbent and Co as they pressed on at the top of the First Division. Soon afterwards early pacesetters Nottingham Forest were seen off 2–0 at Molineux, despite the fact several of the side, Broadbent included, were suffering with heavy colds – a fact manager Cullis did not reveal until after the match.

As in their 1953–54 title-winning season, the key to success in 1957–58 was an 18-game unbeaten run, but it nearly came to an end in the 13th of the sequence when old rivals Albion came to Molineux. The Baggies, who had lost only one of their 17 League games so far that season, were breathing down Wolves' neck on 24 points, just two behind their neighbours. A pulsating game before 55,418 spectators saw Albion give Wolves a mighty scare, as they took the lead through Derek Kevan nine minutes into the second half. A foul by Barlow five minutes from time enabled Eddie Clamp to level for Wolves from the penalty spot. It was a close call and, for once, the clubs' traditional styles were reversed as Albion were the more direct. Once again Broadbent caught the eye as Phil Morgan confirmed 'In their respective styles I reckoned Broadbent and Kevan the best forwards in the game although, as a line, Albion often had the more eager look than the Wolves, whose partiality for dalliance gave the quick-tackling Albion defenders just the moments of grace they needed.'

Two days after the Albion game, Broadbent could add another country to the growing list of those he had visited since joining Wolverhampton Wanderers. Wolves took a party of 14 players to Belgium to play RSC Anderlecht and were beaten 2–0 on Wednesday 20 November 1957, before a sell-out 40,000 crowd. It was not a game for Broadbent to remember, but it did see him team up once more with Harry Hooper. The out-of-favour ex-Hammer, who had asked for a transfer a couple of weeks earlier, was named on the left-wing with Bobby Thomson at inside-left. After half an hour, Hooper, not looking at home on the left, swopped places with right-winger Norman Deeley. Thomson also failed to impress and at half-time Colin Booth was substituted for him. Nine days later Hooper was transferred to Birmingham City for a fee reported at £19,000, but it was not until June 1959 that Thomson finally gave up trying to break into the Wolves first team and moved to Aston Villa.

Another departure quickly followed that of Hooper. Unlike Hooper, schoolteacher Dennis Wilshaw had enjoyed a lengthy Molineux career and created football history by becoming, in 1955, the only man to score four goals in an England v Scotland game. Wilshaw had great respect for Stan Cullis but always suspected the manager was never completely happy that he remained a part-time player throughout his career. A move to Stoke City suited Wilshaw fine, as the Potteries were where his scholastic duties lay. His departure meant Broadbent was the lone survivor of the forward line, who had played in the epics against Spartak and Honved – Leslie Smith having joined Villa in February 1956.

Broadbent helped Wolves to a remarkable comeback victory on their return from Belgium. Trailing 3–1 with 13 minutes to play against Manchester City at Maine Road, Wolves rattled in three late goals to win 4–3. Broadbent hit the winner, but how he got it was not clear to the men in the press box at the time. It was such a misty day that only afterwards were reporters able to confirm that Broadbent had dived, almost horizontally, to head home a Jimmy Mullen centre from the left.

The title pursuit would soon take a back seat once more as Wolves flew out to Spain for the return game with Real Madrid, who had not lost at home to foreign opposition for five years. Wolves came close to ending that record and had the better of things in a 2–2 draw. They had registered a 5–4 aggregate against the European champions and in a team of gold and black stars, on a rainy night in the Spanish capital, none shone more brightly than Broadbent as Phil Morgan recorded 'There were times when Broadbent, despite the surface and the rain, gave examples of ball mastery which were better even than that shown by the accepted artists, Real Madrid, themselves.'

Wolves took the lead on the half-hour, with a bullet-like header by Bobby Mason to a Jimmy Mullen centre. Real's equaliser on 54 minutes came from Mateo, who looked a clear four yards offside. Rial struck 20 minutes from time to turn home a Kopa centre but Wolves were not to be denied, the veteran Mullen scoring nine minutes from the end – his centre eluding the goalkeeper and going in with the help of a defender's foot. Manager Cullis did not declare his men were 'champions of the world' as he had done in the heady atmosphere after the Honved game, but did say 'I would like to strike a medal for all of them'. He may not have been so charitable the following morning when he found out the players had gone out on the town to celebrate after the match. The teams on 11 December 1957 were:

Real Madrid: Alonzo; Becarril, Atienza; Santisteban, Santamaria, Zarraga; Kopa, Marsal, Di Stefano, Rial, Gento (Mateo 14).

Wolves: Finlayson; Stuart, Harris; Clamp (Showell 51), Wright, Flowers; Deeley, Broadbent, Murray, Mason, Mullen.

Referee: M. Hartzoc (France). Attendance: 60,000.

Mason confirmed it was a very special night in Madrid 'Peter played well but we all played well that night. I was lucky enough to get a good goal and we never felt as though we would lose. We thought we could win it. The particular memory I have about that match was at the end, when there was no cheering and after the floodlights had gone out, you could see lots of candles in the crowd. It was a remarkable sight. I think people had lit them before going to church – perhaps they went to pray for Real Madrid!

'Before that game Stan Cullis did not say much to us. He rarely did before kick-off. He always knew we were well prepared and that we knew what we had to do. He could rant and rave at half-time if he felt he needed to but if you'd played well he would not make a big thing about it. He'd come up to you and whisper "Well played". That was his way. Peter was usually quiet before a game. He'd not say much, perhaps look up at the ceiling, now and then at the rest of us, just thinking about the game. Nobody had much to say in the dressing room before a game – apart from Eddie Clamp – then, before we went out, we'd all wish each other luck.'

Wolves' long unbeaten League run came to an end on Boxing Day 1957 when they lost to Spurs at White Hart Lane, home centre-forward Bobby Smith scoring the game's only goal after eight minutes. However, Wolves, were soon back on track in the New Year and, having established themselves as favourites for the First Division title, started to think in terms of the double. After a 1–0 win at Lincoln in the third round, Wolves met Portsmouth at Molineux in the fourth. It may have been nearly 19 years since Wolves' shock 4–1 Cup Final defeat by Pompey, but it still rankled with older Wolves fans. So this first Cup meeting since that dismal Wembley day brought a measure of satisfaction in that some revenge was extracted and by one goal more – Wolves won 5–1, with Broadbent on target twice, after half an hour and then two minutes into the second half, to crown another top-class display. Phil Morgan yet again heaped praise upon him in the *Express & Star*, 'Star of the piece, without a shadow of doubt, was Broadbent, capping an outstanding performance of ball control and body swerve with two capital goals and a near thing, which might have made it three. His second goal was one of the best of his career, a right-footed volley to a Deeley corner.'

A week later, Wolves again won 5–1 at Molineux, this time against Leicester City in the League, with Broadbent again among the scorers. That set the scene for a meeting with champions Manchester United at Old Trafford on Saturday 8 February 1958. Matt Busby's team had revived their season to some effect and were by then six points behind leaders Wolves. The match could be decisive but first United had to complete their European Cup quarter-final tie with Red Star Belgrade. A 3–3 draw saw them into the semi-final but a day later English football – indeed, world football – was numb with shock, after the plane bringing them home crashed on the snowy runway of Munich airport. Wonderful players like Roger Byrne, Eddie Colman, Mark Jones, David Pegg, Tommy Taylor and Liam Whelan as well as reserve Geoff Bent died in the crash on 6 February. The great Duncan Edwards would die a few days later. The crash also took the lives of many others, including several leading press men, one of whom was former England goalkeeper Frank Swift.

Broadbent and the other Wolves players were in Blackpool when they learned of the awful events in Germany. They had gone to the seaside resort for a week's training and relaxation to build up to the big match at Old Trafford. The day of the disaster should have been a happy one – Billy Wright's 34th birthday – but he, Broadbent and the rest were devastated as news filtered through. Instead of stepping out into an Old Trafford packed to the seams for the biggest match of the League season, the Wolves squad made a sad trip to

Molineux for a minute's silence, a gesture repeated at football grounds throughout the land that day. Wolves were playing Leeds in the Central League and the first-team players, in civvies, joined the reserves to line up on the touchline facing the Waterloo Road stand for the act of remembrance. The eerie silence was broken only by the odd click of a press photographer's camera shutter and the whirr of a cine camera in the hands of another newsman.

A week later Wolves again turned their attention to the Cup, meeting Third Division North giantkillers Darlington, who had beaten Chelsea in a fourth-round replay to reach the fifth round for the first time in their history. The dream of another upset lasted for 32 minutes before Wolves broke the deadlock and went on to win 6–1. Broadbent scored twice and struck after only three minutes when Wolves beat Leeds 3–2 in the League four days later. Broadbent had thus scored in four successive matches for a second season running and was obviously in a purple patch, as Phil Morgan confirmed in his description of Wolves' third goal. 'Broadbent crowned his impeccable personal performance with the sweetest of swerves and an in-your-path pass, which Deeley drove well wide of Wood.' After the next match, a 5–1 home win over Birmingham, with all Wolves' scoring done before half-time, Morgan was purring again. 'The mastermind of the attack was Broadbent once again – he was as cheeky as he was brilliant.' Jimmy Murray hit a hat-trick for a second successive Saturday and Wolves might easily have doubled their score, had it not been for the form of Blues' ex-England goalkeeper Gil Merrick.

A telling sideline on those successive Saturday wins is provided by the gates. The FA Cup still had a certain magic and was a far bigger attraction than League fare. That is why there was a gate of 55,778 to see lowly Darlington, while 36,941 turned up for the derby clash with Birmingham.

Broadbent was now confident enough to mix in the odd bit of showboating with his midfield grafting, but was wise enough not to overdo it and risk a rollicking from Stan Cullis. Any talk of the double would have been banished by the boss, but, with their impressive lead in the League, Broadbent and his colleagues must have had it at the back of their minds. Alas, the dream of a Wembley appearance at the end of the season was shattered in the Burnden

Park mud when they were beaten 2–1 by Bolton in the sixth round of the Cup. It was clearly not Wolves' day. Twice they almost scored and each time Bolton punished them with a goal.

First Broadbent went up with goalkeeper Eddie Hopkinson and the ball ran loose to Jimmy Mullen, whose shot was cleared off the line by Brian Edwards. Immediately, Bolton took the lead through Dennis Stevens, only for Bobby Mason to level within two minutes. In the second half, Norman Deeley drove in a hard low shot after Hopkinson had punched the ball out only to see the ball rebound from the foot of a post. Again Bolton hit back to score and the muddy pitch played its part. Malcolm Finlayson, with bravery typical of the Wolves 'keeper, dived to take the ball at the feet of Bolton's marauding centre-forward Nat Lofthouse, only to slide outside his penalty area still holding the ball. From the free-kick, so unluckily conceded, Ray Parry turned the ball in for the winner.

Broadbent was not at his best but he had his moments. He glided past hefty full-back Tommy Banks on the left, took the ball almost to the byeline before laying on a perfect cross for Jimmy Mullen, who snatched at the chance and scooped the ball high over the bar. When Broadbent dropped another perfect centre into the goalmouth, Bolton's other sizeable full-back, Roy Hartle, headed off the line first a Mullen header and then Mason's follow-up shot. It was that sort of day, typified by a late hectic scramble in the home goalmouth when Mullen, Murray, Deeley and Broadbent all failed to get the ball past flailing arms and legs as Hopkinson lay helpless on the ground.

Wolves were thus left with the lone target of trying to clinch a second First Division title, and this they did in style. Preston were now leading the chasing pack but were six points behind Wolves while Albion were third, four points further back. The lead was also extended in a midweek clash with Chelsea at Stamford Bridge, which saw Broadbent again showing his defensive qualities in an emergency. After Norman Deeley's goal had been cancelled out by Jimmy Greaves, full-back George Showell, preferred to a briefly out-of-form Gerry Harris, suffered concussion after being hit in the face by a shot from John Mortimore. To compensate, Wolves moved Eddie Clamp to full-back and

Broadbent dropped back to the half-back line, with Showell going first to the right-wing and later to centre-forward where, dramatically, he volleyed Wolves' winner seven minutes from time. As he had done a few years earlier at Portsmouth, Broadbent took to his role in style. Phil Morgan wrote 'Clamp played as if born to be a back and Broadbent showed himself a more than useful middle line operator.'

Showell recalled 'I just did not know where I was after getting struck by that shot in the face. I could see two of everything. When I scored the winner, the ball came across and I could see two of that as well – I swung my leg and luckily I hit the right one!'

Soon came the second meeting of the season with Black Country rivals Albion. When the sides met earlier in the season Albion were breathing down Wolves' neck. Now they were still third in the table but eight points behind Stan Cullis's runaway leaders. Such was the huge interest in the game that it made history by being the first Football League game to be all-ticket, some 56,000 cramming into The Hawthorns. It proved no contest, as Wolves won 3–0 thanks to goals from Bobby Mason and Jimmy Murray (two). Mason had improved with every game and this was probably his best so far. Bill Slater, in the form that would lead England to name him successor to the ill-fated Duncan Edwards, was the star of the show, but the whole team rose to the big Hawthorns occasion with, according to Phil Morgan, 'some of the most compelling football I have ever seen them produce'.

When the match was virtually over, Wolves played 'keep ball' just outside the Albion penalty area, with Broadbent and the irrepressible Eddie Clamp the ringleaders. It might have been seen as rubbing their noses in it, but perhaps Wolves could be excused for doing so. After all, it was Albion!

So Wolves stormed on with an Easter Monday victory at Arsenal, prompting Phil Morgan to declare that the brightest sparks in Wolves' attack were 'the brilliant Broadbent and the dazzling Deeley'. Such is football, that Arsenal came to Molineux the next day and won 2–1. That could not make a serious impact on Wolves' Championship bid, but it did have a significant effect on their chances of setting a new First Division points record, 66 having been posted by Arsenal in 1931.

Wolves clinched the title with two games to spare, fittingly at Molineux and, equally fitting, against the side who were their nearest challengers – Preston. There was a similarity to Wolves' previous title win. Just as the crunch match with Albion in 1954 had been robbed of four key players through international calls, so it was this time. The game still had to go ahead, even though the Scotland-England game the same day had claimed Wolves' Billy Wright and Bill Slater, and Preston's Tom Finney and Tommy Docherty. While England were hammering the Scots 4–0, Wolves won a tense encounter with North End 2–0 and were champions again. It was not the best of games but Broadbent had the satisfaction of having a hand in both goals. His pass in the 38th minute reached Norman Deeley, despite a defender's attempt to intercept, and the little winger fired the ball home. The second goal did not arrive until two minutes from the end. This time Broadbent's chip into the penalty area caused panic and Gordon Milne, Docherty's deputy, turned the ball into his own net as he tried to scoop it to safety.

After the final whistle, Wolves supporters, who formed the vast majority of a 46,001 crowd, swarmed on to the pitch. The players duly appeared in the directors' box and skipper Eddie Stuart thanked the fans for their support, assuring them that though Billy Wright, the man for whom he was deputising, was up in Glasgow, he was with them in spirit and would no doubt be celebrating as they intended to do. Chairman Jim Baker told the happy throng 'We are proud of this team, for, from the point of view of teamwork and spirit, they are the best Wolves have ever had.'

Two days later, Wolves fulfilled the fixture cancelled through the awful happenings at Munich and visited Manchester United, whom they beat 4–0. Broadbent collected his 21st League and Cup goal of the campaign but in an unlikely way. Eddie Clamp, Wolves' regular spot-kick expert, was limping when United centre-half Ronnie Cope handled the ball in the penalty area and so Broadbent was called on to deputise as penalty-taker. Knowing the nature of Broadbent's game, most had expected a subtle approach to the task. Instead, he discarded all finesse, took a couple of paces back, turned and thumped the ball as hard as he could. It flew into the net before home goalkeeper David Gaskell could move. Before kick-off Wolves had received a gesture from United that was as gracious as it was unexpected. They made sure they left their dressing room first – teams did not walk out together in those days – and formed themselves into two lines between which Wolves could run out. As they did, the United players applauded them in a salute from the old champions to the new.

Wolves' four goals took their total for the season to 102, to which Broadbent had contributed 17 and his wing partner Deeley 23. Wolves managed one more goal in their final game but lost 2–1 to relegated Sheffield Wednesday at Hillsborough, missing the chance to equal Arsenal's record 66 points. Broadbent had taken a knock at Old Trafford and so Jackie Henderson, recently signed from Portsmouth, made his debut. Despite the defeat, Wolves had still won the title by a five-point margin. Writing in the *News of the World* annual, skipper Billy Wright said why he thought Wolves had won the Championship so impressively after finishing only sixth the season before, 'I think the real answer lies in the soccer maturity found by several players at one time. Norman Deeley settled to fill the troublesome right-wing position; Peter Broadbent had his best season since joining Wolves; Eddie Clamp became a force internationally as well as at club level, and the full-backs Stuart and Harris gave Wolves stability, where for years there had been a problem.'

Confirmation that Broadbent had reached his peak came in his inclusion in the England squad to take part in the World Cup Finals in Sweden that summer, along with his club's half-back line of Eddie Clamp, Billy Wright and Bill Slater. All of them would feature in the tournament.

The Wolves quartet returned from Sweden disappointed after England's exit at the group Play-off stage but would soon get down to training for the new season, determined to try to retain their Championship crown. Broadbent, along with Chelsea's Peter Brabrook, had made his England debut in the World Cup group Play-off against the USSR, and the right-wing pair got an early chance to renew acquaintances at Stamford Bridge on Saturday 30 August 1958.

However, the limelight was stolen in dramatic fashion by Jimmy Greaves, Broadbent's 18-year-old opposite number in the Chelsea side. The crew-cutted striker struck twice to wipe out Bobby Mason's early goal for Wolves and hit three more in the second half. The press had a field day, though it was England skipper Billy Wright who came in for most criticism as the champions were humbled 6–2 by five-goal wonder boy Greaves. It was a good week for London as, five days earlier, First Division newcomers West Ham had beaten Wolves 2–0 at Upton Park.

Broadbent's partnership with Norman Deeley had been a feature of the title-winning season and had been very much in evidence when Wolves got the 1958–59 campaign under way, with a 5–1 Molineux trouncing of Nottingham Forest in front of 52,636, spectators. Phil Morgan wrote that the pair were a constant menace. 'They popped up everywhere and were always in the game from the time they scored the first two goals. And it was their scheming that laid on the chances for Mason, in the right places at the right times, to get his first hat-trick in top-class football.'

After the Chelsea debacle it was Broadbent who helped get Wolves back in business. In an away win over Villa, Wolves were described as 'Broadbent inspired' and he received even higher praise when Villa lost 4–0 at Molineux a week later. He was said to have had 'another brilliant ball-playing night', making two goals for Henderson. This was clearly a man on top of his game and pulling the strings for his side.

While Broadbent was enjoying a fine season, his fellow Elvington man Jimmy Murray, whose 29 goals had done so much to bring the title back to Molineux, was going through an indifferent spell at centre-forward. Having failed to settle at Molineux, Jackie Henderson had been transferred to Arsenal and so Stan Cullis asked defender George Showell to wear the number-nine shirt. Though he scored a couple of goals, Showell was not the answer. This disruption could not have come at a worse time, as Wolves were about to play in the European Cup for the first time.

For the big game against West German champions Schalke 04 Stan Cullis turned to Alan Jackson, whose only previous first-team games had been on the left-wing. It was a tough task for Jackson to shine on such an important occasion and it was left to Broadbent to create a bit of history by becoming Wolves' first scorer in the European Cup when the West German side came to Molineux, for the first leg of their second-round clash. Jackson was among the Wolves men who went close after the Germans had taken a shock lead, but it was Broadbent who equalised early in the second half. To complete a good game for him personally, Broadbent's neatly-taken flick header put his side in front on 65 minutes. It was not a good night for Wolves, however, and the Germans equalised three minutes from time.

Broadbent had the boost, before the second leg, of being recalled to the England side to face Wales, but the news failed to inspire him as Wolves lost 2–1 in Gelsenkirchen and were out of Europe. Broadbent, for once, was not at his best. The difference between the sides was that the Germans made the most of their chances, despite creating fewer than Wolves. Koerdel and Siebert were first-half scorers and Wolves went close several times, with Jimmy Mullen and Bobby Mason unlucky to see shots hit the post. Young Jackson did his best and pulled back a goal for Wolves, but he looked the inexperienced player he was.

Wolves were then beaten by the same score at home to Bolton, with Phil Morgan in the *Express & Star* bemoaning the fact that the team had forgotten their forthright direct attacking policy and were employing a tip-tap technique that was getting them nowhere. This was the signal to recall Jimmy Murray to lead the attack, but when, after just three games back, he went down with a cold before the game at Nottingham Forest it led to an interesting diversion in the career of Peter Broadbent – he became a centre-forward.

For the game at the City Ground, on Saturday 20 December 1958, manager Cullis decided to recall striker Colin Booth and give the number-nine shirt to Broadbent. It paid off in the first minute, as Forest seemed determined to give Wolves a goal. Skipper Jack Burkitt tried to walk the ball out of his penalty area instead of clearing, Norman Deeley robbed him of the ball and when he pushed it into the middle, goalkeeper Chick Thomson and full-back Bill Whare collided. The ball ran loose to Broadbent who had a simple task to score. It was a farcical goal but an ideal start for the new centre-forward. Six minutes later a far better executed goal saw Broadbent neatly flick the ball sideways from left-winger Des Horne's centre and Mason was able to slot it home. Wolves went on to win 3–1 and the new-look attack then scored 12 goals in two games against Portsmouth.

In the Boxing Day match at Fratton Park, Broadbent scored the first, and only, League hat-trick of his career. He did so as Wolves revived from being 3–1 down to win 5–3 and take over at the top of the table. A day later, Broadbent failed to score but Wolves completed a double over Pompey by hammering them 7–0 at Molineux – Booth and Norman Deeley each collecting hat-tricks. The final six goals came in the last 29 minutes. It might seem that Broadbent had discovered a new role, but the report of the Fratton Park match in the *Birmingham Post* cast doubts on that. 'It seems unlikely that the Wolves will continue long with Broadbent in the centre-forward position, despite his success as a goal getter. He showed that he is much more at home in an inside berth, where his scoring powers will not be affected.'

Such was the closeness of the race for the title that Bolton, who went into the two-game holiday period as leaders by a point from Wolves, found themselves in fifth spot and three points adrift of the Molineux men after their two holiday matches. Everton had done to them what they did to Wolves three years earlier and beat Bolton both home and away. Wolves were suddenly three points clear of Albion, Arsenal, Manchester United and Bolton, who were all on 29 points, though Albion did have a game in hand.

Cullis stuck with the new look for three more games. The first saw Chelsea, struggling well down the table, gain a shock 2–1 win at Molineux; then Wolves beat lowly Barrow 4–2 in the FA Cup third round to be greeted by the inevitable *Sporting Star* headline 'Wolves wheel-Barrow out'. Finally they faced Bolton, their bogey team at the time, in the next round of the FA Cup and were beaten 2–1. That was enough! Jimmy Murray was recalled to lead the attack and Broadbent went back to being the mastermind.

Wolves fan Malcolm Cookson remembers the game at Barrow well. 'It was freezing. My dad went to a shop and bought me one of those Kangol caps to keep my head warm. The pitch was poor. They'd put sand on it so it was really rough. I thought Peter did well. He did not play like an old-fashioned centre-forward but he kept the line together.'

After the Cup exit, the return of Murray was not the only switch. Broadbent and Deeley became the left-wing pairing as Micky Lill, a scorer at Barrow, was given his chance at outside-right. The new-look forward line was an instant hit, as Blackburn and Leeds were beaten 5–0 and 6–2 respectively at Molineux and Newcastle 4–3 at St James' Park – 15 goals in three games. Broadbent almost collected a second hat-trick in the win over Leeds. Having scored Wolves' fourth and sixth goals he powered in a shot that was so hard, goalkeeper Ted Burgin could not get his hands to it, was hit full in the face and briefly knocked out. Broadbent's first goal was the stuff on which reputations are built. Phil Morgan's *Sporting Star* description was 'A long clearance down the wing by Wright went to Murray. He slipped the ball inside to Broadbent and with one of his twinkle-toe movements the inside-left brought the ball back, turned sharply and in the same movement let fly a fierce left-foot shot that passed just inside the post.'

By this time the Championship chase had developed into a three-horse race between Wolves, Manchester United and Arsenal, United blowing it wide open when they beat Wolves 2–1 at Old Trafford thanks to a last-minute Bobby Charlton goal. Broadbent missed a great chance to put the visitors ahead before Charlton's late strike but fired past the post when ideally placed. Every player has a bad spell during a season and this may have been Broadbent's, because a rearranged home game saw Wolves held 1–1 by Tottenham, who were among the relegation strugglers at the time. The wily Danny Blanchflower, made to chase shadows by Broadbent in the corresponding fixture the previous season, had clearly learned from the experience. This time he took charge of midfield and Broadbent had to play second fiddle. It was Spurs' own version of Broadbent, the tiny Tommy Harmer, who completed a frustrating night for the home fans by equalising in the last minute.

Annoying as the setback might have been, it set the scene perfectly for one of those games that sticks in the memory of all of us who saw it. Wolves and Arsenal met at Molineux on Saturday 7 March 1959 and going into the match both had 41 points, though leaders Wolves had a game in hand and a better goal average. United were a point behind these two. Title showdowns are supposed to be close encounters but this was not. Wolves and Broadbent rose to the occasion beyond all their fans' dreams and dispatched the Gunners 6–1.

Norman Deeley scored in the second minute and Broadbent made it two with a goal that emphasised the Wolves forwards' ability to interchange. It was centre-forward Jimmy Murray who turned up on the left-wing, beat two men and then centred for Broadbent to glide a header past Jim Standen in the Arsenal goal.

After Micky Lill had made it three before the half-hour there was some Broadbent showboating – back-heels, flicks, the sort of things that helped make his reputation. He was revelling in it and on one occasion stood still before calmly back-heeling the ball for Norman Deeley to run on to. Then he left full-back Len Wills flat-footed with an arrogant body swerve, before centring to Murray whose shot was held by Standen. Broadbent, Murray and Deeley were on target in the second half and Phil Morgan's *Express & Star* verdict was that the performance was almost flawless, only some late slackness giving Joe Haverty a consolation goal for Arsenal. Morgan added 'The crowd loved it, from the brilliant, sometimes almost insolent, soccer skill of Peter Broadbent, to the eager determination of Londoner Mick Lill to be in on this, the "kill" of his young soccer lifetime. But Norman Deeley, Jimmy Murray and Bobby Mason all played their part in this exhibition of high-power, entertaining, but utterly lethal forward play that simply tore the amazed Arsenal to shreds.'

What Morgan did not emphasise – perhaps he did not need to – was that the chance for Broadbent and the rest to sparkle was only made possible by the ability of the Wolves half-backs Eddie Clamp and Ron Flowers to dominate the opposition, backed by the leadership of veteran Billy Wright, the two uncompromising full-backs in Eddie Stuart and Gerry Harris, and an inspirational goalkeeper in Malcolm Finlayson.

It was virtually all plain sailing after that, the Arsenal victory being the first of five in a row for Wolves, including beating Albion 5–2. The season ended with a four-match winning sequence. When Luton were beaten 5–0 at Molineux, Broadbent scoring the first and last goals, the title was as good as won. Mathematically, United could still catch Wolves, but the swing in goal average would need to be huge. United themselves had no illusions and, with typical Matt Busby grace, sent Wolves a telegram of congratulations a few minutes after the game. A 3–0 home defeat of Leicester four days later saw Billy Wright presented with the Football League Championship trophy by Leicester chairman Len Shipman, a member of the League management committee. By then the crowd had invaded the pitch as they had done in 1954, and also a year earlier and prematurely after the Luton game. Then it was champagne time in the boardroom for Broadbent and the rest.

A 1–0 win at Everton on the final day of the season took Wolves' final goals total to 110, which admirably reflected their emphasis on attacking football. Jimmy Murray, his renaissance complete, was the scorer at Goodison. He had ended the season by scoring in seven successive matches to reach 21 goals and pip Broadbent by one for the distinction of being the club's top League scorer. Broadbent, with 22, was top marksman in all competitions, a remarkable total for a man so often dismissed as a goal maker rather than goal taker.

Wembley Delight

If Wolves thought they would have a low-key build-up to the new season, then they were rocked, as indeed was the football world, by the shock announcement just before the start of the 1959–60 season that Billy Wright was retiring.

When Wright had been on international duty his deputy George Showell had turned in some faultless displays and manager Stan Cullis clearly felt that, with Wright now 35, Showell could not be denied his first-team chance. Many of the team sheets printed for the traditional pre-season public practice match at Molineux had George Showell at number-five in the Colours, the first team, while Wright was in the Whites XI, the reserves.

When Wright made his dramatic decision, he was switched from the Whites to the Colours and so his memorable career came to an end at his beloved Molineux in a game of little consequence. Broadbent and the others formed a guard of honour to applaud him on to the field. He left at the end with a wave to the thousands who had turned up for what was usually a sparsely-attended occasion.

Wright's departure meant Broadbent was then the longest-serving first-team player at Molineux. Eddie Stuart had signed for the club a month before him but his first-team debut had come after Broadbent's. The South African was much respected and was greatly honoured when Stan Cullis asked him to take over the club captaincy.

Wolves got the season off to a good start when they won the Charity Shield – now known as the Community Shield – by beating Nottingham Forest 3–1 at Molineux. This traditional meeting of the previous season's champions and FA Cup winners had, up to then, been played during the season, but now it was decided to try it as an intro to the new campaign. The idea was voted a success as it attracted a larger than usual crowd – 32,329. Wolves' win brought them the shield outright at the fourth attempt. They had drawn 2–2 with Portsmouth in 1949, 4–4 with Albion in 1954 and lost 4–1 to Bolton in 1958. Forest led after 27 minutes through centre-forward Tommy Wilson, but Jimmy Murray equalised within a minute. Broadbent's goal gave Wolves the lead and Micky Lill, the discovery of the latter half of the 1958–59 season, sealed the success nine minutes from time.

It looked like a good omen for Broadbent and Wolves as they began their bid to win the title for a third successive season, a feat then previously achieved only by Huddersfield and Arsenal. The short trip to St Andrew's to face Birmingham City opened Wolves' 1959–60 campaign. Wolves made a habit of doing well there and Bobby Mason's goal after 27 minutes was enough to make it three wins in a row on Blues' turf. However, it was a miserable day for Broadbent. It started with him looking at his sharpest and one sweet through ball to Mason almost brought an early goal, but with only 14 minutes gone Broadbent was hurt in a collision with Blues' burly centre-half Trevor Smith – the man destined to get the first chance to succeed Billy Wright as England's centre-half. Broadbent was left limping but managed to continue out on the left-wing, until half-time. He did not emerge after the break and it was discovered after the game that he had sustained ligament damage.

Broadbent was missing, as was injured England skipper Johnny Haynes, when newly-promoted Fulham took on champions Wolves at Craven Cottage and won 3–1. They were the better team and Wolves, with Bill Slater playing in Broadbent's place, could have no complaints. The London press loved it. The Fulham chairman at the time was one of the last of the old music hall-style comedians, Tommy Trinder. He had a great time in the directors' box, joking with fellow directors and nearby fans as his beloved team humbled the mighty Wolves. Trinder's antics received plenty of coverage in the morning newspapers.

Weekly newspaper the *Wolverhampton Chronicle* sounded a warning to joker Trinder however, 'While Fulham chairman Tommy Trinder wore a mile-long smile and wisecracked with delighted spectators, Stan Cullis suffered in passionate exasperation. Only drastic changes, if not cheque-book action, will give the team the chance of honours this season… so said the painful pundits yesterday morning after the Fulham reverse.

'This is Tommy rot. One swallow of defeat never did make a soccer catastrophe. We say – wait for next Wednesday. Fulham come to Molineux. Will Trinder be wisecracking then? Or will the wolfish grin be on Cullis's face?'

How those words in the *Chronicle* would ring true! The writer ought to have added that there was likely to be one significant difference between Wolves at Craven Cottage and Wolves at Molineux – Peter Broadbent.

Broadbent returned to action in the 3–1 home win over Blackburn and four days later was ready to play his part in one of the biggest wins in Wolves' history. Poor Fulham did not know what hit them in the return encounter at Molineux on Wednesday 16 September 1959, as Cullis's men rattled in no fewer than nine goals without reply. Parodying the words of Congreve, Phil Morgan wrote in his *Express & Star* report 'Unfortunate Fulham, knocked for nine in the massacre of Molineux last night, now know football hath no fury like Wolves scorned.'

That lovely line from Morgan was, incidentally, mirrored a few years later when pop singer Billy Fury had to cancel his appearance at Wolverhampton Civic Hall. 'Hall hath no Fury' screamed the *Express & Star* headline, courtesy of sub-editor John Ogden who also doubled as the paper's music writer. The headline on Morgan's match report was not quite in the same class but 'An all-star show had Fulham nineplussed' was still a neat line.

As for the match itself, Morgan had the returning Broadbent, Norman Deeley and Ron Flowers as the star performers. Flowers scored one of the best goals Molineux has witnessed. Running diagonally across the field he suddenly drew back his left foot and powered in a 25-yard shot that left Fulham goalkeeper Tony Macedo groping. Deeley had the best scoring spree of his career, hitting four goals – one a penalty – while Broadbent was content to pull the strings. Phil Morgan made the point that the difference between this display and that at Craven Cottage was the return of Broadbent. In the first half he reported that Broadbent and Deeley bamboozled the Fulham defence time after time. 'Some of Broadbent's passes,' wrote Morgan, 'were academic pieces of accurate and intelligent ball placing as, for instance, when, with Lill possibly off-side, he pulled the ball back for Deeley to score his second goal.'

It may have been a Fulham side without Haynes but it still contained future World-Cup hero George Cohen, future England stalwart Alan Mullery, Scottish international winger Graham Leggat and Broadbent's old Brentford teammate Jimmy Hill. Yet Wolves just swept them aside. Another abiding memory of the game was the groan when Bobby Mason, in the final minutes, missed an easy chance that would have taken the goal tally into double figures. They were a demanding lot, Wolves fans.

While Wolves' League form was shaky – after the Fulham match they lost 3–1 at Blackpool and 5–1 at Tottenham – they made a successful start to their European Cup campaign with Broadbent in scoring mood in the competition as he had been the previous season. In the first leg of the first-round tie against East German champions Vorwaerts, he gave Wolves the lead in Berlin after the home goalkeeper had failed to hang on to the ball and he was on the spot in the second leg when the 'keeper erred again. The Germans came back to win the first leg 2–1, but Broadbent's goal at Molineux paved the way for a 2–0 second-leg win to see Wolves through on aggregate. Four goals for Broadbent in four European Cup games was not a bad record.

That visit to Berlin brought an example of how manager Cullis looked after his players. Bobby Mason explains 'We went through the Brandenburg Gate, past the soldiers with guns, it was all a bit scary. We eventually got to what looked like an army barracks – huts, no hot water, awful. Stan told the interpreter "There is no way my players are staying here" and he made the coach driver turn round, take us back into the West zone and he made sure we were put up in one of the best hotels. It's only when you go to another club that you realise just how good Wolves were. Stan ensured we had the best of everything.'

Broadbent returned from Germany with, among other things, a doll bought for young daughter Debbie and a framed picture of the Brandenburg Gate – a souvenir given to all players at the banquet after the match.

An injury in the Vorwaerts game at Molineux meant Broadbent missed the heavy defeat at Tottenham on 10 October 1959, but he was back in action a week later. While a new-look England team were failing to impress in a 1–1 draw in Cardiff, Broadbent was helping Wolves beat a Manchester United side (which included a young Johnny Giles) 3–2. Broadbent scored another goal of high quality, described by Phil Morgan in the *Express & Star* as a 'masterpiece of quick action.' Morgan wrote 'Taking a short pass from Norman Deeley he transferred the ball from his right foot to his left in one movement, before beating Irish international goalkeeper Harry Gregg with a fierce rising drive just inside the angle of bar and post.'

Fan Brian Daniels also remembered it, 'I reckon that was one of the best goals Peter ever scored. The ball just flew past Harry Gregg. I'd always admired Peter. I lived in Penn and as a young lad I used to see him meet Shirley because she used to work at Timothy White and Taylor's, the chemist, at the corner of Owen Road and Lea Road. I used to get so excited and run home and say "I've seen Peter Broadbent." One Sunday they read the banns out at St Chad's and we looked at one another – Peter Broadbent was getting married in our church. We were so excited. When he and Shirley got married I was head choirboy and in the choir who sang at their wedding. Their best man gave us a pound. That was a lot of money in those days, we did not often get that much.'

Next stop on the European Cup trail for Broadbent and Wolves was Belgrade, to meet Red Star. The city had an unhappy memory for Broadbent. He had played there with an RAF side and lost 7–0. This time the visit was far higher profile, as 45,000 packed into the Partizan Stadium. Norman Deeley headed Wolves in front on 29 minutes and Kostic equalised from a free-kick for Red Star, but Broadbent had little chance to flourish in a highly-physical game, with West German referee Willhelm Ommerborn being particularly severe on Wolves. Stan Cullis was an angry man afterwards, saying 'I do not think the European Cup management can be satisfied with the referee, whose handling of the game was deplorable.' Phil Morgan described the referee as 'almost a Red Star 12th man' and said he got tired of counting the free-kicks in the second half. The national press were also outspoken…

Roy Peskett (*Daily Mail*): 'Wolves were opposed by a strong team of marked striking power, a referee who gave them nothing and their rivals much and a most partisan crowd.'

Arnold Saunders (*Daily Telegraph*): 'The crowd did not like some of Wolves' tough football, yet most of it was fair enough by the standards of our League games.'

Desmond Hackett (*Daily Express*): 'Wolves were hacked, hurled down, rough-housed and yet never once lost their poise nor determination.'

Bill Holden (*Daily Mirror*): 'Wolves played not only against Red Star but also against the crowd – obviously partisan – and the referee who penalised many completely fair tackles.'

Peter Lorenzo (*Daily Herald*): 'Wolves scraped a draw in spite of the wickedest display of refereeing I have seen. This was booked to be a tough match. It was tough but it should have been fair. Instead, the referee's outrageous decisions paved the way for Red Star. In the second half matters got so bad that they had only to fall to the ground for a free-kick to be awarded.'

John Camkin (*News Chronicle*): 'Wolves stalked from the Partizan Stadium to a storm of angry boos. Peel, cartons and other flotsam fell on to the heads of England's champions. It was a miserable reward for a team denied victory only by a fantastic display from Herr Ommerborn. Never before have I seen a side so completely baffled by the whistle.'

Yugoslavia's main sports paper, *Sport*, said, 'The English played very grossly and incorrectly and have shattered the belief in traditional British fair play.' Other Yugoslav papers were similarly critical.

Broadbent joined in the debate in his weekly article in the *Birmingham Evening Mail*. He said the game was one of the toughest he had ever played in and added 'I claim, without any hesitation, that we were not at fault. We were pulled up 53 times for fouls. Yet all but a handful of tackles would have gone by without a murmur in an English League game... refereed by an English official. Red Star, like so many Continental sides, were past masters of the body-checking type of foul. The West German referee, like so many Continental officials, took no notice.' Broadbent conceded, however, that Red Star had held Wolves not just because of their tactics, 'They're a good team, a very good team'.

There were some lighter moments in Belgrade, one being when the Wolves players saw the match programme that had struggled with their names.

Showell, Murray, Clamp and Deeley appeared as 'Souel, Marej, Klepp and Dili', while Broadbent was 'Brodbent'.

It seemed fashionable to criticise Wolves around this time. Their defenders were certainly tough and dominated opposing attacks, but they were always fair. Manager Cullis liked his players to be uncompromising but he would never have condoned anything that went beyond the bounds of fairness. Eddie Stuart, one of Wolves' finest defenders, put it this way 'We were hard, I would not deny it, but we were clean. We played the ball – that was what Stan taught us. We certainly never did some of the things that go on today, such as kicking a player from behind. I was never sent off in my career and nobody else was during my time with Wolves.'

Norman Deeley shares Stuart's view, 'We wanted to win the ball but we never went out to deliberately kick anyone. We had strong defenders and forwards who just wanted to attack and score goals. That's what we aimed to do, and that's why people liked to watch us and why we just could not wait for the next match to come along. I just loved playing in that team.'

Another West German official Erik Asmussen did not seem to have a problem in the second leg with the way Wolves played in booking a quarter-final place, thanks to a 3–0 victory in front of 55,519 at Molineux. A Jimmy Murray centre, which goalkeeper Beara misjudged, gave Wolves a lead after seven minutes and then Bobby Mason struck twice in the last five minutes, the second from a perfectly-weighted Broadbent centre from the left-wing. Phil Morgan noted that Broadbent, Mason and Murray had tackled with the same tenacity as Eddie Clamp and Ron Flowers – and none of their efforts seemed to fall foul of the referee.

Despite reaching the last eight of the European Cup, Wolves were showing erratic form in the League, as evidenced when they met their bogey side Bolton home and away after Christmas. The Lancashire Wanderers won 2–1 at Burnden Park and 1–0 at Molineux a couple of days later. Wolves thus slipped to sixth in the table, four points behind leaders Tottenham. Wolves had enough chances in the second game with Bolton to have won easily and Broadbent was among those who failed to take advantage. The first game of the new year saw Wolves share eight goals with Arsenal at Highbury, a handball by Gerry Harris enabling Len Wills to equalise with a penalty for the Gunners in the final minute. These points that got away would cost Wolves dear in the final analysis as the season reached a thrilling climax. It had been a disappointing end to the first half of the season, but the second half would be incident-packed for Broadbent and his colleagues.

The FA Cup quest began with the long journey to the North East to face Newcastle. Wolves earned a 2–2 draw with half-backs Ron Flowers and Eddie Clamp the scorers, the latter from the penalty spot. Bill Slater had by then been recalled in the unfamiliar role of centre-half and he would adapt to it brilliantly. Broadbent also played a key role in the game after Ivor Allchurch had given the Geordies an early lead on the muddy St James' Park pitch. It was Broadbent who helped calm things down after a frenetic start and he began to use the pace of left-winger Des Horne, which worried the home defence.

Snow covered the Molineux pitch for the replay four days later, Wednesday 13 January 1960. The game had a similar pattern to the first meeting. Newcastle led on nine minutes through centre-forward Len White, only for his opposite number Jimmy Murray to level within a minute. Deeley made it 2–1 but George Eastham equalised for Newcastle just as he had done at St James' Park. Then Ron Flowers scored with a powerful long-range drive – just as he had done at St James' Park. Once again the wonderful Wolves half-back line were the key factor, and their dominance enabled Broadbent to pull the strings in the second half after Horne had made it 4–2 on 50 minutes.

Broadbent's goalscoring had taken a back seat for most of the season, but he regained his touch when Wolves beat Manchester City in the League 4–2 at Molineux and was unlucky not to collect a hat-trick. He gave Wolves the lead on 13 minutes when, with typical coolness, he ran on to a Murray through ball and rounded goalkeeper Bert Trautmann to drive a cross shot into the net. He scored a second to make it 4–0 when he turned home what Eddie Clamp had intended as a shot at goal. His chance of a third goal saw him one on one with Trautmann again, but he hesitated a fraction and the 'keeper dived to snatch the ball from his feet. Despite the win, Wolves, though third, were five points behind leaders Spurs with the Cup seeming their best bet for success.

Broadbent's rediscovered goal touch took Wolves further along the road to Wembley when they beat Second Division Charlton 2–1, on a Molineux pitch that was a sea of mud. The Londoners rocked Wolves when Johnny Summers gave them the lead midway through the first half, but Des Horne equalised on the stroke of half-time to set up a second-half onslaught. Standing between Wolves and a rout was goalkeeper Willie Duff who, often more by luck than judgment, kept out everything. It looked like another replay until Broadbent struck 10 minutes from time. Murray's neat footwork near the corner flag enabled Norman Deeley to centre from the right and Broadbent bravely bent low to head the ball under the falling body of Duff. Even then the ball stuck in the mud but clearly over the line. Broadbent looked certain to score again when he raced clear into the penalty area, only to be unceremoniously brought down by big centre-half Gordon Jago. Such had been Duff's good fortune that it was no surprise when he saved the resultant Eddie Clamp penalty.

In a season of highs and lows, Wolves were due one of the latter and it could not have been more dramatic or shattering to their morale. They knew they had a tough task against Barcelona in the quarter-final of the European Cup. Any side who had beaten Real Madrid to the Spanish League title by four points had to be good. But just how good, Wolves found out in the first leg at the Nou Camp. They were beaten 4–0, the score no exaggeration of the difference between the sides and the man who dominated the proceedings was a player much admired by Broadbent – Luis Suarez.

The game had seen Wolves start brightly, with Deeley and Mason going close and then Broadbent heading narrowly wide. It was a false omen, the Spanish side outplayed them. Villaverde and Kubala put them two up inside 15 minutes. Evaristo and Villaverde, again, completed the rout. The man pulling the strings for the home side was Suarez, the one Spaniard in their forward line. His four colleagues, incidentally, came from Paraguay, Hungary, Brazil and Uruguay. Phil Morgan's match report began 'After the battle of Belgrade it was the ballet of Barcelona' and that just about summed it up. He said Jimmy Murray, Ron Flowers and Broadbent were the only Wolves men who looked likely to measure up to the standard that success against Barcelona inevitably demanded. Stan Cullis held his hands up 'I can have no complaints. We were beaten by a better side.'

Among all Barcelona's foreign forward talent there was one name ominously missing – Sandor Kocsis, a star of the great Hungarian side of 1953. However, he was fit for the return at Molineux and helped himself to four goals as the Spanish champions won 5–2. It was a sensational end to Wolves' invincibility against foreign opposition under the Molineux lights, though, in fairness, at four goals down after the first leg Wolves had to take the game to the opposition and paid dearly for the risk that involved. Yet Kocsis did not open the scoring until 29 minutes and his goal was soon cancelled out by Jimmy Murray. That gave Wolves false hope and Kocsis struck three more times before Bobby Mason made it 4–2 on 78 minutes, only for Villaverde to reply within a minute. Broadbent, like the 55,535 sell-out crowd, could only concede afterwards that Wolves had been outclassed.

Leon Hickman was still cutting his journalistic teeth with a Wolverhampton news agency when the second leg took place. He recalled 'Before the game all the national press were in the Sir Tatton Sykes pub. I was just a kid listening to them and the general consensus was "If Broadbent plays at his best and everything happens right, they might just get back in." As it happened, Barcelona were a vastly better side, better drilled and with two or three magnificent players. After the match the Barcelona manager said there were only two Wolves players he thought might enhance his team – one was Broadbent, the other was Slater. And Peter would have enhanced their team and it would have suited him over there.'

Wolves could have been forgiven if such a body blow knocked the stuffing out of them. That it did not says great things about their resilience. They were out of Europe in devastating fashion, but before the Barcelona match at Molineux they had reached the last eight of the FA Cup with a 4–1 win over Luton – where the ever-reliable Bobby Mason had scored twice and where Broadbent had done his best to keep the attacks flowing. Immediately after the Barcelona debacle, Wolves went up to Old Trafford and beat Manchester United 2–0. Right-winger Gerry Mannion and centre-forward Barry Stobart made their League debuts and were nursed along expertly by Broadbent – Stobart crowning his big day with a headed goal as he out-jumped goalkeeper Harry Gregg.

Thus did Wolves warm up for their bid to secure a place in the semi-final. Standing in their way were Leicester City at Filbert Street. Broadbent got Wolves off to a dream start with a goal after 11 minutes. He ran on to an Eddie Clamp pass, took the ball wide of future England 'keeper Gordon Banks and scored with a cross shot. It would be good to report that this well-taken goal set the pattern for the game. Alas, it did not; it was a dour, hard, tough Cup tie, which drew comparisons to the Battle of Belgrade earlier in the season. Let's get the scoring over with first. A Clamp centre was headed on by Stobart and Leicester full-back Len Chalmers, not realising Banks had come off his line, headed the ball back into his own net. When Bill Slater could not cut out a lobbed pass from Ken Leek, Leicester pulled a goal back through Tommy McDonald, the man who had partnered Broadbent briefly on the right-wing in Moscow nearly five years earlier.

So the match ended 2–1 to Wolves. They were in the semi-final but once again Broadbent found some grim reading in the Sunday and Monday editions of the national papers. Denis Compton, England cricket legend and, as a footballer, a winner of League and Cup medals with Arsenal as well as wartime international caps, led the way in the *Sunday Express*: 'This was a grim, savage and relentless battle. Wolves won simply because they were tougher than Leicester. Certainly, neither side were particularly interested in playing football. Furthermore, on the rare occasions that the players endeavoured to show us how the game was meant to be played they were promptly brought to the ground with fierce and dangerous tackles.' Others had their say…

J.R. Chambers (*Sunday Dispatch*): 'Wolves reached the semi-finals with the most ruthless tackling I have seen this season. And Leicester were not a long way behind them in their methods to stop a man at any cost.'

Peter Lorenzo (*Daily Herald*): 'The soccer saying goes "You've got to get one bad game out of your system to win the Cup." By that token, Wolves will be Wembley winners for the next five years. This was spoiling soccer at its worst, with victory rightly going to the better spoilers.'

Broadbent aged five.

SCHOOL DAYS

1938

Young Broadbent with elder brother Jack and their maternal grandfather Matthew Wightman.

The Broadbent boys, goalkeeper Jack and budding inside-forward Peter.

A Football League player – Brentford's 17-year-old signing.

Welcome to Molineux... manager Stan Cullis greets the teenager signed from Brentford.

Leading a raid on the Liverpool goal during his early days with Wolves. In the background, extreme left, is future Liverpool boss Bob Paisley.

South African tourists. Lining up during the 1951 tour, Broadbent is in the centre of the front row with Billy Wright extreme left.

His first FA Cup goal… Broadbent beats Bert Trautmann to give Wolves the lead against Manchester City in the 1952 third-round tie at Maine Road.

Back in Elvington to play for the local cricket club in July 1953. Broadbent is second left in the back row with his brother Jack seated in front of him. At the end of the back row is their father Jack.

Champions at last! The 1953–54 side who completed the run in to the club's first-ever First Division title. Back row (left to right): Flowers, Shorthouse, Stuart, manager Stan Cullis, Williams, trainer Joe Gardiner, Mullen, Slater, Swinbourne. Front: Broadbent, Wright, Hancocks, Wilshaw.

The lighter shirts indicate Wolves have ditched old gold as their colour in this 1954–55 line up. Back row (left to right): Flowers, Shorthouse, Williams, Stuart, Clamp. Front: Hancocks, Broadbent, Wright, Swinbourne, Wilshaw, Mullen.

Action from the famous 4–0 win over Spartak in 1954 as Broadbent watches a Roy Swinbourne header go close.

In the net... Broadbent is foiled by Arsenal goalkeeper Jack Kelsey during the 1955 FA Cup tie at Molineux.

Opposite: His first car... Broadbent admires his Ford Prefect.

Getting fit the Wolves way. Nearest camera is Leslie Smith.

Broadbent often played well against Arsenal at Highbury, but this time he is thwarted by Gunners goalkeeper Jack Kelsey.

Wedding day in 1956 for the Broadbents at St Chad's, Wolverhampton.

Peter and wife Shirley.

Broadbent scored both goals in Wolves' first-ever European Cup match. Here he heads his second in the 2–2 first-leg clash with Shalke 04 at Molineux in November 1958.

So close to a Wembley goal… Broadbent is denied by Scotland goalkeeper Bill Brown during the 1959 international.

Taking a break from England training in 1959 with Manchester United pair Warren Bradley (left) and Bobby Charlton.

Rio next stop... England players ready to fly out for their 1959 trip to Brazil, Peru, Mexico and the US. Sporting a straw hat at the head of the steps is Bobby Charlton. In front of him are Ronnie Clayton, Billy Wright, Don Howe, Johnny Haynes, Wilf McGuinness, Jimmy Armfield and Broadbent, with Norman Deeley in front of him. A young Jimmy Greaves is also in the picture.

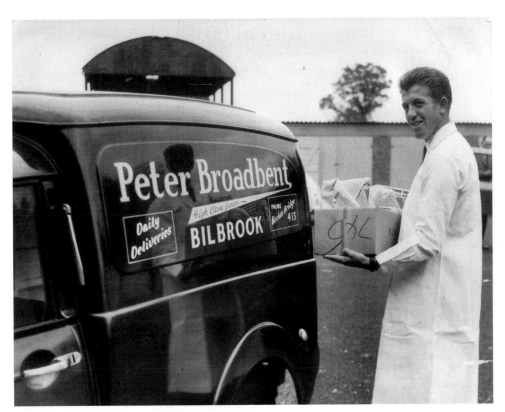

Delivering the goods…
Broadbent the Bilbrook
grocer.

Taking care of business…
Broadbent outside his
grocery shop in Bilbrook.

If he wasn't on the football field, a golf course was often where you would find Broadbent.

Always ready to party, Broadbent and wife Shirley.

A gathering of former Wolves heroes at the dinner to celebrate the club's centenary in 1977. Standing (left to right) are: Roy Swinbourne, Mike Bailey, Broadbent, Billy Wright, Stan Cullis, Ron Flowers, Jesse Pye, Bert Williams and Derek Parkin. In front are: Frank Munro and John Richards.

Smiling as Norman Deeley emphasises a point during conversations for the Breedon Books publication, *Talking With Wolves*. Malcolm Finlayson's fist is probably hiding a smile, too.

Ken Jones (*Daily Mirror*): 'For the whole 90 minutes it was crash-bang soccer with hardly one breath of imagination or intelligence to break the monotony of crash tackles and aimless passes.'

Ian Wooldridge (*News Chronicle*): 'The result was little more edifying than an all-in wrestling match between two gross women in a mud-bath which I once saw in a German night club.'

Desmond Hackett (*Daily Express*): 'If this is the best that can be wrung from a sixth-round FA Cup tie the Football Association, who are currently hot-gospelling for a higher and nobler form of soccer, would do the sport a service by scrapping this competition. Through the crude pattern of the game there ran a horror strip of bumping, thumping, tripping and mauling.'

Laurie Pignon (*Daily Sketch*) did not go along with the rest, however, saying, 'The game has been slated as a disgrace to British soccer but to me this was a Cup tie that was as British as fish and chips and Dunkirk. Men took their knocks, foul and fair, like men.' Gordon Banks tended to agree. In his autobiography, he said it was 'a classic quarter-final full of cut and thrust'.

Back in the League, Broadbent showed his goalscoring form again to help Wolves cruise into a 3–1 lead against Preston at Molineux, only for Wolves to slacken their pace and allow Preston to draw 3–3. Three days later, it was back to Filbert Street and though the game was a much better advert for football, and though Wolves led through a Jimmy Murray goal, Leicester gained revenge for their Cup defeat with a 2–1 win.

Now all eyes turned to the semi-final with Aston Villa. This was the closest Broadbent had been to what was then still the showpiece game of the English domestic season – the FA Cup Final. As ambitions went in those days, only being capped for your country came close. Broadbent had always nursed the dream of appearing at Wembley on that special day. On their way to winning the Second Division title, Villa were managed by Stan Cullis's old pal Joe Mercer. Both born in Ellesmere Port they could hardly have been more different, Mercer the jovial and Cullis the intense, but both highly-successful football men as players and managers. Friends they may have been but both were desperate for success. Cullis gambled and it paid off. He recalled Malcolm Finlayson for his first game in goal since being injured in Barcelona, he took a risk with Norman Deeley who was not fully fit and decided to play 19-year-old winger Gerry Mannion in the white-hot atmosphere of a semi-final, despite his not having made a Cup appearance before. Cullis's decisions paid handsome dividends at The Hawthorns, West Bromwich, as Finlayson made several brave saves at the feet of Villa forwards, Deeley hit the game's only goal on 32 minutes and Mannion showed no nerves whatsoever.

Broadbent kept Mannion well fed with the ball and gave him the sort of passes that could make best use of his speed, and Broadbent himself did as much as anybody to earn Wolves a date with Blackburn Rovers at Wembley. Phil Morgan reported that the goal had come from an attack down the right-wing, which created a chance for Jimmy Murray. When Villa 'keeper Nigel Sims could not hold his shot, Deeley was there to hit home the rebound. The *Express & Star* man wrote 'It was to the beginning of that goal-producing move one had to go to find the man who did more than anybody else to bring to Wolves' line a little less tension than marked the Villa attack. That man was Peter Broadbent. In this almost electric atmosphere, he showed the touch of class needed to calm things down when everybody, it seemed, was prepared to tear around regardless.' The teams at West Bromwich on Saturday 26 March 1960 were:

Wolves: Finlayson; Showell, Harris; Clamp, Slater, Flowers; Mannion, Mason, Murray, Broadbent, Deeley.

Villa: Sims; Lynn, Neal; Crowe, Dugdale, Saward; MacEwan, Thomson, Hitchens, Wylie, McParland.

Referee: J.S. Jobling (Morecambe). Attendance: 55,596 (receipts: £11,150).

Having put themselves in the Final, Wolves could look to the League and Broadbent was again in scintillating form when, four days after the semi-final, title rivals Burnley came to Molineux and were dismissed summarily 6–1. All the critics who had slammed Wolves' display at Leicester ought to have seen this match. They would have seen what made them so attractive to watch. True, half-backs Eddie Clamp and Ron Flowers dominated midfield but the whole team played a brand of attacking football that left Burnley shattered, as it had done to many other teams. Orchestrating it all was Broadbent, bringing the best out of young Mannion, who scored twice, and collecting the goal that made it 4–1 10 minutes before half-time. The *Express & Star* headline said it all, 'Wolves must go for the double now'.

Go for the double is what Wolves then did, as a 3–0 win at Leeds, courtesy of a Mannion hat-trick, and then a 5–0 defeat of West Ham at Molineux saw Wolves top of the table. They had 49 points, two ahead of Spurs, and four more than Burnley who had two games in hand. Against the Hammers Broadbent was once again in top form, just a couple of days after he had failed to sparkle on his recall to the England side for the game against Scotland. Broadbent was now a key figure in the double bid, so it was a body blow when he got injured in training two days before the trip to St James' Park to face Newcastle. Young South African Cliff Durandt did his best as deputy, but Broadbent was sorely missed. Len White's goal, the only one of the game, gave Newcastle victory and the title race was wide open once more. Spurs, Wolves and Burnley each had 49 points from 39, 38 and 37 games respectively.

Thankfully, Broadbent's injury was just a knock and with him back for the next match, the race suddenly swung back in Wolves' favour on Easter Monday. Two goals in the first 11 minutes from Jimmy Murray paved the way for a 3–1 home win over Nottingham Forest at Molineux. The third goal took Wolves' League total to 100, the third season in a row they had reached three figures. More importantly, Spurs were beaten 1–0 at home by Chelsea and Burnley lost 2–1 at Leicester. Alas, Broadbent had been injured again, as had two other vital members of the side – Ron Flowers and Norman Deeley – and the return clash with Forest was the next day. In the circumstances, without that international trio Wolves did well to draw 0–0 at the City Ground, Jim Iley sending a first-half penalty wide of Malcolm Finlayson's right-hand post.

Four days later, Saturday 23 April 1960, Wolves' bid for a third successive League title, not to mention the double, lay virtually in tatters when arch rivals Tottenham won 3–1 at Molineux. The injured threesome were able to return and Broadbent was soon in the action when he equalised Bobby Smith's early headed goal. The Wolves maestro powered in a shot to an Eddie Clamp centre and when Spurs 'keeper Bill Brown could not hold the ball, Broadbent was able to score from the rebound. Tottenham had Scottish hard man Dave Mackay at inside-left instead of his usual left-half role, and it was he who restored the lead before half-time with a glancing header. Soon after half-time Broadbent went close to a second equaliser, but Brown dived to save his fierce shot. That set the pattern for the remaining 40 minutes, with Wolves failing to impose themselves. Almost inevitably, Cliff Jones scored with a flying header to a Terry Dyson centre. The vital goals had come from a Scot and a Welshman, while the architect of the win was an Irishman – Danny Blanchflower. It just had to be St George's Day, the day of the patron saint of the English. Blanchflower had got the better of Broadbent at Molineux for a second year running. It was almost as if Blanchflower made a special effort to do well against him there after his humiliating night at the hands of Broadbent in 1958.

Wolves, despite this shock defeat in front of 56,283 fans, were still a point ahead of Spurs but were no longer in control of their fate, as Burnley were only two points behind them but with two games to play. Wolves were still determined to win their final game of the season, against Chelsea at Stamford Bridge, in order to make the Lancastrians fight all the way for the title. This Wolves duly did, with an impressive 5–1 victory. The win itself was significant but equally so was the line-up that achieved it. Manager Cullis boldly decided to drop Gerry Mannion, who was struggling after his sensational introduction into the team, and his right-wing partner Bobby Mason, who had done so much for Wolves over the past three seasons. Norman Deeley was switched to his old position of outside-right but Broadbent remained in the number-10 shirt to partner Des Horne on the left-wing. Barry Stobart took Mason's place at inside-right. It was a brave move by Cullis, but it paid off handsomely. The big question was: would he stick with the same team for the Cup Final against Blackburn?

Cullis did not name his Wembley line-up until after he had seen Burnley win 2–1 against Manchester City at Maine Road, to pinch the League title from under Wolves' noses. Cullis may well have already made up his mind, but he waited a couple more days before making it public – the team who beat Chelsea would play at Wembley. I wondered if Cullis had had a quiet word with those left out and those included. It seems not. Bobby Mason said 'It was only when the team went up on the noticeboard that I knew I wasn't playing. Stan never said a word to me but once the team was up Eddie Stuart and I went to see him. We wanted reasons but he did not really give us any. He just said the team who had scored five at Chelsea would be playing at Wembley.'

The first Barry Stobart knew of his shock inclusion after just five first-team games was when trainer Joe Gardiner told him, in confidence, that he would be in the team. Then he saw the team pinned up. 'It was a nice feeling, I could hardly believe it when I saw my name there. I went to find my wife Maureen – she was my girlfriend then – to tell her the news and we rang round the family.'

Maureen would watch the Final from the terraces – Wembley was still not all-seats in those days – because Stobart's mother Elsie decided at the last minute she would travel down from Doncaster to watch the big match.

Broadbent and the rest had been busy doing what players in the Cup Final did in those days – trying to make the most commercially out of the occasion. In the days when there was still a maximum wage it was a chance to cash in on their success. A souvenir brochure, *The Wembley Wolves*, was produced and went on sale for two shillings (20p), and there were various other functions and raffles of signed footballs. Stobart recalled 'We also had to go round businesses and shops asking for sponsorship. I went round three or four places but I hated it. It was embarrassing. I'd never had to do anything like that before.'

Another way of raising money for the players' pool was to ask all newspapers to pay a fee to guarantee interviews in the build-up to the big match. Recalled sportswriter Leon Hickman 'Peter was a kind of shop steward and was in charge of the money pot. The news agency I was with in the town would not pay the money so they sent me down to try to talk to the players. I was still a kid, the same age as, or younger than, the players. Bill Slater, being an ex-amateur, I thought might give me a few words but he said Peter was in charge of the pool and the players wouldn't like it if I spoke to you. Then he looked at me and I was kind of pleading and he said "Oh, all right, go in the corner and we'll have a quick chat." So I got one interview but you could understand the players' view. It was their one big chance to make some money but I think there was a Wolverhampton-wide thing not to put any money in. I think the players would have done a lot better if they had got an outside person to be chairman of their committee.'

The Wembley brochure included an advert for the Broadbents' business, proclaiming 'Peter Broadbent, high class grocer, Bilbrook Shopping Centre, Duck Lane. Daily deliveries – frozen foods a speciality. Satisfaction guaranteed'.

The match itself, like so many Cup Finals, was not a classic, which Broadbent readily conceded afterwards. At a sweltering, sun-kissed Empire Stadium, Wolves cruised home 3–0 to collect their third major trophy in three years, but the game, on Saturday 7 May 1960, was spoiled as a spectacle by injury. Stobart had made the most of his big chance and his cross from the left had been turned into his own net by Mick McGrath on 41 minutes. A couple of minutes later, full-back Dave Whelan fell awkwardly as he and Norman Deeley challenged for the ball. The Blackburn full-back had broken his leg and Rovers had to play the rest of the game with 10 men.

Many years later the same Dave Whelan, now millionaire owner of Wigan Athletic, had occasion in the *Daily Mail* to comment on a bad tackle by Michael Essien of Chelsea on Dietmar Hamann of Liverpool. Amazingly, he compared it to that by Deeley. Having been at the Final, I was certain Whelan's injury had not been the result of any illegal action by the Wolves winger. A look at my DVD of the game proved my point. I wrote to the *Daily Mail*, calling on Whelan to look at the same DVD, and then he would see his memory had failed him and that he owed Deeley an apology. I also wrote to Whelan himself. The *Daily Mail* published my letter but I received no reply from Whelan. Deeley chose not to go public but I know he was most hurt by Whelan's claims. Deeley was Wolves' Wembley hero, scoring two second-half goals. Without a doubt this was the high point of a fine Wolves career. He was a close friend of Broadbent's and, like him, Deeley always played the game fairly.

Broadbent did not sparkle at Wembley but he did not have to. He had a steady game as Wolves were clearly superior to their handicapped opponents, who had been rocked before the game when centre-forward Derek Dougan, later to become a Wolves legend, put in a transfer request. As Wolves left the pitch some

Rovers fans unkindly pelted them with orange peel and other rubbish, which prompted one national newspaper to dub it 'The Dustbin Final'. It was a proud Broadbent who followed skipper Bill Slater up the famous Wembley steps to the royal box to collect the trophy from the Duchess of Gloucester.

After the match, Broadbent gave an exclusive interview in the dressing room to *News of the World* reporter Arthur Osman. It is a typically-ghosted piece of writing, done as if Broadbent himself was talking, but it does convey the joy of the Wembley triumph.

'What a truly wonderful feeling! We've won,' the article begins. It goes on, 'Yet it still seems like a dream. If you could see us weary Wolves, jubilant in our South dressing room, as I write this, you would know just what I mean. Now I have collected every honour the game can possibly give me, and believe me this gold winner's medal will be the star exhibit in my collection. In nine fabulous years with Wolves I rate it even above my international caps.

'Ronnie Clayton, Blackburn Rovers' skipper, has just been in to offer his congratulations to us and we all agreed that it was the purest accident that put Dave Whelan out of the game. He and Norman Deeley had seemed to brush together, their legs touched, and down he went. Bad luck, Dave, and bad luck also Rovers. Mind you, I feel we had the game sewn up before that. True, Rovers looked dangerous at times, but it wasn't a sustained challenge at all. I know some will say it was not a good Final but we felt we did well enough to earn the Cup.'

I well remember seeing Cullis being interviewed in the dressing room in the Sunday TV review of the game. What amused me and my dad was that the manager had a towel wrapped around him – he, too, had taken a shower. It was not surprising as it was such a hot day and Cullis was always so animated whether sat on the touchline, as he was at Wembley, or in the stand.

Broadbent touched upon the conditions in his *News of the World* column 'Before the game our manager, Mr Cullis, ordered us to take salt tablets to beat the heat. He repeated the dose at half-time. Phew, how glad we were we had had them! I have played in some pretty hot places in my time, but this was a real roaster.'

The dressing room verdict ends 'Young Barry Stobart, who was seeing Wembley for the first time, is sitting here beside me right now, and I would like to be the first to say that I think he was great, just great. Eddie Clamp had a fine game, too, but to go out for the first time at Wembley and play a real blinder, as Barry did, is quite something.'

Back in the village of Bilbrook, where the Broadbents had their grocery shop, wife Shirley had to watch the game on television. She was expecting their second child and her doctor had advised her not to travel to London, but her parents, Len and Florrie, were at Wembley with Peter's family. 'I watched the game from the flat above the shop, where we lived,' recalled Shirley. 'My friend Joan (McIlreath) was with me and I was crying most of the time – because I wasn't there, because I was proud of Peter and then because we had won. We toasted them with champagne afterwards. They didn't tell you not to drink when you were pregnant in those days. As it turned out, I went about a month past my due date before I gave birth to Gary. It was June 2. If I'd known he was going to be that late, I'd have gone to the match!'

The drama for Shirley was not only at Wembley, 'Our daughter Debbie was about three and she was in the kitchen playing with her toys while I was watching the game. Then we looked out of the window and she was by the Woodman pub, which was opposite our shop. How she got out, I don't know, it had never happened before. That was a real scare.

'Peter rang me as soon as he could after the game. He was so thrilled. I went up to the station to meet the train on the Sunday when they came home and I travelled back through the town on the coach. I've never seen so many people lining the streets and there were thousands outside the Town Hall when the players came out on to the balcony to show them the Cup.'

After the match Wolves' celebration party had been at the Café Royal in the West End, with a cabaret including popular singer of the day Marion Ryan, mother of the singing Ryan twins Paul and Barry. Marion used to sing a song called Norman, and full-back George Showell said she made a point of singing it specially for Norman Deeley. Left-back Gerry Harris said 'She asked for somebody to come up on stage to sing with her and we all shouted out

Norman's name and he did sing with her.' Deeley himself confirmed 'Yes, they made me get up on stage with Marion Ryan and I think we sang Diamonds Are A Girl's Best Friend together. It was a great night.'

Players were allowed to take their wives to the post-final shindig and Maureen Stobart, though not then married to Barry, was also allowed along thanks to director John Ireland, who would later become Wolves' chairman. 'He was always good to the players,' Maureen said. 'As soon as he knew Barry had a regular girlfriend he told him I could come to the party.'

Another special memory for Maureen came after she and Barry left the Café Royal. 'We walked down Regent Street and made our way to Trafalgar Square. It must have been one or two o'clock in the morning but we found this little café that was still open. We got a cup of coffee each and we just sat there, kept getting Barry's Cup-winners' medal out of the box and looking at it. We just could not believe it.'

The teams in the Final on Saturday 7 May 1960 were:

Wolves: Finlayson; Showell, Harris; Clamp, Slater, Flowers; Deeley, Stobart, Murray, Broadbent, Deeley. Goals: McGrath, own-goal (41), Deeley (67, 88).

Blackburn: Leyland; Bray, Whelan; Clayton, Woods, McGrath; Bimpson, Dobing, Dougan, Douglas, McLeod.

Referee: K. Howley (Middlesbrough). Attendance: 98,776 (receipts: £49,816).

After the Glory

Having climbed to the summit of English football Broadbent and Wolves had stayed there quite a while, but now there was only one direction they could go. Their descent was not a rapid one – at first. When the 1960–61 season began they were still regarded as one of the top three or four teams in the land, but, after a useful season, things began to go wrong quickly. Broadbent and some of the others were not veterans but were at the wrong end of their careers and the supply of young talent, while still there, was not quite of the supremely-high standard that had made the side so special.

There was also a very good team waiting in the wings to do what Wolves had just failed to do the previous season. Tottenham Hotspur became the first team in the 20th century to complete the double of League and Cup in the same season and they did it with some style. Yet, despite their glorious season, Spurs did not win the title again and did not enjoy the sort of dominance of English football that had been Wolves' in the 1950s. However, for that one wonderful season they were virtually unstoppable.

Wolves met them at Molineux on Saturday 1 October 1960. Spurs had won 10 successive games from the start of season and 53,036 turned up to see if Wolves could prevent them making it 11. I could not watch this one from the start as I had to play rugby for my school. After my afternoon of chasing around Tettenhall College's pitch at Henwood Road, Wolverhampton, myself and one or two others threw on our clothes over barely washed arms and legs to get the bus into Wolverhampton. We rushed down to Molineux and were amazed, as we ran down Molineux Alley, to see the South Bank terrace packed yet to hear no noise. The gates were always opened 20 minutes from time to let the early leavers out, so we were able to get in and find out the reason for the silence. Spurs were 3–0 up. The match was over as a contest. Before the end, little winger Terry Dyson added a fourth goal to those scored by Cliff Jones and Danny Blanchflower in the first half and by Les Allen on 52 minutes.

Clearly, Spurs were – for a season at least – one of the greatest sides English football had seen, yet there was still a feeling that Wolves had frozen on the big day. So often Broadbent and the rest had risen to the occasion, but not this time. Phil Morgan wrote 'The forwards were extremely off key, even the better touches of Peter Broadbent being wasted in a mix-up of players who once more carried positional switches to a bewildering degree of exaggeration.' The *Express & Star* man added 'This defeat has not changed my opinion that the Wolves style can still bring success and the task of manager Stan Cullis now seems to be to try to ensure his team, whatever the composition, stick to it.'

A week before the Spurs debacle, Wolves had given a League debut to centre-forward Ted Farmer against Manchester United and he had scored twice in a 3–1 win at Old Trafford. His goalscoring just went on and on until, famously, on 21 January 1961, he scored his 21st goal of the season on his 21st birthday. It was also his 21st competitive first-team match. Farmer's career was, a few years later, sadly cut short by injury, but he was brilliant in that first season and told me he owed much of his success to Broadbent. 'Peter appreciated how to get the best out of people. When he knew your style he would always play the ball you wanted. When I got into the team he realised that I was quick so he would play the ball in front of me to run on to.'

Soon after the Tottenham game Wolves embarked on another European adventure. UEFA had decided to introduce a competition for national Cup winners. The Cup-winners' Cup would grow in importance, but the initial competition saw only 10 clubs enter. So Wolves began at the quarter-final stage where they met FK Austria, losing the first leg 2–0 at the Prater Stadium in Vienna. Wolves were not in luck and hit the woodwork no fewer than four times, while Broadbent looked certain to score only for his second-half shot to hit the home 'keeper Gartner in the face. Austria then struck twice late in the game.

The return leg, not until seven weeks later, saw Wolves cruise home 5–0, with Broadbent at his best and scoring twice in the space of three minutes midway through the second half. By then, Wolves were 3–2 up on aggregate. Young wing-half Johnny Kirkham had scored in the first minute with a long-range shot and added a second on 26 minutes when he nodded in a Cliff

Durandt centre. Goalkeeper Gartner then presented Bobby Mason with the third goal. The 'keeper's throw went straight to the Wolves man, who calmly lobbed the ball into the net. Gartner looked to have redeemed himself when he leaped to take a goalbound Broadbent header, but he was beaten by a similar effort on 70 minutes. Broadbent got his second with a low drive to a Mason pass.

Between the two European games there had been a revival in Wolves' fortunes, not least a 4–1 home win over Sheffield Wednesday, who had been desperately trying to keep in touch with League leaders Spurs. They had been unbeaten in their opening 12 matches, nine of which were wins, and had conceded only seven goals. Yet Wolves just blew them away in a whirlwind start, which saw Norman Deeley and Jimmy Murray score in the first two minutes and Murray add a third on 12 minutes. Broadbent was the star forward, with the others responding splendidly to his promptings. He added the fourth goal himself when Ron Flowers's cross-field pass was headed back into the middle by Deeley for Broadbent to tap the ball home.

More evidence of Broadbent at his best came when Wolves beat Nottingham Forest 5–3 at the beginning of November. His goal that put Wolves 4–1 up on 74 minutes was vintage Broadbent. He brought the ball from a deep position right into the heart of the Forest defence. He then exchanged passes with Farmer and found himself clear with only Forest 'keeper Thomson in front of him. He took the ball right up to Thomson and calmly walked it round him before almost nonchalantly side-footing it home.

That game was the first in a remarkable sequence of three Wolves games in eight days, which produced an amazing 26 goals. Ten came when Tbilisi Dynamo played a floodlit friendly. The men from the USSR led 5–2 with 12 minutes to go, but Wolves then scored three times to make it a 5–5 draw. The action then switched to Turf Moor, where Broadbent rocked Burnley with a goal timed at 35 seconds after kick-off. He beat two men before firing in a cross shot. Farmer made it two on nine minutes and scored again after Ray Pointer had reduced the arrears for Burnley. However, 3–1 was as good as it got for Wolves and the champions scored four times without reply to win 5–3.

Wolves' next away game gave Broadbent a chance he had been awaiting. For the first time in a League game he played opposite Fulham's Johnny Haynes, the man whom England's selectors had for so long rated better than Broadbent. In fairness, that season Haynes and Jimmy Greaves had formed a superb partnership for England, who were scoring goals galore. At Craven Cottage, Broadbent had a point to prove. Ted Farmer scored a couple of early goals and then a beautifully-weighted Broadbent pass put Bobby Mason through for a third. Haynes, who was wearing the number-six shirt, did pull a goal back in the second half but he had been outshone.

Let Clive Toye of the *Daily Express* take up the story: 'Peter Broadbent doesn't know it but he has made history. This highly-skilled Wolves inside-forward had the citizens of SW6 – otherwise known as Haynes's Country – muttering "This bloke's as good as Johnny". Today – after another performance of the Fulham Follies – I add that Broadbent is a lot better off than Haynes. For Broadbent was the brilliant brain behind the force and considerable football of Wolves, while Haynes had to play the straight man to a bunch of comedians.'

By this time, Broadbent had been establishing a left-wing partnership with chunky Cliff Durandt, and these two helped Wolves beat Villa at Villa Park on Christmas Eve and again at Molineux on Boxing Day. This was the best period in Wolves' League season as they won nine out of 10 games. The exception came at West Ham where they lost 5–0, goalkeeper Geoff Sidebottom having to be carried off after being badly injured trying to prevent the third goal.

Wolves' next encounter with London opposition would see Broadbent in even better form than in his display at Fulham. Chelsea came to Molineux on New Year's Eve 1960 and were beaten 6–1. Jimmy Murray scored twice in the first half and completed his hat-trick four minutes after half-time, before Johnny Kirkham, Ted Farmer and Durandt added more goals, with right-half Sylvan Anderton hitting a later consolation for Chelsea. Yet again Broadbent was the star of the show.

Harry Langton in the *Daily Express* first mocked Chelsea for planning to build a 'super colossal world-beating stadium' when they hadn't a team fit to grace it. 'It's like building a gold-plated Rolls-Royce without an engine,' wrote Langton before getting on to the main point of his report. 'Enough of Chelsea. You can't kick a clown when he's down so let us sing instead the praise of one of the finest inside-forwards in the world – Peter Broadbent. Broadbent backheeled the ball, flicked it over his head, caught it on his instep, stroked it, spun it, lobbed it, rolled it, swung it 50 yards at a time or stabbed it five yards without making one mistake.'

Langton added that Wolves boss Stan Cullis had said afterwards, 'If Broadbent was playing for a team like Real Madrid he would be an international figure like Puskas or Di Stefano. I don't know why he isn't a regular England player. I won't mention any names, but it seems he doesn't fit in with somebody else's ideas.' Another report said that it had been a long time since the Molineux terraces had resounded with so much laughter. Broadbent tantalised the Chelsea defence into mistakes galore.

Football has a habit of bringing you quickly down to earth and that is what happened. Just a week after Broadbent had sparkled in that wonderful win, Wolves, the FA Cup holders, were surprisingly held 1–1 at home in the third round of the competition by Huddersfield Town, who were struggling near the foot of the Second Division. With Cliff Durandt injured, Broadbent had a new left-wing partner – Alan Hinton, adding a third Wednesbury man to the team alongside Kirkham and Norman Deeley. The newcomer, with Broadbent nursing him along, had a useful debut but the strikers were off key. It was left to Kirkham to hit the face-saving goal after Derek Stokes had given the Yorkshire side a shock first-half lead.

The replay four days later saw Stokes rock Wolves with a third-minute goal and, though Jimmy Murray's penalty made it 1–1, Huddersfield, urged on by a crowd of over 46,000, won the match with a goal from winger Mike O'Grady 15 minutes from the end. Phil Morgan's match report said the freezing cold conditions and resultant hard ground were all against the craft of Broadbent. It was a poor excuse.

Broadbent and his colleagues were in need of a lift after that and it came on a memorable night at White Hart Lane, where few had given them a chance of halting Spurs' gallop. It was four days after Spurs had beaten Villa 2–0 away in the fifth round of the Cup. They were way out in front in the League, talk of the double was rife and they began the game like a team who were going to fulfil their destiny. Not only did burly centre-forward Bobby Smith give Spurs a ninth-minute lead, in doing so his elbow caught Bill Slater a hefty blow in the ribs that rendered him a passenger for the rest of the game.

Broadbent had to switch to right-half, Eddie Clamp moved to full-back and George Showell took over from Slater at centre-half. It was while Slater was off the field having treatment that Wolves equalised and Broadbent probably took some pleasure in the fact he cashed in on a mistake by his nemesis Danny Blanchflower to lay on the goal. The Spurs skipper had plenty of time to clear but delayed and was robbed. Broadbent was on to the ball in a flash and slipped a perfect through pass for Ted Farmer, who, despite the attention of two defenders and the advancing goalkeeper Bill Brown, fired in a shot as he fell, the ball going in via the underside of the bar.

With an attendance of 62,261, as well as thousands outside – unable to get in when the gates were closed – the traffic around White Hart Lane was horrendous and Wolves' coach did not arrive at the ground until half an hour before kick-off. Yet, despite this and the Slater blow, Wolves rose magnificently to the occasion as Farmer testifies: 'Everybody played well that night but Peter was a revelation at right-half. He sprayed the ball around and he outshone Blanchflower and John White in midfield, Norman Deeley and I were alone up front but we still caused Spurs problems. I nearly won it, too – unfairly. Jimmy Murray put across a centre from the left and I was running as fast as I could to meet the cross. I couldn't quite get to it but flicked the ball in with my hand. The referee did not spot it but a linesman did and raised his flag. I always remember Stan Cullis on the touchline and he was going crazy, dancing up and down. He thought it was a good goal. He was still pleased with us all afterwards, though.'

After the early Cup exit, Wembley suddenly seemed a distant memory for Broadbent and for his Cup Final wing-partner Des Horne. Broadbent was still a key man but Horne was unhappy at not being in the first team and was sold to Blackpool in March 1961.

March was also the month Broadbent damaged his ankle in a game against Newcastle at Molineux. He soldiered on and even scored the winning goal in a 2–1 triumph, but he was ruled out for several games, including the first leg of the European Cup-winners' Cup semi-final against Rangers. The Scots won 2–0 before a crowd of 79,229 at Ibrox and brought some 10,000 fans to Molineux for the return leg. The Scots virtually took over Wolverhampton town centre but it was a good-natured invasion. Their country needed a morale boost as, four days earlier, England had inflicted upon them their heaviest ever defeat – 9–3 at Wembley. Rangers proved a match for Wolves on a rainy Molineux night, taking the lead just before half-time through winger Alex Scott, who was being played at centre-forward. Broadbent, according to Phil Morgan, was still not back to top form after his injury, but he did grab an equaliser after 64 minutes.

Wolves' season appeared to be tailing off, but, despite an injury to Farmer, they ended with a flourish by beating Arsenal 5–1 at Highbury. Barry Stobart scored twice in the first half and early in the second Jimmy Murray and Norman Deeley created the opportunity for Broadbent to score with a low left-foot shot. That took Wolves' total of League goals to 99 and Bobby Mason completed the century after Wolves old boy Jackie Henderson had reduced the arrears. Murray's goal on 74 minutes made it 101 for the season. Four successive seasons and a century of League goals each time – whatever the critics might say, watching Wolves was never dull.

Still the season held one last twist. Fulham came to Molineux on the final day, having just persuaded Johnny Haynes not to move to an Italian club. The imminent abolition of the maximum wage in English football would see the Londoners' chairman Tommy Trinder put his money where his mouth was and make the England skipper the country's first £100-a-week footballer. Maybe it was this prospect that inspired Haynes, but he was as influential at Molineux as Broadbent had been at Craven Cottage earlier in the season. Fulham won 4–2 with right-winger Maurice Cook scoring three times.

Defeat was bad enough but on the same day Sheffield Wednesday had lost 4–1 at Villa Park, where Villa legend Johnny Dixon marked his farewell appearance with a goal. Wednesday's defeat meant that if Wolves had beaten

Fulham, they, not the Yorkshiremen, would have finished runners-up to runaway champions Tottenham.

If Broadbent took time to reflect, he could be fairly satisfied that Wolves' final League positions since he had become a first-team regular were: 1 2 3 6 1 1 2 3. However, from what Shirley Broadbent has told me, Broadbent was not one to sit back and contemplate his football successes and failures. At this particular stage of his life, there was plenty to occupy him once the season was over. He could help more with the business, they had a young family and there was plenty of golf to be played.

After a pleasant summer, Broadbent had to get down to the new season, hoping Wolves might be able to maintain their position among the top three teams in the top flight. Instead, you needed to look at the table from the bottom upwards for the quickest way to find the name of the Molineux club as the season unfolded. Broadbent would have the first average season of his career, which must have affected the team's performances. The inevitable consequence was the beginning of the break-up of the great team of the late 1950s. All this at a time when footballers were able to receive greater rewards for their efforts as the maximum wage limit had been lifted.

It was an unhappy start for Broadbent. He suffered a thigh injury in a pre-season practice match and though he played in the opening two League matches, he was clearly not at his best. He looked to be struggling in the 3–2 home win over West Ham and was omitted from the side for the next four games. While Broadbent had every chance to recover his fitness, another Wolves man suffered a far more serious injury. Young Gornal-born full-back Johnny Harris, who made a promising League debut against the Hammers, had the misfortune to break his leg in the very next game, as Villa came back from 2–0 down to draw 2–2 thanks to two goals from the shaven-headed Derek Dougan.

By the time Broadbent returned, only goal average was keeping Wolves above bottom-placed Birmingham City in the First Division table. A report in the *Daily Express* reckoned his absence was one of the reasons for Wolves' poor start. Cullis told the paper that Broadbent had played in the opening two games when not completely fit and added 'He's now getting match fit with the reserves, but, of course, he's been badly missed.'

Broadbent's return did not bring about an immediate improvement and his comeback was soon overshadowed by an excursion into the transfer market by Cullis. Since the inspired signing of Broadbent and goalkeeper Malcolm Finlayson, the manager's dealings had not proved too successful – Harry Hooper had one season; Jackie Henderson went after just a few games; centre-forward Joe McBride, later to play with distinction for Celtic where he won Scottish caps, was bought from Kilmarnock and sold on to Luton without making a first-team appearance; goalkeeper Chick Brodie, signed from Aldershot, would soon be leaving the club after a six-month stay and a lone appearance.

Now Cullis signed Queen's Park Rangers winger Mark Lazarus for £27,000. The Londoner's arrival would have a direct effect on Broadbent, though after his debut in a 1–1 home draw with Cardiff Lazarus had to serve a two-match suspension picked up while with QPR. During his absence, Broadbent showed a glimpse of his old powers when Wolves beat Manchester United 2–0 at Old Trafford. He scored the second goal, racing on to Norman Deeley's pass down the middle of the field and then coolly beating the advancing Harry Gregg.

Lazarus, signed as an outside-right, would find himself fielded at centre-forward for three games before reverting to the wing. He got injured, which meant young Terry Wharton was given a debut. Wharton scored against Ipswich and fans wondered why Cullis had bothered to sign Lazarus in the first place. Wharton did not look out of place alongside some household Wolves names but admits he had to pinch himself, 'Peter, Ron Flowers, Eddie Clamp, Jimmy Murray – when you get into the side at 19 and you see these sort of players, it was very special. Peter was just great to me, he asked me how I liked to have the ball played, whether I liked it to my feet or in front of me. He helped both me and Alan Hinton.'

During the continued absence of Lazarus, Broadbent had the satisfaction of again getting the better of Johnny Haynes's side when Wolves won 1–0 at Fulham. However, it was a hollow victory as the Cottagers had played most of the game with goalkeeper Tony Macedo a limping passenger. He had been hurt in making a flying save to the sort of pile-driving shot that would become a Wharton trademark. Cullis was far from pleased with the performance. Broadbent was dropped, along with Murray, Ted Farmer and left-back Gerry Harris. Broadbent's place duly went to Lazarus, who celebrated his new role as an inside-forward by scoring the first goal in a 3–0 home win over Sheffield Wednesday.

On previous occasions when he had been dropped, Broadbent had taken only one view – to do his very best in the reserves to earn a recall. Now, though, he was rated one of the best players in the land and if Cullis did not want him in his first team, other managers certainly did. Foremost among them were Joe Mercer at Villa and ex-England goalkeeper Gil Merrick, then managing his old club Birmingham City. Both inquired but got short shrift according to the *Daily Herald*, whose headline proclaimed 'Cullis is hanging on to Broadbent'. Cullis told the paper 'Peter is not for sale – at any price'.

If Broadbent had spent some time in the reserves, the bids would, without doubt, have been renewed along with more from other clubs. However, Wolves looked out of touch in losing 1–0 at home to Sheffield United and it was Lazarus's turn to be dropped. Despite his name, his reaction was not to try to rise again into the first-team reckoning. He immediately demanded a transfer. He never played another first-team game for the club and was sold back to QPR early in the New Year.

Cullis's signing of the winger had a few questioning the manager's judgment. They had done so, too, when he felt young wing-half Johnny Kirkham was a good enough prospect to enable him to sell the experienced England international Eddie Clamp to Arsenal. Clamp's second game with his new club brought him quickly back to his old stamping ground, the Gunners winning 3–2 at Molineux. It was around this time that Wolves had let a schoolboy trialist go, believing he was too small ever to make the grade. The lad in question? Alan Ball.

Young Alan Hinton had established himself on the left-wing but an injury enabled Norman Deeley to return to the side when Wolves met Carlisle in a postponed third round FA Cup tie on Wednesday 8 January 1962. Appropriately, he was able once more to team up with Broadbent, his good friend and the player with whom he had built up such a great rapport. Sadly, it was their last outing together. Cullis sold Deeley to Leyton Orient the following month. The little winger arrived in time to help the unfashionable London club successfully complete a remarkable promotion push from the Second Division. Deeley had been Broadbent's wing partner 104 times in League matches – more than any other winger. They also partnered each other in a total of 11 FA Cup and European games.

The Cup game was won 3–1 thanks to two goals from Wharton and one from Broadbent, who showed some of his old trickery as Phil Morgan reported 'Peter Broadbent, purveyor of many a pretty piece during the evening, drew on all his skill to send his opponent the wrong way and then beat George Thompson with a searing left-foot shot.' Carlisle had made Wolves struggle, but the *Express & Star* man added 'At least there were instances when Broadbent demonstrated that quickness of thought and action can work wonders.'

There was hardly a dull moment at Molineux and, having seen Wharton and Hinton prove their worth when given their chance, Cullis decided to throw more youngsters into the team – and to do so in a high profile match. For the visit of arch-rivals Albion in the fourth round of the FA Cup, he gave first-team debuts to no fewer than three of the younger generation – goalkeeper Fred Davies, full-back Bobby Thomson and half-back Freddie Goodwin. Such boldness deserved to be rewarded. It was not. Albion won 2–1. The reason for Cullis's wholesale changes was not only a desire to give youth its fling. He had to do something after what had happened at Blackpool a week earlier. In a not very illuminating display Wolves had been made light work of by the Seasiders, losing 7–2 – the first time since 1934 that they had let in seven goals in a match.

Cullis had been prompted by that humiliating defeat, not only to make changes but also to bring in some experienced new blood. Two days before the Albion Cup tie he paid Villa £30,000 for Peter McParland. A left-winger who had starred for Northern Ireland in the same 1958 World Cup Finals that saw Broadbent belatedly make his England debut, McParland could also play centre-forward. Cullis was not done. On 1 February 1962 he signed England under-23 international Chris Crowe from Blackburn for £25,000.

Broadbent kept his place when the new pair made their debuts against a star-studded Tottenham side at Molineux. Their arrival had the desired effect, both of them scoring as Spurs were beaten 3–1, the first of three successive Wolves victories. Terry Wharton struck the first goal against Spurs and said that, despite the two new signings, it was Broadbent who stole the limelight. 'For me, that display against Spurs was the best I saw Peter play. The marking was one against one in those days so he was up against Danny Blanchflower nearly all the time, but Blanchflower just couldn't live with Peter that day.'

Wolves eventually achieved First Division safety but that was all. Typical of their in-and-out form was a 5–1 home defeat by Albion and then a win at Stamford Bridge, which should have been by the same score. I write 'should have been', because Wolves led Chelsea 5–1 with seven minutes to play only to concede three goals and have to hang on for a 5–4 victory.

After a lean goalscoring start to the season, Broadbent did contribute a few more after the arrival of Crowe and McParland, but his seasonal total of five was his lowest since 1955. After the glory years, this was a lean one for Broadbent as the team finished 18th in the table. To rub it in, a Haynes-inspired Fulham won at Molineux for the second year running, as the campaign drew to a close. Haynes was off to Chile in the summer for the World Cup Finals and, to emphasise Broadbent's fall down the pecking order, the man taken as reserve to the England skipper was Arsenal's uncapped George Eastham.

As ever, the golf course proved a welcoming place for Broadbent to forget what had definitely been a season to forget. The *Sunday Express* reported that he was now a three-handicapper and by shooting 74 in the July Medal on the Oxley Park course in Wolverhampton, he earned himself six free golf balls in the paper's 'Keep a six off your card' competition. The report noted he had gone out in 40 but shot 34 for inward half, helped by three birdies.

Broadbent had already seen Eddie Clamp and Norman Deeley leave Molineux, and the summer of 1962 brought the departure of two more of the players who had helped him to reach the heights with Wolves. Former skipper Eddie Stuart moved to Stoke, where he would play his part in a Stanley

Matthews-inspired renaissance. Bobby Mason joined non-League Chelmsford City, but only briefly, before teaming up with Deeley in a vain bid to keep Orient in the top flight.

The big question, as the 1962–63 season unfolded, was: would Broadbent be next out of Molineux? For Cullis decided to make Chris Crowe his midfield schemer, while letting youth have its opportunity elsewhere in the team – Fred Davies in goal, Bobby Thomson, Freddie Goodwin and David Woodfield in defence, and Terry Wharton, Ted Farmer and Alan Hinton in attack. That left only George Showell, Ron Flowers and Jimmy Murray of the old brigade. Broadbent had once more been dropped and this time it was different. The season had not even begun. When it did, the new-look team hit the ground running.

On day one they trounced Manchester City 8–1 at Molineux as they made an 11-match unbeaten start, including a memorable 2–1 victory at Tottenham, to top the First Division. Cullis was again being hailed a master manager, and one national paper even suggested the whole Wolves forward line should play against France in the first leg of the knockout tournament known as the European Nations Cup, the forerunner of the European Championship. With Walter Winterbottom about to hand over the England managerial reins to Alf Ramsey, it would have been a bold way to mark the end of an era of erratic national selection. It did not happen, of course, though Crowe and Hinton were both capped against the French at Hillsborough.

While all this was going on, Broadbent was out of the team but certainly not out of the limelight. He was not the only skilful forward out of favour. George Eastham was being omitted from an Arsenal side, now managed by Billy Wright. As football became more defence-minded, the days of the traditional inside-forward seemed numbered. An article in the *Daily Worker*, of all places, posed that very theory. 'The traditional sight of a slight figure tantalising defences as he weaves this way and that while keeping the ball was a spectacle to delight,' said the *Worker*, 'but blanket defences based on new tactics are making it more difficult for men who live on skill alone. If this is the case and team plans are based on bigness and toughness it will be a sorry day indeed.'

Whether Broadbent had thought deeply about the broader picture of how football was changing is questionable. All he had thought about, one suspects, is that he was out of the Wolves team and that team were doing very well without him. He told Bob Pennington in the *News of the World* of 16 September that his phone had never stopped ringing, with press men and friends all wanting to know how long it would be before he asked for a move. Broadbent admitted he could not let the situation continue, but Pennington stressed it was not the familiar story about an experienced international being dropped into the reserves and then bleating for a transfer.

Pennington related how Broadbent saw it, 'When the team sheet went up for the first game I was surprised and disappointed to find I was only 12th man. I decided to bide my time and say nothing, thinking I'd probably get back. Well, blow me down, just look at the results they've had. Fabulous, how can you change a team like that? How can I suggest they should do so? I couldn't be happier about it, except that it leaves me right out in the cold. I'm 29 and at that age you can't be content with just reserve football. There would be something wrong if you were.'

Other clubs still rated him. Villa, as in the previous season, would have loved to sign him to bring a touch of experience to their young side. Also keen were Derby County, who had in the summer appointed their old player and former England international Tim Ward as boss.

Broadbent, the *Daily Herald* reported at the end of September, had asked Cullis for a move and had been given short shrift. Cullis was quoted as saying 'I will not be stampeded by clubs tapping at the back door. Broadbent is not for sale at the moment – if we ever decide to let him go, the move must be suitable to us as well as Broadbent.' The paper reckoned that a week earlier, Broadbent had said 'I intend to give things another month before reconsidering my future. I am a signed Wolves player and have no pay grumble.' The *People* reported on 30 September, however, that Derby were all set to sign Broadbent.

A week after these initial reports, the *Daily Express* said Wolves had formally rejected a Broadbent transfer request and said Broadbent was shocked by the club's decision. 'I can no longer stand reserve soccer,' he told the paper. The report said Broadbent had felt that in view of his lengthy service, the club would agree to his request. He said 'I'm disappointed and shaken. I thought they'd let me go after what I've done here.'

So how close was he to leaving Molineux at that stage? Shirley Broadbent has no doubt that a move was on the cards. 'Derby were definitely interested but he did not want to go there,' she told me, 'but he did have secret meetings with Joe Mercer, the Villa manager. Mercer thought the world of Peter. I think Peter would have gone to Villa but Cullis told him "You can go anywhere you want – but you're not going there." He was adamant.'

The day after news broke of Broadbent's rejected transfer request, something happened to pave the way for a reconciliation – table-topping Wolves lost. They were beaten at home by an Everton side who looked Championship material, as indeed they were. There followed a defeat at Bolton, where Wolves surrendered their 100 percent away record for the season, and then lowly-placed Birmingham came to Molineux and won 2–0. Broadbent's exile was about to end.

Cullis reshaped his forward line for the trip to Arsenal and back came Broadbent. Gunners boss Billy Wright had, a couple of games earlier, recalled his Broadbent equivalent – George Eastham. Both inside men impressed in a thrilling Highbury match, which saw Wolves trail 2–0 and 3–2 before roaring back to lead 4–3 – Broadbent's finely-taken volley putting them in front. Arsenal were not done and centre-forward Joe Baker completed his hat-trick, Eastham having the last word with his second goal of the game to make it 5–4.

Peter Lorenzo, in the *Daily Mirror*, said the part played in the game by Eastham and Broadbent had proved that craft conquers crunch. Eastham, he wrote, had produced his greatest display since joining Arsenal, while Broadbent was only a short head behind him when it came to effectiveness and achievement. 'In his first League game of the season, the England inside-left, scored one cracking goal and laid on two others,' wrote Lorenzo, adding 'If he did fade a little towards the end it was only to be expected in this, his first vigorous League outing, after so many appearances in the Central League side.

The moral of this story… that there is no substitute for skill. Eastham and Broadbent showed that they can do more with one flash of supreme ball control than most players can produce in 90 minutes despite all the energy they may use up.'

That last sentence probably summed up what Broadbent was all about and he would go on to prove that he could still bring that touch of special class to the side, getting the best out of young wingers Terry Wharton and Alan Hinton, the latter quickly returning to the team to displace the veteran McParland who was eventually transferred to Plymouth early in the New Year. Wolves finally got back to their winning ways, after seven games without a win, when they beat Leyton Orient at Brisbane Road. The Londoners included Broadbent's old buddy Norman Deeley. When they visited Molineux later in the season, by which time they were well on their way to an immediate return to the Second Division, Orient gave Deeley the honour of skippering the side.

London visits seemed to suit Wolves that season and, having beaten Spurs, West Ham and Orient there, they collected a fourth London scalp when, with Broadbent wearing the number-seven shirt, they beat Fulham 5–0 on 8 December 1962. Phil Morgan wrote in the *Express & Star* that Broadbent had laid on the first two goals, for Barry Stobart and teenage debutant John Galley, and it was 'part of a brainy contribution that made his appearance with number seven on his back merely nominal while he turned up in odd spots to direct operations.' Alan Hinton scored three goals that day.

Broadbent also wore number seven when Wolves bowed out of the FA Cup against Nottingham Forest. In the year of the 'Big Freeze', the game at the City Ground finally went ahead at the fifth attempt. Broadbent seems to have played much of the game as an orthodox right-winger and had a hand in each of his side's three goals as they lost 4–3. Broadbent's pass had enabled Barry Stobart to reduce the arrears after two early Forest goals, and it was Broadbent who inspired a Wolves revival after Forest had made it 3–1 just after half-time. He took a Chris Crowe pass, cut inside full-back Dennis Mochan and beat goalkeeper Peter Grummitt with a stinging left-foot shot. Three times Alan Hinton broke clear as Broadbent continued to fire Wolves but twice he hesitated and was robbed, and the third time saw his goal-bound shot diverted for a corner by centre-half Bob McKinlay. Broadbent was still not finished and after Dick Le Flem had made it 4–2, he lifted the ball accurately into the middle for Stobart to score again. By then, however, time had run out.

The highlights, as Wolves' League season revived, were a 7–0 home win over Albion, Terry Wharton being the hat-trick man this time, and a 7–2 Molineux win over Burnley when Broadbent contributed two goals. The only game Broadbent missed after his return to the side was the very last one of the season, when Wolves slumped, inexplicably, to their heaviest defeat of the campaign – 5–1 at Blackburn. Broadbent had, however, been able to play in the final Molineux match of the season, which saw another of his stalwart teammates take his leave of the club. Bill Slater was made captain for the day, against his former club Blackpool, and Broadbent joined the players at the end of the game in applauding the greatly admired and respected former England half-back all the way back to the dressing room. Slater, by then 36, was leaving Wolves to take up the post of deputy director at National Recreation Centre at Crystal Palace. Slater had made just seven League appearances that season while Broadbent's total of 27 was his lowest in 10 seasons, as Wolves finished a creditable fifth in the First Division.

Broadbent barely had time to celebrate his 30th birthday before Wolves embarked on another overseas trip as fabulous as anything he had been on during his 12 years in Wolverhampton. A 24-strong party set off on May 20 to play 10 games in Canada and the US. Missing from the squad were Ron Flowers, on tour with England, and full-back Bobby Thomson and left-winger Alan Hinton, both chosen to go on an end-of-season England Under-23 tour. However, Wolves took along another youngster of great promise, Peter Knowles.

By the time the tour ended, just over a month later, Wolves had visited New York, San Francisco, St Louis, Vancouver and Toronto. It was highly successful with nine games won, the only draw being against Brazilian side Bangu, whom they beat 4–1 when they met again in the final game of the tour. There was also a 4–2 win in New York over their first ever European Cup opponents Schalke 04, and Broadbent scored against them, just as he had done in 1958.

Centre-forward Ted Farmer remembers 'We had some great times out there and Peter really enjoyed the hospitality and the friendship they showed us. Peter was always young at heart and always joined in the fun.'

Barry Stobart also has fond memories of that trip 'Because they were friendly games and because of the standard of some of the opposition, Peter could do more of his tricks. He would really turn it on and the fans loved it.'

Defender George Showell confirmed Broadbent had enjoyed putting on the style in some of the games. 'There were one or two tough games but quite a few were comfortable and Peter could do things like trapping the ball with his backside. We started off in Montreal and had quite a few days in New York as well as going to St Louis and San Francisco. We were able to see the sights. We went up the Empire State Building, visited Radio City and some of them took a boat trip around the Statue of Liberty. In Canada we had a coach trip to see Niagara Falls. The hospitality was excellent. It was a brilliant tour.'

Left-back Gerry Harris said 'They treated us very well on that tour. We had the best of everything. There was also a bloke who had a huge yacht and he took us on a tour of the lakes. That was the highlight for me. It was wonderful.'

'I think Peter liked Canada better than America,' said Shirley Broadbent. 'I know he said to a reporter over there, as you do, "If ever you're in England, come and see us." Well there was a knock on the door on Boxing Day and it was this reporter. We asked him in, of course, and he stayed a week. We were having a party when he called and, being that time of year, there were one or two other dos as well. I bet he thought that's all we did.'

Pastures New

Broadbent was the longest-serving Wolves player, having completed 12 years at Molineux, as the 1963–64 season began. He again found himself in the reserves on the opening Saturday and did not play until the third game of the season, a 4–3 defeat at Tottenham. A couple of games later, he was switched to right-half and although Wolves were beaten 3–1 by Liverpool at Molineux, he impressed Phil Morgan. The *Express & Star* man wrote 'Out of all the darkness into which Wolves lapsed there came the ray of light – the way the immaculate Broadbent took to the role of wing-half. His constructive use of the ball – crisp, accurate passes and to-the-foot chips – particularly in the first half, was enough in itself to have inspired livelier forwards to greater effort.'

Despite that glowing report, Broadbent was quickly back to an inside-forward role as Wolves lost 5–1 at home to Blackburn. Manager Cullis had decided he needed an established half-back and was trying to sign Calvin Palmer from Nottingham Forest, but before pursuing that possible deal he splashed out a club-record £55,000 for Ipswich's Ray Crawford. The former England centre-forward signed in the morning in time to play against Liverpool at Anfield in the evening. What a debut! Wolves lost 6–0, their fifth successive defeat. They were not helped by an injury to goalkeeper Malcolm Finlayson. Wolves were four down at the time Finlayson had to go off but it might easily have been more had it not been for the heroics of the 'keeper, who would retire at the end of the season.

Crawford soon showed his worth with two goals that stopped the rot in a 2–1 win at Blackpool and he was on target again when Chelsea were beaten 4–1 at Molineux. Broadbent stole the show, however, when he scored the fourth goal late on. Wolves were awarded a free-kick, which in those days was not automatically used for a potshot at goal. On this occasion, Broadbent chose to do just that, in the way he had taken that penalty at Old Trafford a few years earlier. His rocket shot flew past Peter Bonetti in the Chelsea goal and, according to Phil Morgan, would have done credit to former Molineux hotshot Johnny Hancocks.

Peter Knowles was catching the eye with his displays in the reserve team and could not be denied. He made his debut in a 1–0 win at Leicester. Knowles had made Broadbent his role model and recalls 'When I was told by Stan Cullis I was picked to play in the first team at Leicester, I asked him whose place I was taking. When he said it was Peter's, what a shock! The man I was modelling myself on, played for England, a gifted footballer and I was taking his place. It was so embarrassing for me and I found it difficult to look at Peter but, just like the person he was, he was very kind to me and wished me all the best.'

The youngster then had to be given a run in the side after that, but Broadbent was recalled to fill the other inside berth ahead of the likes of Chris Crowe, Jimmy Murray and Barry Stobart. In just a few months, all three would leave Molineux. Broadbent's fellow Elvington man Murray was first to go, joining Manchester City in November 1963. There was a familiar link, as the City manager who signed Murray was George Poyser, the man who had been such a big early influence on Broadbent's career. Murray, who had scored 155 League goals for Wolves, made an immediate impact at City with 21 goals in 19 games.

Broadbent would soon find himself with a new left-wing partner early in the New Year. A week after Wolves had bowed out of the FA Cup at the first hurdle at Arsenal, Wolves lost 3–2 at home to Nottingham Forest, despite Broadbent and Chris Crowe putting them 2–0 up. Alan Hinton, never a particularly combative player, had an unhappy afternoon against Forest's rugged right-back Joe Wilson and received a lot of stick from a section of the crowd. Before January was out Cullis swopped Hinton for Forest's Channel Islander Dick Le Flem. It proved not to be one of the manager's better deals. Le Flem failed to make an impact while Hinton would give fine service to Forest, where he gained two more England caps, and to Derby, where he helped them win the First Division title twice.

Another Broadbent outing at right-half in February brought him a glowing report and a 3–2 win for Wolves over Chelsea at Stamford Bridge. He also did well in that position two days later, though Wolves lost 2–0 at home to West Ham. A new role looked possible for Broadbent but Cullis must not have thought so. Having failed to sign Calvin Palmer, he signed wing-half Bobby

Woodruff from Swindon. Then, in March 1964, Cullis signed a high-profile inside-forward – Liverpool's England international Jimmy Melia. Initially, Cullis kept faith with Broadbent but Wolves were struggling and a run of 11 games towards the end of the season brought only one win. Broadbent was dropped, Knowles took his place and scored in each of the last two matches, which brought a home win over Fulham and an away win at Bolton, both 4–0.

Wolves had finished 16th but their displays in the final two games had raised hopes of better things. However, the writing looked to be on the wall for inside forwards at Molineux if you weren't either Knowles or Melia. Chris Crowe signed for Nottingham Forest in the close season but Broadbent opted to stay with Wolves and for three weeks in the summer accompanied them on an eight-match trip to the Caribbean. Chelsea made the tour with them and the clubs met five times, with the Londoners three-time winners and Wolves triumphing twice. Wolves' other games brought a 4–0 win over Trinidad in Port of Spain, an 8–4 win over Jamaica in Kingston and a 1–1 draw against Haiti in Port-au-Prince. Broadbent did not play too many games as Knowles and Melia cemented the places they had gained towards the end of the season. Barry Stobart went on tour but joined the inside-forward exodus when he got home, as George Poyser took him to Maine Road to join Jimmy Murray. The Caribbean had provided a sunny and fun-filled trip for Broadbent, but the storm clouds were about to gather over Molineux…

It would have been appropriate, given the affection in which he was held, for Broadbent to have bowed out from Wolverhampton Wanderers in a blaze of glory. Sadly, he left quietly, early in 1965, after some dramatic events at Molineux that saw the club slump to the bottom of the table and manager Stan Cullis pay the price. One knew that Broadbent could not go on for ever, but one thought he might have figured in the club's unexpected fight against relegation. No player was ever guaranteed his place under Cullis, but Broadbent came very close. He had been dropped during 11 seasons, but only rarely, and it was clear that Cullis saw him as a key member of his squad. Broadbent always gave 100 percent and as much as anyone heeded the sign that the boss had hung in the home dressing room – 'there is no substitute for hard work'.

When the 1964–65 season opened, Wolves fans had probably accepted that the team were no longer one of the First Division's big guns. Their old rivals Manchester United were still up there but now the challenge was coming from Bill Shankly's Liverpool, Don Revie's Leeds and Tommy Docherty's Chelsea. However, there was no reason why the Molineux regulars could not expect an improvement on the 1963–64 finish of 16th. As for Broadbent, he looked set for a role as the squad's senior citizen, nursing along younger players.

Alas, Wolves did not head for calmer waters but found themselves in a sea of troubles. The new kid on the block, Peter Knowles, was champing at the bit – and it is 'champing' not 'chomping' as I keep hearing so many radio and TV presenters say – and so Broadbent was in the reserve team when the annual public practice game was staged at Molineux. It proved an embarrassing day for Cullis as the reserves triumphed 4–3.

Philip Osborn wrote in the *Daily Sketch* 'Don't start writing Peter Broadbent off yet. This is the decisive message from Wolves' practice match. Manager Stan Cullis chose the men who appeared in the closing two games of last season as the first team, indicating that he is thinking of relegating Broadbent to the reserves. The former England forward replied by producing all his old skills to prove he is still good enough for the First Division.' Osborn also said that Knowles, despite scoring, did not look in the same class, spending too much time waiting, instead of working, for opportunities.

So, for the opening game of the season Broadbent got the vote ahead of the youngster. Alas, the writing was on the wall for Wolves and Cullis from the first day when Tommy Docherty's lively Chelsea youngsters won 3–0 at Molineux. Of the home forward line who took the field that day – Terry Wharton, Jimmy Melia, Ray Crawford, Broadbent and 19-year-old debutant Clive Ford – only Wharton would still be with the club at the end of the season. Chelsea, parading their new all-blue strip, led through Bobby Tambling from the fourth minute and completely outclassed Wolves. So bad were the home team that there were even sporadic outbursts of slow hand-clapping – on the opening day of the season.

The defeat meant an early exit for Ford, who joined Walsall in December, as Knowles was recalled to the side for the visit to Leicester City and Broadbent switched to outside right. In the game at Filbert Street it was Broadbent's flighted pass that saw Knowles hook the ball past Gordon Banks to open the scoring. It was a false omen, as Leicester went on to win 3–2. It did not get any better when Wolves visited Leeds three days later. The story was similar – Knowles gave Wolves the lead early on but the result was a 3–2 defeat. The return game with Leicester brought Wolves their first point of the season in a 1–1 draw, but an injury to Knowles meant Broadbent was back in his old inside-right position when Arsenal visited Molineux early in September, with the home side giving a debut to another 19-year-old winger, David Thompson. A late goal from Gunners winger Alan Skirton decided the match and two days later Broadbent was back on the wing as Wolves' form went from bad to worse, with a 5–0 pounding by West Ham at Upton Park. Broadbent was one of several who paid the price for this latest setback and missed out on the 4–1 defeat at Blackburn.

What a start for Wolves! Seven games, six defeats and one point – the club had not made a poorer beginning to a season since 1926–27, though that was in the Second Division. This was their worst ever start to a top-flight campaign. Broadbent and fellow stalwarts like Ron Flowers, George Showell and Gerry Harris, so used to success after success during the 1950s, had never known anything like it. All of which set the scene for one of Molineux's most memorable games, when West Ham came to town for the return fixture on Monday 14 September 1964. Broadbent played his part in it, recalled to the inside-left spot at the expense of Melia.

Hopes were high of that elusive win when Ray Crawford headed Wolves in front after just three minutes and Knowles made it 2–0. The match then changed dramatically in the space of 22 minutes, starting with Peter Brabrook's hooked goal in the 39th. Six minutes after the break Gerry Harris put the ball into his own net and on 61 minutes Harris was penalised for a challenge, which enabled Johnny Byrne to give the Hammers the lead from the resultant penalty. Harris did not let his mishaps get him down. With 13 minutes left he raced down the left-wing and sent in a drive so powerful that the Londoners' goalkeeper Jim Standen, also a useful cricketer for Worcestershire, could not hang on to the ball. Crawford was on hand to put home the rebound. Harris was not finished. With four minutes to go he slammed a long-range ball into the visitors' goalmouth where Standen misjudged the flight and was beaten.

The returning Broadbent had done as much as anyone to bring about the overdue victory. In the *Express & Star*, Phil Morgan referred to 'top-form Broadbent reaching the heights nearly 14 years after his first game for the club'. The teams that night were:

Wolves: Davies; Thomson, Harris; Goodwin, Showell, Woodruff; Thompson, Knowles, Crawford, Broadbent, Wharton.

West Ham: Standen; Bond, Burkett; Bovington, Peters, Moore; Sealey, Boyce, Byrne, Hurst, Brabrook.

Referee: F. Schofield (Morecambe). Attendance: 19,405.

This superbly dramatic match set Wolves fans buzzing, but events were about to unfold that would not only shock them but also the whole of the English game. Manager Stan Cullis had not been well and on doctor's orders he had taken a holiday, but had returned in time to see the win over the Hammers. The following day the football world was stunned. Wolves sacked him. Cullis had been at the club as player, assistant manager and manager for 30 years. In their brief statement after his sacking, the club said 'The Wolves board of directors have informed their manager, Stanley Cullis, they wish to be released from their contract arrangements with him. This he has consented to do.'

Shirley Broadbent recalls that the decision came out of the blue. 'I think Peter was very sad about it all. Cullis had given him his big chance. I would not say Peter was fond of him but he certainly respected him, far more as he got older. The phone never stopped ringing with reporters trying to find out what the players thought but Peter said to me "Don't get saying anything to them, they'll only twist it round and make it up into something sensational." So I'd put the phone down.'

Defender George Showell confirmed that the sacking took the players by surprise. 'It must have been announced in the afternoon because I was on the bus and remember seeing a newspaper placard. I know there was some aggro between him and John Ireland but it was still a big shock.' What did Showell think of the Molineux maestro? 'I have to say I found him all right. Stan used to tell me what he thought if I needed to be told. If we'd had a poor game it was a case of not wanting to be first in the dressing room afterwards. If you were, you'd be the one to get it, though he never swore. He used to say "flipping" or "flopping".'

Gerry Harris, hero of the win over West Ham, was as surprised as the other players when he learned next day of Cullis's departure. 'I think it was Peter who told me, and I was also told that Stan had collapsed in his office and they had to send for the physio George Palmer to bring him round.'

Clearly the directors felt something had to be done after Wolves' dreadful start. In such circumstances there is only one person who carries the can – the manager, even if that manager happens to be one of the greatest names in English football. Cup Final hero Barry Stobart, who had moved to Manchester City in the close season, had a prediction of the Cullis sacking from an unlikely source. 'There was a chap who ran a fishing tackle shop, I just can't recall his name, but he seemed to know everything that was going on at Molineux. When I told him I wanted to go he said "I'm telling you, another six months and Cullis'll be gone." I did not give it much credit but, my goodness, he was right. But by then I'd made up my mind I was going.'

Gerry Harris reluctantly felt the club had been right to end Cullis's reign. 'Stan's record speaks for itself but I think time had caught up with him. He did not adapt to modern football. I remember that in the game at West Ham, a few weeks before he was sacked, they were running us ragged and Stan went berserk at half-time. He set about young Freddie Goodwin and Freddie said "But, boss, they're playing four-two-four," and Stan just went quiet. Then Stan said "Yes, yes, I know," but really I don't think he knew what Freddie was talking about.'

Harris continued: 'At that club we had every type of player, young and experienced, who could have played in any formation but Stan insisted we carry on playing the same way, even though the game had changed. When we played Barcelona a few years before I bet they rubbed their hands when they saw Eddie Clamp and Ron Flowers getting forward in attack and leaving three of us at the back. That's what they'd been told to do but it was just not the way to play the away leg of a European Cup quarter-final. We were attacking them from the first whistle, no wonder we lost 4–0. I reckon if Stan had been tactically more aware we could have won the double three times on the trot.'

Some might take issue with Harris but one can appreciate his view. The Barcelona mauling should have been a wake-up call. The all-out attacking style that had brought so much success and excitement to Molineux was being countered by a more subtle brand of football. Cullis always had great vision of how football should go – smaller top division, floodlights, televised League games – and perhaps he could have changed his on-field ways, too. Wolves never gave him the chance.

The Harris view is shared by winger Norman Deeley, who had left the club over two years earlier, 'I think Stan was great in his time but when the team who had done so well started to split up, he lost the plot as a manager.' Deeley may be right, but the way Cullis left Wolves upset a host of fans.

It was left to the training staff in consultation with the directors to name the team to face Blackpool at Molineux four days after Cullis's dismissal. Only one change was made, fit-again Ron Flowers replacing Freddie Goodwin. Blackpool, who included former Wolves winger Des Horne, added to Wolves' woes by winning 2–1, but their success owed much to the display of their England goalkeeper Tony Waiters. Broadbent, with a screaming first-half drive, was one of those denied by him. In that Blackpool side was young Alan Ball, who could so easily have been a Wolves player, had Cullis and his coaching staff paid more attention to his skill and potential rather than his physique.

So Wolves boasted only three points from nine games. It would get worse before it got better. After Blackpool, Wolves lost another six games in a row, including a 5–1 defeat by arch-rivals Albion at The Hawthorns, where Jeff Astle made his home debut after two away games since being signed from Notts County. Astle showed a hint of the scoring prowess that would make him one of Albion's all-time greats when he put them two up with goals after 25 and 49 minutes. Broadbent was fortunate enough to miss that one, as Wolves had again made changes. He was recalled, at Melia's expense, for the visit of Manchester

United a week later. It was not a happy return, as the United side, on their way to winning the First Division title and parading Bobby Charlton, Denis Law and George Best, won 4–2.

Three days after United's Molineux win, Wolves signed Carlisle striker Hugh McIlmoyle on 20 October. Times were changing and Broadbent's time at Wolverhampton Wanderers was running out. Melia took Broadbent's place and McIlmoyle was given the number-10 shirt. It took another Molineux arrival, however, before Wolves at last managed their second win of the season. That came at Stoke on Saturday 7 November, three days after Wolves had appointed Andy Beattie the caretaker team manager. Beattie had helped Nottingham Forest avoid relegation in 1960–61 and did a similar job for Plymouth in 1963–64. However, the task at Molineux looked to be the toughest yet for the pre-war Preston and Scotland star. More significantly, in the Broadbent story he would soon decide which players he thought might get Wolves out of trouble.

Wolves followed up the win at Stoke with a 3–1 home win over Tottenham, a 1–1 draw at Burnley and a 1–0 win over Sheffield United at Molineux. Four games without defeat seemed too good to last – and it was. There followed five successive defeats as the gloom descended once more over Molineux. In the reserves, despite the first-team's struggles, Broadbent got an unexpected return to action following the departure of Jimmy Melia. The ex-Liverpool man had not really settled in the Midlands and on 16 December, four days after he had figured in Wolves' 2–1 defeat at Chelsea, he was sold to Southampton for £30,000.

Broadbent's recall came when Leeds visited Molineux on Saturday 19 December 1964 when yet another Molineux youngster, Fred Kemp, was given his Football League debut. Leeds won by the only goal of the game from reserve centre-forward Rodney Johnson.

Wolves' fate looked settled, but the side certainly wasn't and there came another addition to their ranks on Boxing Day morning. David Wagstaffe was signed from Manchester City in time to face Aston Villa at Molineux in the afternoon. Still only 21, Wagstaffe had plenty of football under his belt, with 161 League and Cup appearances for the Lancashire side. With Wagstaffe's dramatic transfer to Molineux, the name of George Poyser would crop up once again. He had intentionally done Wolves a favour by recommending Broadbent to them, now he would unwillingly do them another good turn. It was Poyser who sold Wagstaffe to Wolves to provide another piece in the jigsaw that became Wolves' very useful side of the 1970s, a team who reached the UEFA Cup Final in 1972 and won the League Cup in 1974.

Waggy would stay at Molineux for over a decade and prove a firm fans' favourite. He could beat an opponent and whip over pinpoint crosses in the best traditions of good old-fashioned wing play. The great partnership of Derek Dougan and John Richards would owe much to Waggy the provider. Poyser certainly did Wolves another great favour, though Wagstaffe believes the City manager was far from keen to see him go.

'City were in the doldrums and I was ready for a change but the transfer came out of the blue,' said Wagstaffe. 'It was Christmas Eve and I got home and there'd been a phone call from the manager. So I rang him and he said "Wolves want you. I'll drive you down there Boxing Day morning. If you decide you want to sign, fair enough, if not, you can come back to Manchester." So he drove me down to Wolverhampton, I had a chat with Andy Beattie and decided to sign. It was as simple as that. I don't think Poyser wanted me to leave but I think I was ready for a change.'

While Wagstaffe became one of the most-admired players in Wolves' history, the fortunes of Poyser slumped. A week after he sold Wagstaffe, City had their worst ever gate at Maine Road – just 8,015 to see Swindon – and before the season ended he resigned. He never went back into management.

'I liked George Poyser,' Wagtaffe stressed, 'but he was not really a manager. He was obviously a great scout and could spot players but as a manager, he was not really up to it.'

Did Wagstaffe remember that one and only League outing with Broadbent? 'I certainly do – we got beat! The thing I remember most was the pitch. It was rock hard, icy. I'd only brought one pair of boots with me and they were no use for a day like that. Before the kick-off the trainer brought in a big bag of galoshes and baseball boots and he said "Find yourself something to play in." So I played in a pair of baseball boots. No wonder I did not do very well, but none of us did.'

It may surprise many Wolves fans to know that Wagstaffe was not really aware of the club's Fabulous '50s heritage. 'When I was young all I wanted to do was play football, for the school in the morning and for the boys' club in the afternoon. That's all I wanted to do – play.' It was only later that he learned about Wolves' past and the role Broadbent had played in it.

Wagstaffe can shed some light on Broadbent the man, however. When he finally left Wolves for Shrewsbury, Broadbent was allowed to do some of his training at Molineux for a while and so Wagstaffe, who had found himself a house in the Fordhouses area on the outskirts of Wolverhampton, still used to see him. 'After training once he asked me where I and the missus were going on Saturday night and said "Come out with us." He used to go to the Oakley Club at Brewood, just outside Wolverhampton. He and Shirley used to go there every Saturday night. I thought it was lovely of him to invite us because he knew that we did not know anybody in Wolverhampton yet. That's the way he was. He was a smashing bloke and he and Shirley were lovely to me. I'll always remember that.'

Not only were the Boxing Day 1964 fans witnessing the arrival of a player who would became a Molineux cult figure, but, had they but known it, they were also saying farewell to the great Peter Broadbent. The match would prove to be his last First Division outing in the gold shirt. There was no happy ending as Villa, who had a few weeks earlier signed Barry Stobart from Manchester City, won 1–0. It was a controversial goal, Wolves 'keeper Fred Davies claiming he had been pushed as he went up to collect a Villa corner before Alan Baker bundled the ball in. Broadbent was dropped after the Villa game and would be gone from Molineux within a month.

Clearly, Andy Beattie did not see Broadbent as part of his blueprint for the relegation battle. After selling Broadbent, Beattie told one paper 'We decided that Broadbent's style was not suited to our present difficulties.' One can only wonder if Beattie questioned his judgment at the end of the season, by which time Wolves were preparing for their first season in the Second Division for over 30 years.

Broadbent was sold to Shrewsbury Town on 18 January 1965. Some reports had the fee at £10,000. A player of infinite skill, adored by the fans in his heyday, he was still only 31. He had scored 127 goals in 452 League appearances for Wolves. Clearly, the Salopians' player-boss, Arthur Rowley, whose 434 League goals is still an English football record, believed Broadbent could do a job for him in the Third Division. Yet the transfer was still a shock to Broadbent. Wife Shirley remembers 'He went training on Friday morning and when he came back he said "I've been transferred". He had no idea whatsoever beforehand. That's the way they did things then. But he loved it at Shrewsbury. He was very happy there and I think all the players there respected him.'

If Broadbent was not wanted by the new regime at Molineux, Wolves, to their credit, ensured he left with a star-studded tribute to his talents in the shape of a testimonial game on Wednesday 17 March 1965, when a Wolves Past and Present XI were beaten by an All-Star XI 8–5. Wolves included former Albion and England striker Ronnie Allen, who, a day earlier, had joined Wolves from Crystal Palace to become senior coach. The Past and Present XI also included Arsenal star Ian Ure. Billy Wright, the Gunners' boss, had hoped to make a Molineux return, but when he was unable to he sent along a more than capable deputy in the Scotland centre-half. Tom Finney, the great Preston and England winger, came out of retirement and was the night's star performer, hitting two goals for the All Stars. Derek Dougan then with Peterborough, and Broadbent's new boss Rowley also hit two each, the other goals coming from Arsenal pair Ted Magill and George Eastham. Broadbent fittingly hit two for Wolves, for whom Jimmy Mullen, another retired England winger, collected three.

Phil Morgan said of Broadbent in his report of the game, 'So last night he put on the Wolves strip for the last time after wearing it with distinction for so long. He did not lead this mixed Wolves team to a glowing victory but he did what everybody hoped he would do by getting a couple of goals and played his part in a thoroughly entertaining game.'

The programme for the match said Broadbent had been the club's most consistent forward for 10 seasons. It went on: 'The deceptive body swerve, the swift acceleration and the deft use of the ball were the hallmarks of Broadbent at his best – and that was vintage football. He has given a lot of pleasure to a lot of people and there is no reason why he should not continue to do so for some time to come.' That last remark would prove prophetic, as a career that seemed on a downward trend was destined to be revived with another of English football's great clubs. The teams for the testimonial match were:

Wolves Past and Present: Finlayson; Showell, Harris; Slater, Ure, Flowers (Knighton); Wagstaffe, Allen, Lofthouse, Broadbent, Mullen.

All-Star XI: Barron (Wolves); Armfield (Blackpool), Magill (Arsenal); Whitefoot (Nottingham Forest), Curtis (Coventry), Harris (Coventry); Finney (Preston), Dougan (Peterborough), Rowley (Shrewsbury) Eastham (Arsenal), Hinton (Nottingham Forest).

Referee: Jack Taylor (Wolverhampton).

So Broadbent had to get used to life in a Football League backwater in the quiet surroundings of the quaint Gay Meadow ground alongside the River Severn, a huge contrast to mighty Molineux, even a half-filled Molineux, as it had then become. There was time for him to make 15 appearances for Shrewsbury before the season ended and score a couple of goals.

When Broadbent moved to Gay Meadow, Rowley was in his final season as a player before hanging up his boots to devote himself exclusively to management. Wolverhampton born, he and his brother Jack had not found their way on to the books at Molineux. While Arthur would go on to write his name into English football history, Jack would find fame with Manchester United, where he helped them win the First Division title, the FA Cup and gained England caps too.

Broadbent and Arthur would play only a couple of games together, as the veteran began to take a back seat as a player. Broadbent's first game for his new club was against Walsall. He had gone from one derby game to another, but while nearly 31,000 had seen his Wolves farewell against Villa, there were only just over 8,000 at Fellows Park to see his debut in the blue of Salop. It was not a winning start, as a goal from John Regan gave Shrewsbury a 1–1 draw. Town were still on a high as three days earlier they had beaten Manchester City 3–1 in an FA Cup third-round replay in front of a packed Gay Meadow crowd, all 16,084 of them. City had included Broadbent's old Wolves mate Jimmy Murray in their forward line as well as former England colleague Derek Kevan, but there was no stopping the Shropshire minnows that night. Not surprisingly, Rowley stuck with the same line up for the fourth-round trip to Millwall when Shrewsbury won 2–1 to earn themselves a fifth-round trip to Leeds.

Under Don Revie's managership, Leeds were starting their climb to the top of the English football tree. They had won promotion from the Second Division the previous season and were now top of the First Division. The week before the big game, Town lost 4–0 at home to Hull and Broadbent was unexpectedly given the number-nine shirt for the game at Elland Road on 20 February 1965. Leeds, with their mighty half-back line of Billy Bremner, Jack Charlton and Norman Hunter, proved a tie too far for Town and won 2–0 to end the Shropshire side's best-ever Cup run. A crowd of over 47,000 meant it was a quick return to the big-time football atmosphere for Broadbent. Leeds would go on to do what Wolves had done under Major Buckley in the final season before World War Two – finish runners-up in both League and Cup.

After that it was back to the bread-and-butter football of the Third Division for Broadbent, as the old maestro showed he had lost none of his skills. Town finished only 16th but had some spectacular results, such as a club-record away win – 7–2 at Luton when George Boardman scored four goals. Broadbent himself even managed a couple of goals by scoring in successive matches, first at Queen's Park Rangers when Town came from 2–0 down at half-time to win 3–2 and then in a 4–0 win at relegation-bound Colchester. He may have been out of the limelight but Broadbent had found new admirers in the homely Gay Meadow.

Broadbent's role as 'senior professional' at Gay Meadow was confirmed when Rowley made him captain the following season, 1965–66. Early in that season there was proof that Broadbent could sparkle at this level. A *Shrewsbury Chronicle* report of Town's 1–0 win at Oxford United said they were masterminded by Broadbent, whom the report described as 'brilliant'. By coincidence the star man in the Oxford side was a powerful half-back named Ron Atkinson – yes, that Ron Atkinson. He had been a groundstaff boy at Molineux and remains a firm admirer of Broadbent. Despite being Oxford's best player, that night Big Ron could not curb Broadbent.

Arthur Rowley then briefly tried Broadbent in the left-half position, which meant playing deeper and having more defensive responsibilities. He kept out young Ted Hemsley, the highly-capable sporting all-rounder who also played cricket for Worcestershire. Broadbent's stint in defence included the third-round League Cup game when Salop were knocked out at Rotherham 5–2. Broadbent was soon back in his more familiar inside-forward role after that. Hemsley returned to defence and they would help the Shropshire side on another epic FA Cup run.

Broadbent grabbed the winning goal when Salop began their Cup campaign with a 2–1 home win over Torquay in the first round. There were only four minutes left when he hit home a Lew Thom centre at the second attempt. Then Town beat Peterborough, also at Gay Meadow, by the odd goal in five to earn a third-round trip to Queen's Park Rangers. Four days before that big game, Broadbent made a happy return to Wolverhampton for a special presentation dinner, organised by the Wolverhampton Sportsmen's Committee. This group of local businessmen had been set up to organise thank yous to stalwart players, as clubs were not allowed to be directly involved. My dad was a member of that committee and it covered a broad cross section. My father had for many years run a hosiery stall in the much-lamented old Wolverhampton Market Hall, while among other members of the committee were bookmaker Bert Bartlam, builder Bill Whittingham and *Express & Star* sports editor George Gillott.

Broadbent's special night was staged at the Victoria Hotel in Wolverhampton town centre on Tuesday 18 January 1966. After a 10-course meal, Broadbent was presented with a silver salver and his testimonial match cheque of £1,777 by committee chairman Charlie Lewis, another local builder. Lewis said that Broadbent had given him much pleasure as a spectator and that the player had carved himself a place in Wolves' history. Wolves chairman John Ireland handed over more cash to Broadbent in the shape of his accrued share of benefit. On the back of the menu for the banquet is a glowing tribute. It's worth repeating some of it:

'When Peter Broadbent was transferred from Wolves to Shrewsbury Town almost exactly a year ago it took many people by surprise. Granted his days in the First Division were drawing to a close, but here was a great artist in footwork, ball control and the ability to cause panic in opposing defences. But Shrewsbury's player-manager Mr Arthur Rowley wanted him to bring out the best in his youngsters at the Gay Meadow, and that he certainly has done, culminating, recently, in his appointment as captain of the side. Many will recall that until his transfer to Arsenal, Bryn Jones was regarded as one of the best-ever inside forwards for Wolves, but Peter was greater.'

Reading between those lines confirms I am not alone in thinking Wolves had been a bit hasty in getting rid of Broadbent, when his vast experience might have been crucial in their battle against relegation.

Broadbent was gracious in his response to the presentations, telling the assembled guests 'I do not think I could have served a finer club and it has thrilled me no end to see them now fighting for promotion. This would be a great thing for England as well as Wolves, for the First Division is the only place where such a club, who have done so much for this country, should be. I wish them success in their efforts.'

Another who backs my theory that Wolves might have found Broadbent valuable in their bid to avoid relegation is full-back Bobby Thomson, who had just won his eighth England cap before his teammate's move to Shrewsbury. 'It was a time of change, new players were coming in but I think it possibly was a mistake to let him go,' Thomson reflected. 'He had a lot of football left in him. I know two players who played with him at clubs after he left Wolves and could not understand why they let him go. Both felt he was an asset to their two teams.'

Winger Terry Wharton shares the Thomson view, 'I think they got rid of him too soon. He still could have done a job for them.'

After the tribute dinner, Broadbent turned his attentions to the business of the FA Cup visit to QPR. Battling Town earned a goalless draw and then won the replay 1–0 thanks to a goal from former Burnley winger Trevor Meredith 12 minutes from time. That set up a fourth-round date with Carlisle United. The sides drew 0–0 at Gay Meadow and then 1–1 at Brunton Park, which in the days before penalty shoot-outs meant a second replay on neutral ground.

Deepdale, Preston, was the venue and Broadbent played his part in an epic match on 21 February 1966. Reward for the winners would be a trip to high-flying First Division outfit Chelsea.

Town were reeling in the first minute when goalkeeper Alan Boswell could not hold a Chris Balderstone free-kick. It was over an hour before Eric Brodie put Town level, only for Shrewsbury to fall behind to a Dave Wilson goal on 85 minutes. As ever, a few fans started to drift away and would miss the late drama. With the tie well into injury time, Broadbent stepped in. Let Mike Jones take up the story as he recorded it in his excellent club history, *Breathe on 'em Salop!* This is how he recalled it: 'Four minutes into injury time Town were awarded a free-kick on the right edge of the penalty area. Trevor Meredith stood over the ball, Peter Broadbent, for some unknown reason, patted his head. Trevor chipped the ball accurately towards Peter, who nonchalantly headed Town level with a goal which rates – with Trevor Brooking's 1980 Cup Final winner – as the game's unlikeliest headed goal.'

Thus dramatically reprieved, Salop took the lead 13 minutes into extra-time only for Frank Clarke's goal to be cancelled out within two minutes by Willie Carlin. The seventh, and winning, goal of a special game came four minutes from the end of extra-time through George Boardman's sweetly-struck shot.

Suddenly, Broadbent was back in the big time as Shrewsbury prepared to meet Chelsea in the fifth round on Saturday 5 March 1966. In previous rounds, Chelsea had beaten both the 1965 finalists, first holders Liverpool and then Leeds. Under Tommy Docherty's managership they had become a much-talked-about side. Shrewsbury supporters among a 51,144 crowd at Stamford Bridge numbered 15,000, but there was no fairytale ending. Chelsea cruised to a three-goal lead then Broadbent and Frank Clarke grabbed goals to rattle the Londoners, who were forced to hang on in the last 10 minutes to edge home 3–2. Bryon Butler's match report in the *Daily Telegraph* said that in Broadbent, Shrewsbury had 'easily the most accomplished forward afield'.

Shirley Broadbent was among the fans shouting on Shrewsbury at Stamford Bridge. 'I drove down so Peter could drive back with me – but I got lost. I followed this Shrewsbury coach and the driver must have lost his way, too. I ended up parking in Hammersmith, I think it was near Woolworth's. I know we had a job after the match trying to find where I'd parked. We eventually found the car but I think Peter was a bit annoyed, though he was pleased about the way they had played.'

Confirmation of the warm welcome Broadbent received at Shrewsbury came from Peter Dolby, a true Salop legend, who played some 350 League and Cup games, mostly as a central defender, for Town. 'We were staggered when Arthur Rowley told us Peter was coming. He arrived at the ground in a Triumph Toledo, which we regarded as quite a car in those days. He ran the show in that Cup tie against Chelsea. After the game I came off and I cried because we had played better than Chelsea. I felt we were worth at least a draw.'

Chatting to Dolby reveals just how well Broadbent fitted in with his new teammates, though he soon found life at Gay Meadow was very different from Molineux. 'Take the training kit, it was awful,' said Dolby. 'I don't know where Arthur got it from but it was very ordinary quality. We had numbers on the kit so we knew whose it was but we were training on mud and in the car park and it was not being laundered. The kit was just hung in the boiler room after training to dry. So after a few weeks it was really tatty and would be just chucked in the middle of the dressing room and everybody used to grab what looked like the best bits of kit. It was every man for himself. Peter could be late at times as he travelled from Codsall so once he found himself left with the worst tracksuit bottom and top, ripped, dirty, terrible. He just lifted it up and said "Bloody hell. An English international and I'm reduced to this." He said it with a wry smile and that just summed up the way he was.'

Dolby cited another example of the dry Broadbent wit. 'We were travelling back from Southend or somewhere – a long journey. We were playing cards, as you do. Peter liked his cards, poker or brag – he was a clever fella – and we got to talking about crowds and who had played before the biggest. I had played at Leeds, Frank Clarke and Trevor Meredith had played at places like Old Trafford. Others were listening and chipping in with theirs until the highest was about 70,000. Peter hadn't said a word so I said "Come on, Broaders, what about you?" Without looking up he said "Hundred and sixty thousand at the

Maracana." That killed the conversation dead. It was just the way he said it with that wry smile of his.'

Another Dolby recollection says much about Broadbent's personality and approach to the game. 'Shrewsbury were very good to us and we always stayed in good hotels. We were down in London one Friday night before a Saturday game and Peter asked me if I fancied a drink that evening. I was a bit surprised but said to Arthur Rowley "Gaffer we're just going out for a stroll." We found a pub and just had a quiet chat. I had half a Guinness and I think Peter had half a bitter, that's all. He just wanted to have a drink and relax. I think it was his way of dealing with any nerves.'

Maybe it was just a 'night before the match' thing with Broadbent, as Shirley Broadbent confirmed 'Peter was always very quiet on a Friday night. He never had a good night's sleep on a Friday before a match. Generally, though, he was very easy going. He would not come home and be in a mood if they'd lost or he'd played badly. He was never like that.'

Sadly, Town's season tailed off after that Chelsea game, but they finished a respectable 10th in the Third Division table, an improvement of six places on the previous season, as the nation turned its focus on to the summer's World Cup action. After Alf Ramsey's 'wingless wonders' had gloriously won the Jules Rimet Trophy the days of the orthodox winger were numbered, so the fact Broadbent was given the number-11 shirt when Shrewsbury opened the new season did not mean he had suddenly become an old-style winger. The numbers still retained some significance but as years went by they became of less relevance until the advent of squad numbers meant they were purely for identification. He played in the opening nine League games and scored his final goal for Town in their 6–1 League Cup win over Wrexham. Town had looked as though they might make a greater impact on the Third Division that season, but fate determined that Broadbent played no further part in it.

Aston Villa, a great name from football's Victorian era, were struggling in the First Division, having lost their most creative midfielder Phil Woosnam during the summer. The Welsh international moved to the US, where he would become manager-coach of Atlanta Chiefs in the North America Soccer League. Without

Woosnam, Villa's slump of the previous season continued. They lost eight of their first 12 matches in the 1966–67 season and manager Dick Taylor could see he needed an old head in the middle of the pitch. That's when he turned to 33-year-old Peter Broadbent. Taylor signed him for a mere £7,500 on 21 October 1966.

Broadbent had played 84 League and Cup matches for Shrewsbury. He had played only one complete season, yet he clearly created a big impression at this football outpost. Mike Jones's list of Town teams for all seasons has Broadbent in the best XI from the 1960s. He is named in the centre of the midfield trio in Jones's fantasy 4-3-3 line up.

To return to the top flight, even with a struggling Villa side, obviously boosted Broadbent's morale. Writing in the much-lamented *Sports Argus*, he said 'Signing for Villa was one of the nicest things that has happened in my football career. It is wonderful to know that after 15 years in soccer you are still appreciated and that there is a place for you in the top flight. Dick Taylor thinks I can do a useful job for Villa. I feel honoured by his faith in me and will do my utmost to carry out whatever role he wishes me to play.'

A forecast that Broadbent would do well for his new club came from an unexpected source – *Coal News*. The mining newspaper quoted his dad Jack: 'I reckon he's got three or four good seasons left in him. I know that Peter will play his very best for Villa and help them fight clear of the bottom of the First Division.' Sadly, the optimism of Broadbent senior proved misplaced.

Broadbent made his Villa debut against Sheffield United at Villa Park on Saturday 22 October 1966 and helped them gain a goalless draw. The next two matches brought a shock 1–0 win at Tottenham and a 3–2 home win over Albion. Maybe Broadbent could spark a revival? For a while it looked like it, as Villa continued to pick up a victory or two to keep their heads above water, intermixed with the odd heavy defeat – 5–1 at Fulham and 6–1 at Stoke. Barry Stobart, Broadbent's fellow 1960 FA Cup-Final hero, was also on Villa's books and his goals helped the survival bid.

Blackpool were rooted to the bottom of the table and certainties for relegation. Who was to join them developed into a contest between Newcastle and Villa. With nine games left, Newcastle looked the likelier to fall, but the Geordies managed to scrape nine points from their remaining fixtures. Villa, in stark contrast, lost seven and drew two. They were down. There was a certain irony for Broadbent as Villa dropped – back into the top flight as Second Division runners-up came his old club Wolves.

The man who had brought Broadbent back to the big time, Dick Taylor, was sacked at the end of a dismal season. Into his place came former Burnley centre-half Tommy Cummings, a man who, as a player, had seen Broadbent in his pomp. Yet the 1967–68 season saw Broadbent injured early on and then fail to win back his place. He made only eight League appearances as Villa struggled to finish an unimpressive 16th. Villa made a poor start to 1968–69 with only seven points from their first 11 games and Cummings at last turned to Broadbent to try to revive his side's fortunes. It was not too late for the veteran to make an impact, but time had run out for Cummings. He was sacked in November and once again Broadbent found himself at a famous old club in the middle of off-field upheaval.

With Cummings's departure, coach Arthur Cox was put in temporary charge, but unrest among the supporters was at a huge level. There was a public meeting of fans and the pressure eventually told on the club's board, who resigned. They were replaced by a new set of directors led by a local travel agent, Doug Ellis. Their first major decision was to find a replacement for Cummings and they certainly went high profile by naming Tommy Docherty. The Scotsman had hit the headlines sensationally earlier in the season when he resigned from the manager's job at QPR, claiming chairman Dick Gregory had refused him money to buy Brian Tiler from Docherty's old club Rotherham. The Doc had been at Loftus Road for just a month. The Scotsman had been led a merry dance by Broadbent on more than one occasion during his playing career and maybe he still rated him, as Broadbent kept his place in the side for virtually all the remaining matches.

Docherty was allowed to do at Villa what he was denied at QPR and duly signed Tiler. Not that there was any improvement in the club's fortunes. Villa finished two places lower in the table. The only relief amid the gloom was an FA

Cup run. The Doc would have taken great pleasure in starting the Cup exploits with a 2–1 away win over QPR. Broadbent missed that one but was in the team who held Southampton 2–2 at The Dell in the fourth round. The replay at Villa Park attracted nearly 60,000. It must have seemed like the old glory days for Broadbent. A big game in front of a huge crowd saw him rise to the occasion, as he scored the first goal in a memorable 2–1 win. He was also on target in the fifth round but could not stop Tottenham triumphing 3–2 at White Hart Lane. Again there was a large crowd – nearly 50,000 – but it was one last taste of the big time for Broadbent.

Villa were a struggling team and the set-up must have been very different from the regime Broadbent had known at Molineux. Stan Cullis had been a disciplinarian but the conduct he demanded from his players had paid dividends. One gets the feeling Villa Park's atmosphere was far more relaxed – and it showed on the field. 'Peter loved it when he went to Villa,' said Shirley Broadbent. 'They were a big club and a good crowd of players but I think they were too fond of a good time. When Docherty came in I think he wanted to be one of the boys and you can't be like that if you want to be a manager.'

In the summer, Docherty signed Bruce Rioch from Luton for £100,000 and clearly did not see Broadbent as part of his plans for getting Villa out of the Second Division. Villa made a dreadful start to the campaign, losing seven of their first nine games and drawing the other two. Yet Docherty did not turn to the wise old head of Broadbent. Instead he sold him in October 1969 to Stockport County. For the record, Docherty did go on to get Villa out of the Second Division that season – they were relegated to the Third!

The man who signed Broadbent for Stockport was a Scotsman, Walter Galbraith, who did not preside over one of the better periods in the history of the Cheshire club. Through no fault of his own he had found himself, earlier in his managerial career, at three clubs who subsequently lost their Football League status – New Brighton, Accrington Stanley and Bradford Park Avenue. Galbraith made an impact in at least one quarter. He was voted by one old Stockport fan, in a *Manchester Evening News* interview, as the club's worst-ever manager.

Broadbent was not a happy man at Edgeley Park and found he had moved from one struggling club to another. County had already played 13 League games when he joined them. They had lost 10 of them and won only one. There was at least one familiar face to greet Broadbent, as the right-half for County was Freddie Goodwin, who had played nearly 50 games for Wolves and left Molineux a year after Broadbent did.

It was not an auspicious start for Broadbent. His debut at home to Mansfield on Saturday 11 October 1969 ended in a 3–1 defeat, but then he saw County enjoy their best run of the season. In eight League and FA Cup games, they lost only once. There were even back-to-back League wins in that spell, but after the 1–0 home win over Bury at the start of November they would win only three more League matches that season. The return game with Mansfield in March saw Broadbent score, in a 4–1 defeat, the final League goal of his career. There were 7,829 fans at Field Mill to see it. His first goal for Wolves, against Albion at The Hawthorns nearly 19 years earlier, had been witnessed by roughly five times that number. County finished bottom of the Third Division with only 23 points and Galbraith took the blame, being sacked in the final few weeks of the season.

Broadbent perhaps should have done what Billy Wright did and retired while still remembered at his best by the fans. Instead, after he was released by Stockport at the end of their woeful season, he chose to play a few more games with non-League Bromsgrove Rovers before finally hanging up his boots. It was not in his nature to be inactive, as wife Shirley confirmed 'Tommy Docherty told him he could have a job in football if he wanted to stay in the game. But that wouldn't have suited Peter. He'd have had a heart attack. He wanted to be a player, though he wasn't very happy at Stockport. They let him train down here on his own and he was a very good trainer, but he didn't like it at Stockport.

'When he finally stopped playing he had his golf to concentrate on. Peter had to be active. Our son Gary was good enough to get on the European tour for about five years and he always said Peter was the best teacher he ever had. Peter was strong-willed though, and when they had to play each other in a local tournament once he really wanted to win, but I think Gary beat him. That was Peter – he always wanted to win, whether it was tennis, table tennis, darts or tiddlywinks. His golf was a big help after he gave up playing football. I think if he had taken it up instead of football, he would have been good enough to have played professionally.'

Many years later, Broadbent's grandson Andrew Smith, son of his daughter Debbie, would show he had inherited the family aptitude for golf when he became World Boys' Champion. He now works, still in the world of golf, in the US.

Back in 1970 Broadbent and Shirley also had a business to run – a babywear shop in Halesowen. 'He used to help in the shop,' said Shirley. 'He was happier selling prams and things like that but he did not like having to sell frilly clothes and such. He kept the books as well. He was very good at that. We had the shop for 30-odd years.'

Family holidays had also featured large in the Broadbents' life. 'It always seemed to be Woolacombe, the Narracott Hotel,' said Shirley. 'The children loved it there, they never wanted to go anywhere else. Quite a few footballers and their families used to go there too – people like George Showell, Johnny Kirkham and even Geoff Hurst. One year, there were 28 of us there. The men would have football games on the beach against the staff and, of course, the staff always wanted to get the better of them. The club managers would have gone mad if they'd have known.'

His Country's Loss

Without doubt Peter Broadbent was a great Wolves player. His doting Molineux fans felt he could also have been a great England player. Many would say his lack of England opportunity owed much to the presence of Fulham's Johnny Haynes. That may have been true in the latter part of Broadbent's career, but does not explain why he was overlooked for so long in the years before Haynes became the darling of the England selectors and of coach Walter Winterbottom.

Broadbent's representative honours amounted to 11 games – seven full caps, two games for the Football League, an England B cap and an England under-23 cap. One might think the blame for that lay solely at the door of Winterbottom, but his role as England 'manager' was vastly different from that of successors like Alf Ramsey, Bobby Robson and Sven Goran Eriksson. Winterbottom had to contend with the FA's selection committee. They came from various League clubs and would often push for their own particular favourites to be selected. There was some continuity but far too many players were discarded after just one or two matches.

Winterbottom, to his credit, fought slowly to get things changed so that the England side could be chosen as a team and players be given a chance to prove their ability over a few games. However, he never achieved full control and the selectors continued to have the last word, always chopping and changing. By the time Alf Ramsey took over and insisted that he alone chose the team, it was too late for Broadbent and his ilk.

There were other problems that beset the choosing of international sides during Broadbent's heyday. In the 1950s, international calls were no excuse for clubs to postpone a game. They could lose two or three players to England or other British Isles teams and still have to field a side in their scheduled League fixture. Understandably, club managers might kick up a fuss if too many of their team were wanted for international games.

So it is no wonder that someone of Broadbent's talent could be overlooked for so long despite some national newspaper writers pushing his claims. As early as October 1952 his name was being touted for a full cap. England had been held 2–2 by Northern Ireland in the first international of the season and the pundits wanted changes to be made. On Saturday 11 October Henry Rose wrote in the *Daily Express:* 'England's soccer selectors will be working off their Belfast hangover this afternoon in a widespread check on established international players and challengers for places in the next national side to meet Wales at Wembley. One of them will be at the Wolves-Newcastle star game to study the possibilities of young Peter Broadbent, the classy Wolves inside-left.'

It had escaped Rose that the dropping of John Taylor in favour of Dennis Wilshaw meant Broadbent had just switched to inside-right. The *Express* man was also wide of the mark in suggesting only one selector would be at Molineux. According to Bob Pennington, reporting in the *Sunday Pictorial* on Wolves' 2–0 win over Newcastle, 'Two selectors will report that 19-year-old RAF equipment assistant Peter Broadbent, Wolves inside-right, is England material.' Pennington praised Broadbent's speed of action when he opened the score. Broadbent was first to react after goalkeeper Bob Robinson fumbled a Leslie Smith shot. Pennington also praised Broadbent's confidence in taking the ball off his skipper Billy Wright when in position to do more with it, and for his stream of defence-splitting passes as well as two 'glorious left-foot drives that deserved to be goals'.

Were the England selectors brave enough to select a 19-year-old for his debut against Wales? They certainly were – they named 19-year-old Redfern Froggatt of Sheffield Wednesday at inside-right! Jackie Sewell, Froggatt's club colleague, and Spurs' Eddie Baily, the inside men in Belfast, were both dropped. The number-10 shirt went to Chelsea's Roy Bentley.

This was the first instance of Broadbent being overlooked and his brother, Jack, feels another influence may have been at work in denying Peter an England cap so early in his career. He believes Stan Cullis may have told Winterbottom – or others at the FA – that Peter was not ready for the England team. 'I spoke to quite a few Wolves players at the time,' said Jack, 'and they told me they felt Cullis had told someone at the FA that Peter was not ready. Cullis probably felt he was looking after him. So England lost interest – they would, wouldn't they? Nothing was ever said but I think Peter had an idea that Cullis had been involved.'

It may be that the Wolves boss, despite winning his first England cap two days short of his 21st birthday, did not want any of those fancy England ways to rub off on his young protégée.

Broadbent had obviously been mightily close to an England cap but, such is football life, a couple of months later he lost form and his place in the Wolves side. He bounced back early in the 1953–54 season and soon the selectors were again taking an interest, though not for the full England side but for the inaugural Under-23 team. There had been B internationals in the past aimed at giving representative experience to players on the fringe of the full England team, whatever their age might be. Now the plan was to give an opportunity to the youngsters, the internationals of the future.

Most of this first-ever England Under-23 team made little impact on the full international scene later on, though one did achieve immortality – Dudley-born Duncan Edwards. At 17, he was the youngest member of the side who faced the Italian youngsters in Bologna on Wednesday 20 January 1954. The Manchester United wing-half, who four years later died as a result of injuries received in the Munich Air Crash, would be a full international just over a year after the Under-23 outing.

Four others, in a team beaten 3–0 by the young Italians, went on to play for the full England side, though none became a permanent choice. Goalkeeper Ray Wood won three caps, Broadbent seven, Johnny Nicholls two and Frank Blunstone five. Wolverhampton-born Nicholls, in the middle of his greatest ever season with West Bromwich Albion, was the first to graduate to the full England side. He and clubmate Ronnie Allen were chosen for the game against Scotland at Hampden Park in April and both scored in England's 4–2 win. Both kept their places for the following game, a 1–0 defeat in Yugoslavia, but Nicholls never played for his country again. Neither he nor Allen was named in the World Cup squad that summer, despite being the most feared goalscoring partnership in the country.

Broadbent's Wolves pal Ron Flowers was a travelling reserve in that inaugural Under-23 squad and four years later became a regular England choice, winning 49 caps and three times captaining the side. He played in the 1962 World Cup and was still good enough to get into England's triumphant 1966 squad.

Italy Under-23: Stefani (Atalanta); Comaschi (Napoli), Zagatti (Milan); Turchi (Bologna), Bernascone (Atalanta), Unvernizzi (Udine); Conti (Sampdoria), Pivatelli (Bologna), Virgili (Udine), Tortui (Sampdoria), Savioni (Novara). Goals: Virgili, Pivatelli, Savioni.

England Under-23: Wood (Manchester United); Gunter (Portsmouth), Ellis (Charlton); Whitefoot (Manchester United), Dodgin (Arsenal), Edwards (Manchester United); Finney (Sheffield Wednesday), Broadbent (Wolves), Leary (Charlton), Nicholls (West Bromwich Albion), Blunstone (Chelsea).

As Wolves went on to make club history and become champions of England for the first time, Broadbent had plenty to celebrate. A Championship medal and an Under-23 cap in his first season as a true first-team regular must have given him reasons to be cheerful when the 1954–55 season opened. Wolves began the defence of their crown by going to the top of the table in the opening months. Broadbent was playing well, so maybe the England selectors would take note.

After England had bowed out at the quarter-final stage of the World Cup Finals in Switzerland during the summer, there was a unanimous call for new blood. The selectors got the message and no fewer than seven players made their debut in the opening international of the new season – against Northern Ireland in Belfast on 2 October 1954. Broadbent was not one of them, despite his bright early-season displays. The number-eight shirt went to Don Revie, better known then for his deep-lying centre-forward role with Manchester City. Revie was one of the newcomers, along with a Manchester United trio of goalkeeper Ray Wood and full-backs Bill Foulkes and Roger Byrne, half-backs John Wheeler of Bolton and the stylish Ray Barlow of Albion, Fulham's Johnny Haynes and Burnley winger Brian Pilkington. Revie and Haynes scored in England's 2–0 win and were promptly dropped for the next match. Foulkes, Wheeler, Barlow and Pilkington were never chosen again. You see the pattern?

Broadbent, a young player of great promise, ought to have been in the thoughts of the selectors. Instead they next turned to veterans Roy Bentley and Len Shackleton for their inside-forwards. These two duly helped England beat Wales and then world champions West Germany at Wembley. Between those two matches, Broadbent and his teammates attracted national acclaim when they beat Moscow Spartak at Molineux, and 12 days after the Germans had lost at Wembley Wolves were in the limelight again as mighty Hungarians Honved went the way of Spartak.

Bentley and Shackleton had every reason to think their part in helping to beat the Germans would guarantee them a run in the England side. Their reward when the showpiece encounter with Scotland came around in April? Both were dropped. Back came Revie and Broadbent's teammate Dennis Wilshaw, the latter scoring four goals as the Scots were whipped 7–2, enabling the selection committee to fend off the criticism hurled at them before the game.

With England due to make a summer tour of France, Spain and Portugal it might have made sense to take Broadbent along as clearly the search was on for someone to fill the number-eight shirt. One suspects that the many vested interests among the FA selectors would be against taking too many players from one club. They had already agreed to take Wolves quartet Bert Williams, Billy Wright, Ron Flowers and Wilshaw. Five from one club was clearly something they baulked at. So as well as Revie and Wilshaw the party included Chelsea's Bentley, who could also play as a centre-forward, and Sheffield Wednesday's Albert Quixall. Dubbed the 'Golden Boy' of football – and this nearly half a century before David Beckham – the fair-haired ball-juggling Quixall had been capped three times as a 20-year-old a couple of years earlier. Typically, he had soon been discarded.

Now Quixall was back in favour. He was similar in some respects to Broadbent, possessing some outrageous ball-juggling skills, but he did not have the creative passing ability of the Wolves man. He collected two more caps on the tour as England drew with Spain but lost the other two games. However, that was that. Quixall was never chosen again.

If Broadbent did not figure in the deliberations for the full side, maybe he could push his case through the Under-23 side, whose programme would be stepped up early in 1955. Alas, a dip in Wolves' form did not help his cause as defeats at home and away to Everton over Christmas saw the champions virtually surrender their title to Chelsea. Whatever the reason, he did not get the call when it came to the return match with Italy at Under-23 level, played at Stamford Bridge in January 1955. The number-eight shirt was given to John Atyeo. He would score 28 League goals that season but was plying his trade with Bristol City in the Third Division South. Broadbent was doing the business two divisions higher, but, as I may have intimated, logic and England selectors did not go hand in hand.

When England beat their young Italian counterparts 5–1, fired by Wolves' Ron Flowers and Manchester United's Duncan Edwards and with Atyeo one of the scorers, not even the perverse selection committee could alter the line up for the game against Scotland Under-23 a month later. The B international against West Germany at Hillsborough in March brought another game for Atyeo, though it was Wolves centre-forward Roy Swinbourne who hit England's goal in a 1–1 draw. It was clear that Atyeo was a selector's favourite. A big lad, with an eye for goal, he is revered at Bristol with one of the stands at City's Ashton Gate home bearing his name. He scored a load of goals but never played top-flight League football. A good player, yes, but in Broadbent's class? No way.

Before Broadbent could set about pushing his England claims or, such was the competition at Molineux, ensuring he stayed in the Wolves first team, there was more of the world to see. He may have missed out on an England trip to Europe but he did go on a far more intriguing trip as a prelude to the new season – Wolves' visit to the USSR to play Moscow giants, Spartak and Dynamo.

After that memorable excursion behind the 'Iron Curtain', it took Wolves a couple of games to get into their stride in the 1955–56 season, and then they struck a purple patch as seven goals were hit against Manchester City and nine against Cardiff. The team were flying, Broadbent was in fine form, while centre-forward Roy Swinbourne could not stop scoring – four against Manchester City, three at Cardiff and three again at home to Huddersfield, all on successive Saturdays.

Swinbourne was too old for the Under-23 side by then but Broadbent was still only 22. Any chance of a call-up disappeared, however, at Blackpool on 17 September 1955 when near the end of the game Broadbent burst an eyebrow in a challenge and had to have a couple of stitches inserted in the wound. He returned with some plaster over his right eye and was clearly struggling. He was not considered fit to play in Wolves' next match, though he did get an outing in the reserves. Any hope of being in the England Under-23 side to face Denmark at Portsmouth on 28 September had gone. Fulham pair Bobby Robson and Johnny Haynes were given the inside-forward berths and made the most of their opportunity, each scoring in a 5–1 win.

Maybe Swinbourne, in the form of his life, and Broadbent, having missed out on the Under-23 match, were destined for higher honours for there seemed every reason for the Wolves men to litter the first full England line up of the new season. Perish the thought. Even if it made sense, the FA had made a bizarre ruling for the friendly against Denmark in Copenhagen to coincide with the British Exhibition being staged there. It was decided that no more than one player per club could play in the game. With Billy Wright a permanent fixture as centre-half and captain, that ruled out any chance Broadbent or Swinbourne might have had. It also meant goalkeeper Bert Williams, who had made a dramatic return to the England side at the age of 32 a year earlier, would have to stand down. The number-eight shirt was given to Geoff Bradford of Bristol Rovers. He scored in an easy 5–1 win but looked out of his depth. He was never chosen again.

As other full internationals came along, Revie was given a one-game recall to the number-eight shirt, as was Haynes. Atyeo, now a Second Division player, Bristol City having been promoted, duly got his first full cap and scored in a 4–1 win over Spain. That match saw Haynes switched to inside-left and the Fulham man was from then on a virtual ever present in the national side.

Albert Quixall was back in favour for an Under-23 game but just when it seemed Broadbent was destined to be a nearly man at international level, he was named in the England B team against Scotland B. It had been over two years since his call-up for that first-ever Under-23 match. Broadbent's selection came as he hit the most successful scoring spell of his entire Wolves career – seven goals in just three games.

The clash with Scotland B on Wednesday 29 February 1956 was at a rain-soaked Dens Park, not the ideal place to try to sparkle, and it seems Broadbent was not alone in finding it heavy going. According to the FA Yearbook the 12,000 present saw 'a mediocre game in which few reputations were enhanced'. As in his Under-23 appearance, Broadbent was partnered on the right-wing by Sheffield Wednesday's Alan Finney. The teams were:

Scotland B: Brown (Dundee); Kerr (Partick Thistle), Rae (Falkirk); Neilson (St Mirren), Malloy (Cardiff), Glen (Aberdeen); Cullen (Luton), Yorston (Aberdeen), Mulkerrin (Hibernian), Turnbull (Hibernian), McCulloch (Airdrieonians).

Goals: Mulkerrin, McCulloch.

England B: Matthews (Coventry); Cummings (Burnley), Langley (Brighton); Wheeler (Bolton), Kennedy (West Bromwich Albion), Shannon (Burnley); Finney (Sheffield Wednesday), Broadbent (Wolves), Taylor (Manchester United), Atyeo (Bristol City), Perry (Blackpool).

Goals: Taylor, Atyeo.

After an early goal from Tommy Taylor, the Scots came back to lead 2–1 only for John Atyeo to snatch a late equaliser. Tommy Taylor kept his place in the next B international against Switzerland B three weeks later, but Broadbent and the other three forwards were dropped. Broadbent's number-eight shirt went to Blackpool veteran Ernie Taylor, who had won his one and only full cap in the infamous 6–3 Wembley defeat at the hands of Hungary three years earlier. The other inside-forward berth went to Leicester's Arthur Rowley. Taylor was 30 and Rowley 29 – hardly forward planning by the selectors and hardly geared to boost the confidence of young Broadbent. Neither Ernie Taylor nor Rowley ever figured in England's reckoning again.

Broadbent may have still been in contention for a full England chance but circumstances at club level did not help his cause. Legendary right-winger Johnny Hancocks was not the power he once was and Stan Cullis had made another excursion into the transfer market by signing Harry Hooper from West Ham to be his successor. The new boy was not eligible to play in the first team, however, so the manager decided to use Broadbent on the right-wing. His chance of playing for England in the prestige game against Scotland at Hampden Park may have gone, but any hopes of reviving his claims weren't helped by this switch. While England were disappointing in a 1–1 draw in Glasgow on 14 April 1956, Broadbent was wearing the number-seven shirt in Wolves' 2–1 win over Preston at Molineux.

The England display against the Scots was unsatisfactory. Tommy Taylor was played at inside-right alongside Nat Lofthouse – two centre-forwards, one the young pretender and the other the old Lion of Vienna. One had to go and Taylor was the man for the future, all of which meant that the number-eight shirt was up for grabs once more. Playing on the right-wing was no way for Broadbent to stake his claim. So when the mighty Brazilians came to Wembley at the end of the season, Taylor was duly moved to centre-forward and the inside-right spot went to John Atyeo. England won that game 4–2 but Atyeo hardly impressed, even missing a penalty – as did Manchester United skipper Roger Byrne. How Broadbent would have loved to have played in that match. As well as it being against the supremely talented Brazilians, who would be world champions two years later, he would have played alongside the legendary Stanley Matthews. Blackpool's 'Wizard of the Dribble' was recalled at 41 and led the South Americans a merry old dance.

Atyeo kept his place in the next game, the first of England's summer tour, but missed at least two good chances in a goalless draw with Sweden. He was promptly dropped and Broadbent may have taken some pleasure in seeing his Wolves colleague Dennis Wilshaw drafted into the team at inside-left, Haynes moving to inside-right.

The England team were enjoying some measure of success – they won the return game with West Germany 3–1 in Berlin – and Walter Winterbottom was at last getting home the message that it paid to have a settled side. Yet that one inside-forward place was still not settled as the 1956–57 season got under way. Alas, Broadbent was not able to take advantage. As is detailed elsewhere in this book, early in the season he lost form and his place in the Wolves team.

He was dropped after the 1–1 draw against Albion at The Hawthorns on Saturday 6 October 1956, the same day England played their opening match of the new season. It provided more evidence of the uncertainty of the number-eight shirt, as Don Revie was given a recall for the trip to face Northern Ireland in Belfast. After that the selectors gave three caps in successive games to Johnny Brooks. He was enjoying a spell of good form in a Tottenham side, who would finish runners-up in the First Division to Manchester United. Those three caps, which did bring him goals in the wins over Wales and Yugoslavia, would be as good as it got for Brooks.

Brooks's third and final game was the World Cup qualifier against Denmark. It was played at Molineux, which would have been a fitting place for Broadbent to win a first full cap. Broadbent, however, was now getting used to life as a Wolves reserve and could only watch as the Danes were beaten 5–2. There was added reason why an in-form Broadbent might have earned a cap. Johnny Haynes had been injured in the 3–0 win over Yugoslavia and it says much for the lack of suitable replacements that Manchester United's Duncan Edwards was moved up to fill the gap. To add to the Edwards legend, the Busby Babe set the fans in his native Black Country buzzing by hitting two goals to add to three by his club colleague Tommy Taylor. It was a magical Molineux night for those of us who saw it with two legends on the wings, Matthews and Finney, and Wolverhampton's own hero Billy Wright leading the team out on his own turf. If only Broadbent could have been part of it all.

Enough of wishful thinking. Broadbent was down the pecking order now and having to bide his time as he tried to win back his Wolves place. This he duly did and started 1957 back at his best. He would end the 1956–57 season with 17 League goals to his name, the best return of his Molineux career so far. Could he now attract the England selectors? Alas, in those days the only thing to be expected of the men who chose the England team was… the unexpected. So for the match against Scotland at Wembley the inside-forwards were one Tommy Thompson of Preston, who had only one previous cap as a Villa player six years earlier, and Derek Kevan, in his first full season as an Albion first-team man.

Kevan opened the scoring in a 2–1 win over the Scots, but neither he nor Thompson featured in the three World Cup qualifiers with which England completed the season. It was back to Atyeo and Haynes, as a win and a draw against the Republic of Ireland and a win in Denmark ensured a place in the Finals in Sweden. England had enjoyed a run of 15 games unbeaten, yet no fewer than six players had worn the number-eight shirt during that sequence.

So Broadbent was still waiting in the wings, though he had not even received a genuine audition. Yet, like the great actors, Broadbent had perfected his technique in the provinces and was ready for the big stage. He had honed his skills, he could take on opponents, spray telling long passes and turn up in the right place at the right time to collect his fair share of goals. He was virtually the complete player, the finished article. England would surely have to take note.

There was no restful close season for Broadbent. He was in the Wolves party who went to South Africa for the tour, which laid the foundations for the club's three-season domination of English football. Wolves made a great start to 1957–58 and Broadbent's form at last attracted wider attention once more. He was selected for the Football League against the League of Ireland at Elland Road, Leeds. None of the players chosen with Broadbent were in the full England side. It was another of those 'pat on the back for good lads' teams, which accounts for why it included men like Liverpool full-back Ronnie Moran, Reg Pearce of Luton and Bristol Rovers winger Peter Hooper (no relation to Harry). For centre-half Jack Charlton it was a rare representative honour before six years later Alf Ramsey plucked him from relative obscurity and moulded him into a World Cup legend. Jimmy Armfield, Ray Parry and Broadbent of this Football League line up would also go on to play for England. Parry hit two goals and Broadbent the other, as the Irish side were beaten 3–1. The teams on 9 October 1957 were:

Football League: Sims (Aston Villa); Armfield (Blackpool), Moran (Liverpool); Barlow (West Bromwich Albion), Charlton (Leeds), Pearce (Luton); Kaye (Barnsley), Broadbent (Wolves), Tindall (Chelsea), Parry (Bolton), P. Hooper (Bristol Rovers).

Goals: Parry (two), Broadbent.

League of Ireland: A. Kelly (Drumcondra); Fullam (Drumcondra), Nolan (Shamrock Rovers); T. Dunne (St Patrick's Athletic), Keogh (Shamrock Rovers), Rowe (Drumcondra); Pownall (Drumcondra), Peyton (Shamrock Rovers), Leahy (Evergreen United), Ambrose (Shamrock Rovers), Tuohy (Shamrock Rovers).

Goals: Nolan.

This proved a one-off for Broadbent. The FA decided to shelve B internationals and use Under-23 games to groom would-be England players. That ruled out Broadbent, who was then 24. No player had made a permanent claim to the number-eight shirt in the England side, but, that apart, the national team looked settled and for the first time real candidates to win the World Cup. For the first two games of the season, Derek Kevan was given his chance in the problem position. He failed to score in a 4–0 win over Wales in Cardiff and, after a shock home defeat by Northern Ireland, he was dropped in favour of his clubmate Bobby Robson, who scored two goals in a 4–0 win at Wembley over France.

Then came an event that cast a shadow over football. The plane bringing home the Manchester United side from their European Cup game against Red Star Belgrade crashed at a snowy Munich airport. United's wonderful young side were shattered and England would lose three of their key players, Roger Byrne, Tommy Taylor and the uniquely-talented Duncan Edwards. Amazingly, Bobby Charlton escaped the wreckage of Munich physically unscathed and would help the makeshift United side to the FA Cup Final at Wembley.

Even before the awful events in Germany, England's selectors must, at long last, have had Broadbent in their thoughts. His displays as Wolves surged towards the First Division title could not be ignored, even by that motley group of FA committeemen. However, Charlton's precocious post-Munich form saw him take over from Robson for the game against Scotland at Hampden Park. He scored a memorable volleyed goal to mark his debut as England won 4–0, and then struck both England goals as Portugal were beaten 2–1 at Wembley.

Before that game there was more proof that Broadbent, having been named in the preliminary group of 40 World Cup possibles, was now a strong candidate to be included in the squad for Sweden – he was selected for what was then a traditional eve-of-Cup Final game between England and Young England. Obviously, players of Cup-finalists Manchester United and Bolton could not be considered for the match and the scope was widened a little by declaring the game would be between England and Young England 'Past and Present'. That enabled the latter team to include players who had passed the Under-23 limit and Broadbent was one of four over-age players chosen. The others were full-backs Jeff Hall and Peter Sillett, and centre-half Maurice Norman.

As for the England team in that game at Stamford Bridge, on Friday 2 May 1958, the only changes from the side who had won at Hampden were enforced by the Cup Final, Bolton goalkeeper Eddie Hopkinson having to drop out along with Charlton. In the Under-23 Past and Present team, the inside-right berth was originally given to Chelsea's Jimmy Greaves, then just 18, with Broadbent playing inside-left. Brian Clough was at centre-forward. It would have been a chance for the precocious talent of Greaves to play alongside Broadbent, but the Chelsea man had to drop out and Manchester City's Joe Hayes played instead. England won 4–2 but the Under-23 Past and Present must have done well, as six of them made the World Cup squad – Sillett, Norman, Eddie Clamp, Peter Brabrook, Alan A'Court... and Peter Broadbent. Sadly, Greaves and Broadbent never did play in the same team.

One report said the scoreline flattered the senior side a little and added that Broadbent and A'Court featured in a late rally by the Under-23 team. This was the Stamford Bridge line up:

England: McDonald (Burnley); Howe (West Bromwich), Langley (Fulham); Clayton (Blackburn), Wright (Wolves), Slater (Wolves); Douglas (Blackburn), Robson (West Bromwich), Kevan (West Bromwich), Haynes (Fulham), Finney (Preston).

Goals: Finney, Haynes, Douglas, Kevan.

England Under-23 Past and Present: Hodgkinson (Sheffield United); Hall (Birmingham), Sillett (Chelsea); Setters (West Bromwich), Norman (Tottenham), Clamp (Wolves); Brabrook (Chelsea), Hayes (Manchester City), Clough (Middlesbrough), Broadbent (Wolves), A'Court (Liverpool).

Goals: A'Court, Clough.

Broadbent was now closer than ever to that deserved England cap. He was named in the England party for World Cup warm-up games against Yugoslavia in Belgrade and the USSR in Moscow. For this two-game trip England also took along Brian Clough, then in his goalscoring prime with Second Division Middlesbrough. He had hit 40 League goals that season and looked sure to be given a chance. He was not and did not even make the World Cup squad. In Belgrade, England were beaten 5–0 and Charlton was one of the players to be dropped for the second warm-up game.

Charlton, in the space of three games, had gone from golden boy to forgotten man. Winterbottom or the selectors, or maybe both, had decided he was hampering the England forward-line. They wanted someone who could create chances, although the 20-year-old Charlton had scored three goals in his first three internationals. So if England had decided such a player was not worth encouraging and wanted someone more creative, surely they need look no further than Broadbent? He could have every reason to think his moment had come, but, no, Robson returned as strike partner to Derek Kevan, who, with Clough's claims apparently dismissed, had taken over at centre-forward from the sadly departed Tommy Taylor. Kevan scored England's goal in the 1–1 draw in Moscow, where there was something for Wolves fans to cheer as the club provided the England half-back line in the shape of Eddie Clamp, Billy Wright and Bill Slater. Yet a great chance had been missed, the chance to take a look at Broadbent. If the selectors had been bold enough to play him in Moscow, the story of England in the 1958 World Cup Finals might have been very different. However, as Bobby Robson himself would say many years later, 'if' is the biggest word in football.

Broadbent may not have been given a look in during the two-match trip but at least, unlike Clough, he made the squad for Sweden. Even the England selectors could not ignore the claims of Wolves players after the way they had stormed to the club's second Football League title and it would have been madness to ignore the players, who had been instrumental in sweeping virtually all before them. Half-backs Clamp, Wright, Slater and Ron Flowers were the engine room of the good ship Wolves, but Broadbent was undoubtedly its navigator. So it was no surprise when four of those five – Flowers was the odd one out – were named in England's party of 20 for Sweden. Such had been the success of Wolves' right-wing that it would have made equal sense for Norman Deeley to have been among the 20. For the record, this was the party for Sweden:

Goalkeepers: Colin McDonald (Burnley), Eddie Hopkinson (Bolton); full-backs: Don Howe (West Bromwich Albion), Tommy Banks (Bolton), Peter Sillett (Chelsea); centre-halves: Billy Wright (Wolves), Maurice Norman (Tottenham); wing-halves: Ronnie Clayton (Blackburn), Eddie Clamp (Wolves), Bill Slater (Wolves); wingers: Tom Finney (Preston), Bryan Douglas (Blackburn), Peter Brabrook (Chelsea), Alan A'Court (Liverpool); centre-forwards: Derek Kevan (West Bromwich Albion), Bobby Smith (Tottenham); inside-forwards: Johnny Haynes (Fulham), Bobby Robson (West Bromwich Albion), Peter Broadbent (Wolves); utility player: Bobby Charlton (Manchester United).

Broadbent was one of four players in the squad yet to win a full cap. Tottenham duo Maurice Norman and Bobby Smith and Chelsea winger Peter Brabrook were the others. A fifth Wolves player might also have gone to Sweden. Left-back Gerry Harris, who had won four Under-23 caps that season, was told to keep himself fit just in case there was an injury to Bolton's Tommy Banks. To many of us, Harris, in the best form of his life at that time, would have been a better bet than Banks to fill the enormous gap left by the death of Roger Byrne.

England's opening World Cup game meant a second successive meeting with the USSR and an unchanged side this time drew 2–2 with them in Gothenburg. Alas, Tom Finney, on target with a penalty equaliser five minutes from time, was injured and would miss the rest of the tournament. A creditable 0–0 draw with Brazil and a not-so-creditable 2–2 draw with Austria meant England finished level on points with the USSR in their group. World Cup rules at that time ordained that there be a Play-off if teams were level. Having previously never played the Soviet Union, England would now meet them for a third time in the space of a month.

Throughout the group games, England's selection had come under much fire. Critics were divided about the effectiveness of Kevan as a centre-forward but they were probably more united in feeling Robson was not up to the task at inside-right. If there was any consensus, it was that a place had to be found for the raw talent of Bobby Charlton. Doing the obvious had never come into consideration as far as England selection was concerned. So Robson was indeed dropped but his place went not to the people's choice Charlton but to Broadbent. Out also went Blackburn's Bryan Douglas so that Broadbent and Peter Brabrook would form an untried right-wing.

Two new caps had been asked to play in a World Cup Play-off. They had not even had the chance for much preparation, as the England selection committee did not meet until lunchtime on the day of the game. Confessing my Midland bias, I have to say that I felt then, and do so now, that there were certain players for whom manager Winterbottom would always fight to be in the team. Johnny Haynes was undoubtedly one – to Broadbent's cost – and Blackburn half-back Ronnie Clayton was another. So it was hardly a surprise that Clayton was reinstated at the expense of Eddie Clamp. Yet, if a gamble was to be taken on Broadbent then keeping his club colleague in the side would surely make sense? Apparently not, even though these two had been star men in Wolves' Championship triumph. At least Broadbent at last had the opportunity that should have been his many years earlier.

This tournament was the first to have England games broadcast live, so my dad and I were able to watch on our black and white TV with a 12-inch (30cm) screen as the drama unfolded. There was the added bonus of seeing how our local men would do. We knew Billy Wright and Bill Slater had what it took, but could Broadbent hack it at this level? We need not have worried.

Broadbent was the star performer on Tuesday 17 June 1958 in Gothenburg and Brabrook, at least, looked an improvement on Douglas. Despite all their efforts, however, the game turned out to be the first of a succession of World Cup nail-biters, which it seems England fans are destined to endure generation after generation. On this occasion the side did everything except score, going close several times. Inevitably, the USSR scored the game's only goal. Broadbent was a revelation, his display proving what so many of us had thought for a long time – that he was international class and should have been given his chance long before this.

A game with so much at stake not surprisingly saw two tired teams playing cat and mouse for the first half hour. Then England burst into life and it was the two fresh faces who stirred things up. Broadbent tried a quick shot from 25 yards, which the redoubtable Lev Yashin held after a leaping save. Broadbent was suddenly inspired. He moved out to the wing and then drew Yashin to his near post before laying on an inch-perfect pass for Brabrook at the far post. It looked a simple tap in but the Chelsea man contrived to lunge at the ball instead of taking his time and merely directed it straight to a grateful Yashin.

If Broadbent, wearing the number-18 shirt, was laying on chances, Brabrook continued to miss them and twice in the second half he raced through to send shots past the Russian 'keeper, only to see the ball hit the far post each time. The first time the ball was cleared and the second it rebounded into the arms of Yashin. Brabrook did eventually get the ball into the net but he had stumbled on his way into the penalty area before he shot and the referee ruled that in keeping his balance Brabrook had handled the ball. The Russians then scored against the run of play. Goalkeeper Colin McDonald made a poor clearance. The ball went to Falin 15 yards inside the England half and he was able to find Voinov, who played centre-forward Simonian through with Ilyin in support and only Billy Wright there to try to stop him. Simonian calmly drew the Wolves skipper into the tackle before squaring the ball to Ilyin, who was then able to beat the advancing McDonald. It was a situation similar to Brabrook's efforts against Yashin as the ball also struck a post. Luck was with the Russians, however, and the ball did not rebound to a thankful 'keeper, but merely rolled into the other corner of the England net. With Broadbent continuing to sparkle, England managed several more chances before the end but it was not their day.

At the end of the game, Broadbent and the other players were taken by skipper Billy Wright to each side of the pitch to salute the fans at the Ullevi Stadium. Wright, at 34, must have known he had played in his last World Cup Final. Broadbent, at nine years his junior, had reason to hope he might play in another.

Had Broadbent been as good as my memory told me from that day nearly 50 years ago when I watched the grainy picture on the TV in our front room in

Bilston? A match report by one of the top sportswriters of the time, *Daily Express* man Desmond Hackett, provides an answer. He wrote:

'Only a man with a heart made of pools coupons could have watched unmoved at the end of the game when the players came to each side of the pitch to salute the Gothenburg crowd. There was something immensely sad about the shirts stained with sweat from their courageous but unskilled labours.

'As the moving-off players forced a trot from their tired limbs, three England selectors walked across the pitch with heads bowed. They were the mourners at the funeral of the team whose chances they killed. These selectors did not see earlier that leaving out men like Bobby Charlton and Peter Broadbent cut down the vital ammunition of skill.

'Broadbent brilliantly proved the point that skill beats slugging soccer. He was England's best forward, an elegant among the brawn boys. He was the man who panicked the Russians, the menace who plagued and probed when England had their finest half hour in the second half.' The headline on Hackett's report said it all, '"Brains" Broadbent capped too late'.

England: McDonald (Burnley); Howe (West Bromwich Albion); Banks (Bolton); Clayton (Blackburn), Wright (Wolves), Slater (Wolves); Brabrook (Chelsea), Broadbent (Wolves), Kevan (West Bromwich Albion), Haynes (Fulham), A'Court (Liverpool).

USSR: Yashin (Moscow Dynamo); Kesraev (Moscow Dynamo), Kuznetsov (Moscow Dynamo); Voinov (Dynamo Kiev), Krijevski (Moscow Dynamo), Tsarev (Moscow Dynamo); Apoukhtin (CSKA), Ivanov (Moscow Torpedo), Simonian (Moscow Spartak), Falin (Moscow Torpedo), Ilyin (Moscow Spartak).

Goal: Ilyin (65).

Attendance: 23,182.

If Hackett's words reinforced the way I remembered Broadbent's virtuoso performance from my ringside seat on our front room settee, the *Daily Express* man also confirmed it had not been the best of competitions for Johnny Haynes. 'As the minutes ebbed away it became clear that the long gruelling run on the England plan of "never stop chasing" had finally snuffed out the bright soccer genius that was once Johnny Haynes.'

The inquests after the tournament were not as intense as after England failures in more recent times, yet questions were still asked – such as why were changes not made sooner? Blackburn winger Bryan Douglas was way below form and Bobby Robson may have been more tactically aware than Bobby Charlton, but he never looked to have the natural striker's instinct that the United man possessed. If the selectors were adamant that Charlton was not the answer, why not give Broadbent his chance before that do-or-die Play-off? More to the point, why had Broadbent not been tried earlier in the season? It seems bizarre that such decisions should be in the hands of a selection committee, which included Harry French of Middlesbrough and Chesterfield's Harold Shentall. One was a fruit merchant and the other a fruit wholesaler, but that hardly guaranteed they knew the pick of the crop when it came to choosing World Cup sides.

Wolves boss Stan Cullis wrote in his autobiography, *All For The Wolves*, that if Brabrook and Broadbent had been brought into the team for the Austria game, England might have gained automatic qualification for the quarter-finals. 'To my mind, the selection committee had violated a fundamental principle of team selection, and I do not base this criticism on wisdom acquired after the event,' wrote Cullis. 'From my experience at Molineux, I would not hesitate to state that there is no policy more disastrous than to persist with a player who has temporarily lost form. If he is retained in the side in the hope that he will find his missing confidence and touch, the team's engine is working on one fewer cylinder and games which should have been drawn will be lost.'

One who did not enhance his reputation was golden boy Haynes. To his credit, he later admitted he had not been on top form though pointed out he was not 100 percent fit. 'One thing was that the hard grounds in Sweden gave me very painful blisters and my feet were cut about rather badly,' said Haynes. He thought he had not played too badly against Brazil but against the USSR in the group match and the Play-off his view was 'I might just as well have stayed in the dressing room.' If Haynes himself knew he was struggling, one can only wonder why the selectors, or manager Winterbottom, did not have the courage to drop him.

A Season with England

Broadbent's debut in the group Play-off in Sweden had virtually guaranteed him a place in England's first post-World Cup international. Furthermore, he had started the new campaign in good form and so his place was assured in the team to meet Northern Ireland in Belfast on Saturday 4 October 1958 in the first match of the Home International Championship – the now defunct competition that involved the four home countries each meeting one another once during the season.

Broadbent would again team up with Peter Brabrook on the right-wing, but centre-forward Derek Kevan was dropped as the clamour to select Bobby Charlton won the day. Charlton, who had been wearing the number-10 shirt for his club, had struck 10 goals in 10 games as Manchester United made it clear they would be among the teams after Wolves' First Division crown. Charlton had also scored a hat-trick a few days earlier, as England's Under-23s defeated their Polish counterparts 4–1 at Hillsborough. United's good start also brought a first cap for Wilf McGuinness, who was preferred, probably on age grounds, to Wolves' Bill Slater.

Another change in the England team was the return of veteran winger Tom Finney. The Preston man deservedly ranks among football's all-time greats, and Broadbent among his many admirers. Finney was looking for the goal that would make him England's outright all-time top goalscorer, a distinction he was, at that time, having to share with Bolton's Nat Lofthouse on 29 goals. When asked many years later who was his favourite player, Broadbent opted for Brazil maestro Pelé, but said Finney was the best ever English player. 'He could play anywhere in the forward line and he didn't seem to have a favoured foot,' said Broadbent, 'he could use them both. You never knew which was his natural one. Yes, Pelé was undoubtedly the World's best player but I'd put Tom Finney second. He was a great player.'

If the game at Gothenburg had been more important than the one in Belfast, there was no comparison in atmosphere. The Ullevi Stadium had been sparsely populated. Windsor Park was bursting at the seams and not even overnight rain and another downpour before kick-off could dampen the spirits of the home fans. Broadbent must have savoured it all as the teams walked out side by side, led by the drums and pipes of the First Battalion Irish Fusiliers.

Northern Ireland had enjoyed a better World Cup than England; they had reached the quarter-finals and were in the middle of possibly their greatest era. They had won at Wembley a year earlier and with players like Harry Gregg, Danny Blanchflower and Jimmy McIlroy, were easily a match for England.

On a greasy pitch, there was plenty of goal entertainment for the crowd of nearly 60,000, as the Irish led three times but were finally held 3–3. Charlton was a success, with two goals to make it five in his first four internationals. Broadbent did have a shot kicked off the line by Newcastle full-back Dick Keith early in the match, but he was given a role totally out of keeping with the way he played for Wolves, as a Press Association report of the game confirms: 'England's plan of attack seemed to be for Haynes and Charlton to do the constructive work with Broadbent the spearhead. These tactics were difficult to understand. Broadbent, a fine constructive player, looked unsuited to his new role.'

Northern Ireland led when Blanchflower and McIlroy sent Wilbur Cush racing through to slip the ball past Colin McDonald on 33 minutes. Six minutes later Charlton fired a right-foot special into the top corner of the net. After 58 minutes the Irish struck again, a centre from Billy Bingham was cleared only as far as Bertie Peacock who scored from long range. Eight minutes later Finney duly posted up his goal record when he made it 2–2. Back came Ireland within two minutes. McDonald could not hold on to Peter McParland's centre under pressure from Tommy Casey, who bundled the ball home. There was a quick response from England with another Charlton special completing the scoring.

Northern Ireland: Gregg (Manchester United); Keith (Newcastle), Graham (Doncaster); Blanchflower (Tottenham), Cunningham (Leicester), Peacock (Celtic); Bingham (Luton), Cush (Leeds), Casey (Portsmouth), McIlroy (Burnley), McParland (Aston Villa).

Goals: Cush, Peacock, Casey.

England: McDonald (Burnley); Howe (West Bromwich Albion), Banks (Bolton); Clayton (Blackburn), Wright (Wolves), McGuinness (Manchester United); Brabrook (Chelsea), Broadbent (Wolves), Charlton (Manchester United), Haynes (Fulham), Finney (Preston).

Goals: Charlton (two), Finney.

Attendance: 58,000.

While Wolves had two players on England duty and Manchester United three, the sides still had to fulfil their League fixture at Molineux and it was the cue for some Wolves innovation which, surprise, surprise, did not go down too well with the Football League. Wolves, with United's agreement, staged the match in the evening. They had hoped to get television interested in broadcasting the match live, but the League moved swiftly to knock those plans on the head. Saturday evening football was pushing it a bit but live TV too – that would never do. How times have changed!

If the League wanted continuity in domestic football, continuity was certainly not a quality that applied to the England team. Broadbent, not allowed to play in the role he fulfilled for his club, had not had the best of games at Windsor Park, but it was hardly surprising. So the saga of perverse England selection went on. Out went Broadbent and his fellow Gothenburg debutant Brabrook. No suggestion of giving them a few games to establish themselves or dropping Haynes after his miserable World Cup. Out, too, went young McGuinness and for the visit of the USSR the selectors recalled Bill Slater at the age of 31. Nat Lofthouse, the old Lion of Vienna himself, was brought back from the international wilderness to lead the forward line at the age of 33. Charlton was given Broadbent's number-eight shirt and Brabrook made way for another of the selectors' favourites, Bryan Douglas.

Johnny Haynes kept his place. He had not sparkled in the World Cup but he was England's golden boy and would have to have a monumental loss of form to be dropped. In those days BBC TV had a midweek programme called *Sportsview,* and the men in charge of it clearly felt Haynes should go – or at least decided it would make good television to suggest his time was up. They did a hatchet job on him, even editing a film of a Fulham match to show only

Haynes's errors. It was all part of their case against Haynes, ending with the suggestion that he should not play against the Russians. It was a cheap piece of journalism, did not help Broadbent's cause and served as superb motivation for the Fulham man. Haynes rattled in three goals as England won 5–0 at Wembley. To their credit, the *Sportsview* crew appeared on the programme the following week in sackcloth and ashes. The Russian match also saw Lofthouse hit his 30th goal for England to draw level with Finney.

Clearly the message to Broadbent was to go back to his club and forget about international football. In any case, Wolves were about to make club history by taking part in the European Cup for the first time.

While Wolves were struggling against the Germans Schalke 04 in the first leg of their European match and were held 2–2, Broadbent scoring twice, events elsewhere on the same night would lead to an unexpected resurrection of his international career. At Anfield the Football League were beating the Irish League 5–2, but Johnny Haynes picked up an injury. He would not be fit to play in England's next game. Who would be his deputy? Even the selectors could not get this one wrong. It was when Broadbent was with Wolves at the Duisberg Sportschule, preparing for the return leg against Schalke at Gelsenkirchen, that he learned that he had been named in the England side to face Wales at Villa Park. So had Ron Flowers, taking over from clubmate Bill Slater. Flowers had previously been capped against France in Paris in 1955, but, by his own admission, had a poor match.

Wolves bowed out of the European Cup in Germany but club problems were put to one side as Broadbent, Wright and Flowers turned their attention to England's second game in the Home International Championship against Wales on Wednesday 26 November 1958. The wingers who had played against the USSR, Bryan Douglas and Tom Finney, were, like Haynes, also on the injured list so there would be no second chance for Broadbent to play in the same team as the Preston legend. Douglas's injury was an ideal opportunity for the selectors; if they were going to include Broadbent why not play him alongside his Wolves right-wing partner Norman Deeley? Don't be silly, that would smack of logic. In came Arsenal winger Danny Clapton. He was enjoying a brief purple patch and – excuse the chip on my Midland shoulder once more – probably had the London soccer experts pushing his cause. To be fair, Clapton had been given an outing in the Football League side at Anfield and had a satisfactory game. So he got the vote over Deeley, but the young Gunner did not make the most of his unexpected chance and never played for England again. In stark contrast, the match at Villa Park was an undisputed triumph for Broadbent.

Wales, another British side who had done better than England in Sweden, took a shock lead after 15 minutes. Goalkeeper Colin McDonald could not hold a Terry Medwin cross shot and Derek Tapscott drove home the rebound. On the half hour, Wales skipper Dave Bowen suffered an arm injury and had to continue as a virtual passenger on the left-wing. Bobby Charlton then went close to an equaliser with a couple of trademark long shots but not as close as Broadbent, whose header struck the bar. The Wolves man was not to be denied and duly levelled with a memorable goal before half-time. He latched on to a Graham Shaw through ball and, though surrounded by Welsh defenders, lobbed the ball sweetly over the head of Jack Kelsey, whom he had spotted off his line.

Wales started to call the tune in the second half with Tapscott, Ivor Allchurch and Phil Woosnam prominent. In contrast, England were struggling. Little was seen of the veteran Nat Lofthouse, Charlton's shots dried up and the wingers were ineffective. Broadbent posed the only home threat. It was no surprise when Allchurch pivoted to send home a shot via a post to give Wales the lead once more. Broadbent, supposedly in the team as the maker of chances, showed once again he could take them, too. A'Court, for once, beat his man and Broadbent leaped high to meet his centre and steer his header into the top corner of the net. The teams in the 2–2 draw were:

England: McDonald (Burnley); Howe (West Bromwich Albion), Shaw (Sheffield United); Clayton (Blackburn), Wright (Wolves), Flowers (Wolves); Clapton (Arsenal), Broadbent (Wolves), Lofthouse (Bolton), Charlton (Manchester United), A'Court (Liverpool).

Goal: Broadbent (two).

Wales: Kelsey (Arsenal); Stuart Williams (West Bromwich Albion), Hopkins (Tottenham); Crowe (Aston Villa), Mel Charles (Swansea), Bowen (Arsenal);

Medwin (Tottenham), Ward (Bristol Rovers), Tapscott (Cardiff), Ivor Allchurch (Newcastle), Woosnam (West Ham).

Goals: Tapscott, Allchurch.

Attendance: 41,581.

A young Wolves fan at that game was Malcolm Cookson, who is still watching Wolves nearly 50 years later. 'I'd just started work at Wolverhampton Council, bricklaying, but I'd got the afternoon off so my dad took me to Villa Park,' he told me. 'We stood on the old kop, the open end, and Peter was brilliant that day. Yet he was only in because Johnny Haynes was injured. They'd dropped Peter after the Ireland match but they couldn't drop him after the way he played against Wales.' Cookson has other thoughts on that match, which tend to coincide with mine. He thought Deeley could have been given a chance on either wing, with both Douglas and Finney sidelined. 'I think Danny Clapton got in because of the old London bias business and as for A'Court – Ron Flowers fed him all afternoon, lovely passes, but he got no change out of Stuart Williams. He just could not beat him.'

Someone else felt Broadbent was the star man. The great Stanley Matthews was at the game and though his words in a national newspaper may have been penned for him by a ghost writer, the views were those of the former England maestro and he was bubbling over with enthusiasm for Broadbent. 'Here is a man we have been searching for since we lost those old inside-forward ball artists,' was the verdict of the Blackpool wing wizard. 'After his great display against Wales, he must be our regular inside-right in future internationals – never again a makeshift deputy. He has earned the right to full England status. He isn't afraid to hold the ball in an era of quick passing and first-time kicking. What a delight it is to see him dribbling through, beating his men with a perfect body swerve.'

After a brief spell wearing the number-nine shirt for Wolves, Broadbent settled down in a new-look forward line who would go on to clinch Wolves' second successive First Division title in style. So he could feel confident of keeping his place in the England team for the annual encounter with the Scots. Before that, there was a little matter of the Football League's visit to Dublin to play the League of Ireland at Dalymount Park. It was a chance to look at one or two likely candidates for the Wembley game, but few enhanced their reputations (apart from Bolton winger Doug Holden), with the Irish rising to the occasion to earn a goalless draw. The line up on 17 March 1959 was:

League of Ireland: Blount (Transport); Blake (Sligo Rovers), Fullam (Drumcondra); McDonagh (Dundalk), Keogh (Shamrock Rovers), Rowe (Drumcondra); Coleman (Drumcondra), Dunne (St Patrick's), Doyle (Shelbourne), Hamilton (Shamrock Rovers), Tuohy (Shamrock Rovers).

Football League: McDonald (Burnley); Howe (West Bromwich Albion), Shaw (Sheffield United); Clayton (Blackburn), Gratrix (Blackpool), Flowers (Wolves); Wilkinson (Sheffield Wednesday), Broadbent (Wolves), Viollet (Manchester United), Haynes (Fulham), Holden (Bolton).

Having taken a look at Dennis Viollet in the number-nine shirt, the selectors decided for the visit of Scotland to revert to the skilful inside trio used against Northern Ireland, Broadbent, Charlton and Haynes, only this time Broadbent would be allowed to play something near his normal style. It was a brave experiment to dispense with the Nat Lofthouse type of leader and one many hoped would be persevered with, irrespective of the odd short-term setback. Some hope!

However, the plan of using three players better known for their skill rather than their strength met with initial success when the Scots were beaten 1–0 at Wembley on Saturday 11 April 1959. Overshadowing the match was the achievement of Broadbent's club colleague Billy Wright, becoming the first man in the history of the game to appear in 100 internationals. To complete his day, Wright was watched by wife Joy, of the famous singing Beverley Sisters. He had been worried she might not be allowed to attend, having given birth to their first child, Victoria, just six days earlier. Joy had her twin sisters, Teddy and Babs, with her at the match.

Broadbent and his one-time fellow lodger Ron Flowers took great pleasure in being at the old stadium on Wright's special day. They, like the rest of the Wolves players, had great affection and admiration for a man who had always played the game hard but fair, who led by example and never got too big for his boots. The distinction of being the first footballer to win a century of caps could not have happened to a lovelier man. There was a note of sadness about the day though. A week earlier, former England full-back Jeff Hall had died after contracting polio. As a mark of respect to the Birmingham City defender, the 22 players wore black armbands. It was barely a month since Hall's last game for Blues before illness struck him down so quickly. Indeed, he had played against Wolves in March.

Although the victory over the Scots was by the narrowest of margins, it was an emphatic one in all other respects as the eminent football correspondent of *The Times*, Geoffrey Green, confirmed 'The truth is obscured by the bare result. Nearer the mark perhaps would have been 4–0. They (England) held the whip hand all through and though the goals did not come as they should, the flow and form of their movement from midfield to the Scottish line had the bloom of water colours as they painted their patterns.'

Billy Wright, in his book *One Hundred Caps And All That*, wrote 'The ball playing abilities of Broadbent, Charlton and Haynes were too much even for such admirable defenders as Dave Mackay and Tommy Docherty. And without centre-half Bobby Evans and the ever-reliable Bill Brown the score might indeed have been 4–0.'

It was goalkeeper Brown who denied Broadbent a first-half goal, as the *Sporting Star* on-the-spot-match report related: 'England almost took the lead after 20 minutes. Beautiful combined play between Haynes, Charlton and Holden, left Broadbent with a golden opportunity only about eight yards out. A goal looked certain but Brown flung himself at the shot and managed to divert the ball for a corner.'

The England plan had nevertheless seemed to be working well and there is a reference earlier in the match report to Haynes and Broadbent combining splendidly. When the goal finally came on the hour, Broadbent played a prominent part. His perfectly-weighted pass sent Douglas away down the right and Charlton came bounding in to meet the winger's high centre. Charlton's powerful downward header gave Brown no chance.

The *Sporting Star* also notes that at the end of the game, England's players 'cheered' Wright from the field. In those days, a reporter would dictate his match report over the phone to a copytaker, taking his words down on to a typewriter. It was never easy trying to hear what a reporter was saying from a press box at a noisy stadium, so what came across as 'cheered' was probably originally dictated as 'chaired' – for that was what happened. At the end of the match Wright was chaired from the field on the shoulders of Ronnie Clayton and Don Howe, with Broadbent in close attendance.

England: Hopkinson (Bolton); Howe (West Bromwich Albion), Shaw (Sheffield United); Clayton (Blackburn), Wright (Wolves), Flowers (Wolves); Douglas (Blackburn), Broadbent (Wolves), Charlton (Manchester United), Haynes (Fulham), Holden (Bolton).

Goal: Charlton.

Scotland: Brown (Dundee); McKay (Celtic), Caldow (Rangers); Docherty (Arsenal), Evans (Celtic), Mackay (Tottenham); Leggat (Fulham), Collins (Everton), Herd (Arsenal), Dick (West Ham), Ormond (Hibernian).

Attendance: 98,329.

Shirley Broadbent was a spectator at Peter's home internationals against Wales and Scotland and remembers them with pride. 'I was just so thrilled. It was an honour to play for your country. When they played the national anthem the tears were rolling down my face. At the Scotland match I sat next to the Beverley Sisters and when they got up at half-time I thought I'd follow them if they were going to have a cup of tea or whatever, but, when I got to the hospitality room they were in, the man on the door would not let me in. Wives weren't included in anything in those days but the Beverley Sisters must have had some special arrangement.'

For the second season running, Broadbent featured in the England v Young England game on the eve of the Cup Final. This time, though, he was in the senior team, who were the same team to beat Scotland with the exception of the injured Bryan Douglas. This would have been an ideal opportunity to have a look at Norman Deeley alongside his club colleague, but instead the England number-seven shirt at Highbury on Friday 1 May 1959 went to Warren Bradley.

The newcomer had been a successful amateur with Bishop Auckland and had joined Manchester United as a professional, as they sought to rebuild the team following the devastation caused to their squad by the Munich Disaster. England led 3–0 at one stage through two Bobby Charlton goals and an own-goal from Fulham 'keeper Tony Macedo, but the Under-23 side fought back to draw 3–3 thanks to goals from Ray Parry, Ray Pointer and Jimmy Greaves.

It had been a happy first appearance at Wembley for Broadbent when he faced the Scots and he returned to the stadium, six days after the Highbury match, when England faced Italy prior to the testing close season tour to South America. The selectors decided to reward Bradley with a cap to go with those he had won as an amateur and once again Wolves fans were left wondering why Deeley, so successful that season as Broadbent's partner, had not been given his chance. If not Deeley, who had played much of the campaign on the left-wing, there was a strong case for another Wolves man. Micky Lill had been brought in on the right-wing for the second half of the season and had received some rave notices, resulting in him being hotly tipped as a future England international. Neither Lill's emergence nor Deeley's continued good form won the day.

The match was an eventful one and was clearly affected by an injury to Ron Flowers. He was carried off, having broken his nose in a collision with an Italian player, and while he was having treatment England surrendered the two-goal lead they had established in the first half. Broadbent's pass had enabled Bobby Charlton to open the scoring and when goalkeeper Buffon could not hold a Haynes volley, Bradley was on the spot to mark his debut with a goal. During the 15 minutes Flowers was off the field, Brighenti and Mariani took advantage of some poor defending to hit back for Italy. Both sides went close before the final whistle, but 2–2 was probably a fair reflection of an entertaining game. The sides at Wembley on Wednesday 6 May 1959 were:

England: Hopkinson (Bolton); Howe (West Bromwich Albion), Shaw (Sheffield United); Clayton (Blackburn), Wright (Wolves), Flowers (Wolves); Bradley (Manchester United), Broadbent (Wolves), Charlton (Manchester United), Haynes (Fulham), Holden (Bolton).

Goals: Charlton, Bradley.

Italy: Buffon (AC Milan); Robotti (Fiorentina), Casteletti (Fiorentina);

Zaglio (Roma), Bernasconi (Sampdoria), Segato (Fiorentina); Mariani (Padova), Brighenti (Padova), Gratton (Fiorentina), Galli (AC Milan), Petris (Fiorentina).

Goals: Brighenti, Mariani.

Attendance: 90,000.

For the exacting South American tour, Broadbent was at last joined by Deeley. Douglas was still injured, Clapton's call-up had been just another quirky selection, Bradley, despite his goal, had not been a hit against Italy and so maybe Deeley was about to be given the chance that his performances had earned.

First port of call was Brazil to meet the world champions. When Broadbent and the rest of the party visited Rio de Janeiro's famous Copacabana beach, they soon discovered that the stories of young Brazilian kids learning their remarkable ball control on the sand were not mythical. As the England men strolled along the promenade they could see for themselves. There were other sights to take in. A steep walk took them to the Corcovado, where the huge monument to Christ dominates Rio.

It was a great compliment to Wolves when the England side were announced. Deeley was indeed preferred to Bradley so that the club had four men in the national side for the first time since Bert Williams, Billy Wright, Ron Flowers and Dennis Wilshaw lined up against France four years earlier. What a place for Deeley to make his debut! The Maracana, football's biggest stadium. The experience was something Broadbent often recalled. The England team were given a motorcycle escort from their hotel to the huge circular stadium. Players changed in dressing rooms below ground level and emerged through a tunnel and then up steps into the vast bowl. The noise that greeted them was fearful – 160,000 spectators and still room for 40,000 more. This was Brazil, the new masters of football against the old masters. Broadbent always regarded it a privilege to have played in the same game as Pelé, the man he rated as the greatest footballer ever. The Brazilian team that day included others not far behind Pelé in world ranking – goalkeeper Gilmar, full-backs Djalma Santos and Nilton Santos, and midfield maestro Didi. Deeley was not the lone debutant. Full-back Graham Shaw was replaced by Blackpool's Jimmy

Armfield, who, with Jimmy Greaves, had been taken off the Under-23 tour to Italy and West Germany to join the senior party.

One legend missing from the Brazilian team on Wednesday 13 May 1959 was right-winger Garrincha, a star of the 1958 World Cup triumph, but his replacement, Julinho, proved just as much of a handful. He opened the scoring after only three minutes, after Canhoteiro and Henrique had attacked down the left. Soon afterwards, Julinho saw a shot hit the post. Deeley and Broadbent were not overawed and both had shots that went over the bar. However, Brazil were calling the tune and that man Julinho danced through England's defence in the 28th minute to set up the second goal for Henrique, who beat Eddie Hopkinson from close range. England attacks were rare, though in one of them Bobby Charlton beat Gilmar only for the ball to strike the post.

In the second half, England continued to play second fiddle and were let off in the 53rd minute when Pelé, of all people, shot wide of the gaping goal. The great man later had to be carried off after a tough tackle from Ronnie Clayton. He soon returned, but the Blackburn man was left in no doubt by the crowd of what they thought of him. Another brief flurry saw Johnny Haynes's shot pushed on to a post by Gilmar, but Brazil ended on top and Julinho (twice) and Canhoteiro sent shots whistling just wide of the England goal.

Brazil: Gilmar (Santos); Djalma Santos (Palmeiras), Nilton Santos (Botafogo); Sani (São Paulo), Bellini (Vasco da Gama), Orlando (Santos); Julinho (Palmeiros), Didi (Botafogo), Henrique (Palmeiros), Pelé (Santos), Canhoteiro (São Paulo).

Goals: Julinho, Henrqiue.

England: Hopkinson (Bolton); Howe (West Bromwich Albion), Armfield (Blackpool); Clayton (Blackburn), Wright (Wolves), Flowers (Wolves); Deeley (Wolves), Broadbent (Wolves), Charlton (Manchester United), Haynes (Fulham), Holden (Bolton).

It was a memorable experience for Broadbent, completed when he swopped shirts with Pelé himself at the final whistle. Shirley Broadbent said some people had suggested that the number-10 shirt was in fact worn by Didi, but Peter was adamant he had swopped with Pelé. 'I can't think Peter would get that wrong. He was always adamant it was Pelé's shirt.'

It was not a bad display against the world champions on their home turf and, after the way the Brazilians had taken the latter stages of the 1958 World Cup by storm, a two-goal margin of defeat was no disgrace. Surely the England team would get another chance when the tour moved on to Lima to face Peru? Ten of the side did get a vote of confidence. Broadbent was the one who did not. If he thought he was the easy choice for scapegoat, he could have been forgiven. He had also been quickly dropped after the Northern Ireland game when what he needed was the encouragement of an extended run in the team.

Jimmy Greaves had been pressing hard for his chance and it was obvious when manager Walter Winterbottom switched him from the Under-23 tour that the Chelsea teenager would get his first senior cap at some stage. Yet it seemed harsh that Broadbent had to make way for him. Was this the same Broadbent around whom, just a few months earlier, the great Stanley Matthews had said England should build their team for years to come? If we had any doubts – and we hardly did – that Johnny Haynes could do no wrong, then they finally disappeared. Winterbottom's steadfast allegiance to Haynes was like Eriksson's to Beckham. So exit Broadbent. Greaves faced Peru and duly scored on his debut, but the team were embarrassingly beaten 4–1.

More changes were made for the game against Mexico. Out went Norman Deeley and Ron Flowers, though the latter did come on as sub for Wilf McGuinness. Derek Kevan, the man who had taken a lot of stick during the World Cup, got a recall, with Bobby Charlton switched to outside-left. This new-look side lost to the unfancied Mexicans 2–1 and an end-of-tour romp against the US, which brought an 8–1 win, was no consolation.

Before the 1959–60 season began, Billy Wright made the shock announcement that he was retiring. In contrast, Broadbent's club career was at its height, though he must have been wondering whether he still had a future at international level. His way back into the side the previous season had been through Haynes's unfortunate injury and he had made the most of his opportunity. Early in the new campaign, Haynes was again sidelined, but, as misfortune would have it, so, too, was Broadbent.

When Broadbent did return to action he had an impressive game against England right-half Ronnie Clayton, as Wolves beat Blackburn 3–1 at Molineux. Norman Deeley on the left-wing benefited from Broadbent's return and outshone Rovers' Bryan Douglas, a man so often favoured by England. Wolves' European Cup first round opponents Vorwaerts had 'spies' at the match, but, more importantly, also there were a couple of England selectors, Major H. Wilson Keys and Lieutenant-Colonel Gerry Mitchell. What the football pedigree of these military men was, who knows, but at least even they should have been impressed, especially as Broadbent ensured a harrowing afternoon for Clayton, the man designated to take over the England captaincy from the retired Billy Wright.

Despite Broadbent's good form after his injury and the continued absence of Haynes, the mysterious men who decided the make-up of the England team could still find no place for him. For the opening international of the season, against Wales in Cardiff, they named five newcomers – Stoke full-back Tony Allen, Birmingham centre-half Trevor Smith, wingers John Connelly of Burnley and Eddie Holliday of Middlesbrough, and Holliday's club colleague Brian Clough as centre-forward – the selectors heeding at last the many calls for his inclusion. With Jimmy Greaves the choice as striker to play off Clough, who was to be the creator in the forward line? Broadbent was the obvious choice to those of us who were watching him frequently and, seeing a man at the peak of his powers, so the selectors turned to Bobby Charlton! In those days he was still considered primarily a goalscorer, though his creative talents would emerge gloriously later. He had been wearing the number-10 shirt in the Manchester United team but was forming a twin-strike force with Dennis Viollet. Albert Quixall was the playmaker, not Charlton.

Not surprisingly, the strange-looking England side did not sparkle. Jimmy Greaves gave them a first-half lead but they rarely looked like adding to it and justice was done when Graham Moore, a Cardiff City striker playing on his home ground, headed a last-minute equaliser. Charlton did his best as the schemer of the side but he was clearly no Broadbent.

After this latest snub, Broadbent must surely have got the message that his face did not fit, but he showed the England hierarchy what they were missing when, on Monday 12 October 1959, he was in the Wolves team who played Celtic as the Scottish giants officially switched on their new floodlights. Before 44,000 fans, Broadbent emphasised what the England selectors had chosen to ignore and a report of the match, which Wolves won 2–0, said there were some 'touches of brilliant football from Broadbent'. He scored the first goal on 20 minutes after good work by Cliff Durandt and Des Horne, his first-time left-foot shot leaving goalkeeper Fallon groping. The other Wolves man who caught the eye was goalkeeper Malcolm Finlayson, playing in his homeland. He made several daring saves and handled the ball cleanly, as he did for virtually all his Wolves career. If Broadbent getting only seven caps was a scandal, so was the excellent Finlayson getting none.

Broadbent's good club form was of little consequence as the England season unfolded. He was obviously out of favour. Six days after the Welsh match, a Football League side beat the Irish League 5–0 in Belfast, Clough memorably scoring all the goals, and the inside-forwards were Blackburn's Peter Dobing and Newcastle's George Eastham. Whatever their contribution to Clough's goal spree, these two did not displace Greaves and Charlton when the England team were named to face Sweden at Wembley. After the Swedes became only the second continental nation to defeat England at home – the score was 3–2 – there was more re-thinking. Brian Clough would never get another chance for his country and was omitted from the Football League side who beat the League of Ireland 2–0. His number-nine shirt went to Dennis Viollet, whose Manchester United teammate Bobby Charlton was ignored. Instead, Ray Parry, who had made his League debut against Wolves as a 15-year-old in 1951, was tried at inside-left. He must have done enough to impress as he was given his first England cap a couple of weeks later when England beat Northern Ireland 2–1 at Wembley. However, Viollet did not join him, England making history by choosing for the first time a player based in Scotland, Joe Baker of Hibernian.

More significant for Broadbent was the return of fit-again Johnny Haynes. Before the season ended, Ronnie Clayton would lose his form under the burden of captaincy and it would be Haynes who took on the leadership role, never to relinquish it, apart from a couple of injury absences, until his unfortunate car crash in Blackpool that ended his international career.

Yet Broadbent's England career was not quite over. Four days after Wolves had beaten Villa 1–0 in the FA Cup semi-final at The Hawthorns to reach Wembley, Burnley, one of their main rivals for the title, came to Molineux and were outclassed 6–1. Broadbent was at his best and watching from the Molineux directors' box was manager Walter Winterbottom. It was no chance visit – his favourite 'son' Haynes was battling to be fit and the annual, and, in those days, much-anticipated clash with Scotland was just nine days away. Broadbent had been expecting, on Saturday 9 April 1960, to have a day off from football, helping in the grocery shop that he and Shirley had opened in Bilbrook on the outskirts of Wolverhampton. Instead, after Haynes had been told by a specialist that his twisted knee should not be risked, Broadbent got a call from Winterbottom to say he was wanted at Hampden Park. Winterbottom told the *Daily Mail* there was no suggestion that Broadbent had been chosen because his club had a blank Saturday. 'Broadbent was first-choice replacement,' stressed the England supremo.

Broadbent was not the lone Wolverhampton representation in the team. Ron Flowers was by then a regular choice at left-half, but the centre-half spot went to veteran Bill Slater. He had switched to the central defensive role to such good effect that he collected the Football Writers' supreme accolade – Footballer of the Year.

It was another new-look forward line. Baker and Parry, who had both scored on their debuts, had earned a second chance, but left-winger Eddie Holliday was dropped in favour of Bobby Charlton, who had only recently been switched to outside-left by his club. Sadly, for Broadbent and Slater, it was a below-par England display as they were held 1–1. Centre-forward Ian St John gave Slater an unhappy afternoon, in stark contrast to the polished displays that had earned the Wolves defender so many plaudits. Yet England should have won. Charlton's penalty cancelled out the Scots' goal from Graham Leggat and the Manchester United man had a chance to win the match when a second spot-kick was awarded. His kick was saved by goalkeeper Frank Haffey but a re-take was ordered. This time Charlton fired the ball wide. After that he would never take another penalty for his country. The role was given to Flowers, who would never fail from the spot for England in six attempts. As for Broadbent, he struggled in the new-look forward line and the limelight was stolen by Scotland's young dynamo Denis Law.

Reasons were given for the lack of skill shown by both sides – the swirling wind, the hard pitch and some pedantic refereeing by the Hungarian official Geno Skranko. They were not the best set of circumstances in which to try to re-establish your international credentials. Broadbent, however, would have been the last to look for excuses. That was not his way, yet he was in an England team, rejigged yet again, who consisted of players largely unfamiliar with each other's play. That mattered not in the eyes of critics and selectors alike.

For Broadbent – and Slater, too – it was the end of the international road. Broadbent's seven caps were scant reward for sustained brilliance over six seasons. He is in good company among players of supreme skill who deserved greater recognition at international level – like Sunderland's irreverent genius Len Shackleton, who played just five times for England, Sheffield United schemer Jimmy Hagan, capped only once, and Stoke's gifted Alan Hudson, chosen only twice.

Scotland: Haffey (Celtic); McKay (Celtic), Caldow (Rangers); Cumming (Hearts), Evans (Celtic), McCann (Motherwell); Leggat (Fulham), Young (Hearts), St John (Motherwell), Law (Manchester City), Weir (Motherwell).

Goal: Leggat (17).

England: Springett (Sheffield Wednesday); Armfield (Blackpool), Wilson (Huddersfield); Clayton (Blackburn), Slater (Wolves), Flowers (Wolves); Connelly (Burnley), Broadbent (Wolves), Baker (Hibernian), Parry (Bolton), Charlton (Manchester United).

Goal: Charlton (50, pen).

Attendance: 129,193.

There was a controversial angle to the match as Scotland were denied the services of three key players, goalkeeper Bill Brown, half-back Dave Mackay and midfield maestro John White. The common denominator? All three played for Tottenham, who were then neck and neck with Wolves and Burnley for the First Division title. While England could force clubs to release Football League players, Scotland could not and Spurs said they wanted the trio for their game against Everton on the same day as the Hampden match. Wolves were due to face West Ham and would be at a disadvantage without Slater and Flowers. In a display of growing enlightenment, the Football League agreed to postpone their game. It was a good job too, with the subsequent call up of Broadbent. Spurs' move did not pay off – while England were floundering against Scotland, the Londoners went down 2–1 at Goodison Park.

Two days later, Wolves duly played West Ham, beat them 5–0 at Molineux and went to the top of the table, two points ahead of Spurs. More to the point, Broadbent chose that match to show in all its glory the talent that had failed to surface in Glasgow. The great pity was that those critics and selectors who had seen him against the Scots were not at Molineux. Had they been, they would have seen a player who was not a spent force. He was in his prime. Phil Morgan was happy to report in the *Express & Star* that Broadbent and Slater, two who had taken much of the blame for England's shortcomings, were the team's inspiration, ably supported by half-backs Eddie Clamp and Ron Flowers. Broadbent had a hand in four of the five goals.

As an antidote to his Hampden hangover this was ideal, but it had no impact on the England selectors. A fit Haynes returned to face Yugoslavia and Broadbent was not in the squad for the tour games against Spain and Hungary. Yet if manager Walter Winterbottom had had his way, he would have been. In his definitive book, *England v Scotland*, Brian James explains that Winterbottom had wanted to keep a squad together for the four matches – Scotland, Yugoslavia, Spain and Hungary. Because the side did not impress when drawing with the Scots, the selectors knocked the idea unceremoniously on the head. They met and discussed players for three hours before declaring they would not be able to announce their party for the next internationals until after Easter because they were going to look at a whole new group of possible England men.

James records Winterbottom's significant, if brief, comment after the selectors' meeting 'I can't now give you a single name for the tour – it's the committee's decision and I have nothing more to say.' Later in the year the Football League further undermined Winterbottom's status when they said he would no longer manage teams for inter-League matches. From then on, the management of the Football League side would be given to various club managers on a match-by-match basis.

Before Winterbottom decided to join the Central Council of Physical Recreation he would have a fine 1960–61 season as England switched to a 4-2-4 formation with Haynes and Bobby Robson, no longer a striker, as the two men pulling the strings in midfield. Surely Broadbent would have been ideal for such a role alongside Haynes? He probably would have been, but others had decreed his international days were over at 27. The sublime skills of Peter Broadbent were never again seen on football's highest stage.

As a postscript to the long years of Broadbent being largely overlooked for England selection, it's worth taking a look at a few significant facts. He truly established himself in the Wolves side at the beginning of the 1953–54 season, yet it was only at the end of his fifth season as a first-team regular that he finally got his England chance in that World Cup showdown. From the start of the 1953–54 season to Broadbent's belated first cap, England played 44 internationals. In that time no fewer than 15 – yes, 15 – players were tried in the number-eight shirt. Here's the list, with the number of games each played at inside-right:

Atyeo (6), Bentley (4), Broadis (5), Brooks (3), Charlton (3), Haynes (3), Kevan (2), Mortensen (1), Quixall (2), Revie (6), Robson (5), Sewell (1), Ernie Taylor (1), Tommy Taylor (1), Thompson (1).

For those of us who think the selectors were wrong not to give Broadbent a chance much earlier to show what he could do, these are damning statistics. Highlighting the selectors' muddled thinking is the fact that the most games any of those 15 was given in the inside-right spot was six.

During the same 44 games, there were also 12 different inside-lefts, with, inevitably, Haynes making the most appearances with 20. Broadbent's Wolves colleague Dennis Wilshaw played 11 times. That highlights how few games the other 10 inside-lefts played.

If Broadbent had been given an extended run in the England team early in his career, he would surely have made the scheming role his for keeps. However, once the selectors, or Winterbottom, or both, had decided Haynes was to be the brains of their team, Broadbent was always fighting an uphill battle for selection.

Wolves' 1960 FA Cup Final star Barry Stobart endorses that view: 'Peter did enough to earn a long run in the England team. If they had given him time and stuck with him he would have produced for England, I've no doubt of that. He needed to be in the team and settled, then he'd produce.'

Back to Leon Hickman, whose views, as the former sports supremo at *Birmingham's Evening Mail*, are worth heeding. He says 'It still makes me angry to think they preferred Haynes. Even now, after all these years, I still want to argue with somebody about it. I was chatting to John Charles once, when he was Hereford manager, and I asked him how he rated Broadbent and he said "The best English player I ever played against." That says it all.'

A final memory from Hickman, 'When they opened one of the new stands at Molineux all the old players were introduced to the fans and I was walking across the pitch with Peter and I said "I have to say, Peter, you're the best player I ever saw on this pitch, certainly consistently." And he did not flinch, he did not say "thank you," he did not say "that's kind of you," he just nodded as though to say "Of course I was." My father said Bryn Jones had the same kind of charisma but Peter's the only Wolves player who transcended mere brilliance to reach genius.'

It has to be a football travesty that the Broadbent talents were never allowed to flourish at international level.

How Others Saw Him

As I said in the foreword, it would have been ideal if this book had been an autobiography and Peter Broadbent could have told his own story. From all that I have learned about him, I am sure he would have related it in a modest self-effacing manner, with plenty of laughs along the way. Alas, the rapid onset of Alzheimer's means he is now in a home on the outskirts of Wolverhampton. He needs one-to-one care. Wife Shirley visits him daily, his family also call regularly and he has other friends and former playing colleagues who look in on him. He has good days and bad days. As time goes by the latter outnumber the former.

All of which explains why, to end this story of a very special footballer, I have assembled the thoughts of a few fans, journalists and some of the men who played alongside him.

Reg Summerfield, a theatrical agent who has booked acts for clubs around the Midlands for many years, is among the many Broadbent admirers. 'He was my idol,' recalled Reg. 'He was so skilful. If he had been a Brazilian or French he'd have won a hundred caps. They used to say he and Johnny Haynes were too alike and could not play in the same team, but they could have played Peter as a striker – though in my opinion he had the edge over Haynes as a schemer. Peter was an entertainer, which Haynes really wasn't. Haynes could certainly pass a ball, but Peter could pass the ball just as well as him and he was a superb striker. A lot of people forget that – just how many goals he scored.

'I remember him playing against Danny Blanchflower and he absolutely bamboozled him and left him sitting on his backside more than once. They switched Blanchflower with Jim Iley, who was also a very good player, but Peter did exactly the same thing with him. Two very good wing-halves and he ran rings round them.

'When he was transferred to Shrewsbury he came to play at Walsall and me and my pals – about six of us – went over to watch him. We saw him in the car park at Fellows Park before the game and shook his hand and wished him well. I don't think he could believe it, that we had made the effort just to go and see him, but that was how much we thought of him.'

Another man eminently qualified to talk about Peter Broadbent is Ron Warrilow. A freelance reporter based in Wolverhampton, Warrilow has covered Wolves through good times and bad for the best part of 50 years. 'Tell me what you thought of him,' I badgered Warrilow and this was his response:

'There is a line in the opening sequence of the 1973 western Cahill US Marshall, where an outlaw tells John Wayne in the title role "I'll say one thing for you JD. You sure got style." That was Peter Broadbent – one of the greatest inside-forwards to grace a football field and a man who had certainly got style.

'I started covering Wolves in the 1960–61 season as a green almost 17-year-old and I only had the pleasure of watching Peter in action for a handful of years before he went to Shrewsbury Town. Since then, having spent nearly 47 years sitting in the Molineux press box, I have seen countless players who possessed great skills – men who could light up a game with a single move. However, there was only one Peter Broadbent and I can say without reservation he is the best player I have ever seen in a Wolves shirt. Peter possessed great vision, his control was superb, he could pass brilliantly, he could dribble and he could find the back of the net with either his feet or his head. He had everything in the recipe needed to make a good footballer.

'Peter Broadbent was, in short, the complete footballer and it is a tragedy he won only seven England caps. Walter Winterbottom had Johnny Haynes, a magnificent player, ahead of Broadbent in the queue for an England slot. I am convinced that if Haynes had not been around at that time Peter Broadbent would have controlled the England midfield for many years.

'Peter Broadbent played with confidence and he was never afraid of hanging on to the ball. There was nothing more entertaining than to see him face an opposing player sideways on. He would then give a shoulder shimmy in a space no bigger than a hoola hoop and you did not know whether he was going to the left or the right. Then, in the blink of an eye, he had gone past his man, leaving him totally bewildered.

'I consider myself fortunate to have seen Peter Broadbent play football because the man truly had style.'

Tony Butler, doyen of Midland sports broadcasters and football phone-in pioneer, who is still going strong on BBC Radio WM, believes Broadbent was a player before his time 'Perhaps his skills would have been put to better use in, say, Spain or Italy. He was never given the credit he deserved in England, his talent wasted by the national team. One game I remember well. I took my son Nick to see Villa play Cardiff. It was a cold winter's day, ice covered at least half the pitch. The game would have been called off today. Broadbent, coming to the end of his career, stood out like a beacon. His control was as good as ever, his passing a joy to watch when players all around him couldn't keep their feet. I don't remember the score or who played in the game. For me, it was a joy to see a genius in action, even if he was slower about the park – a game I have never forgotten and never will.'

Leon Hickman, once the voice of sport at the *Birmingham Evening Mail*, says 'When I was a kid we had a youth club at Pendeford and we would talk for hours about Peter Broadbent – he was that good. A pal of mine from Burnley used to say McIlroy was better but I just laughed at that. I can't think of a player who was better than Peter in his day. Johnny Haynes had got the England place and was a very good player who passed the ball ably, but why they preferred him to Peter is a mystery. I think if Broadbent had played for Spurs, he would have won 70 or 80 caps.'

Bob Davies, another sports journalist of some standing, who worked for the *Shropshire Star* and later the *Express & Star*, reflects 'I suppose I was lucky. I became an avid football fan in the days when virtually all matches kicked off at 3pm on a Saturday and the television moguls didn't dictate when games should be played.

'Saturdays were therefore sacrosanct. It was Gay Meadow one week and Molineux the other. Both very different venues as homes, as they were, to teams at each end of the footballing spectrum. The point of it all is that, as I squeezed on to the Molineux terraces along with many thousands of gold and black fans, I quickly became an admirer of the silky skills of Peter Broadbent.

'After all, it was difficult not to. I had seen Broadbent grace the bigger stage at Wembley as he pulled on the white shirt of England, but it was squashed among the doting fans at Molineux that I really came to appreciate just what exceptional talent he possessed.

'Imagine my delight, therefore, when another legend, Shrewsbury Town's Wolverhampton-born Arthur Rowley, persuaded Broadbent, for some reason surplus to requirements at Molineux at 31, to sign for the Gay Meadow club.

'It's doubtful if, in his managerial career, Rowley ever made a signing which gave the fans more pleasure. Broadbent was an immediate hit with the Gay Meadow faithful, charming them not only with his huge skills with the ball at close quarters but also his ability to despatch penetrating passes to the four corners of the ground.

'He arrived at the Gay Meadow two-thirds of the way through the 1964–65 season and the following campaign was virtually the first name Rowley wrote on the team sheet, as he missed only two League games. To the best of my recollection, he never produced a poor performance.

'Broadbent, of course, was renowned much more for his creative skills, operating as an inside-forward in the days when teams lined up with two full-backs, three half-backs and five forwards, than he was as a striker. Yet he scored a lot of goals for Wolves.

'And there were two goals he notched which have become etched in Gay Meadow folklore. The first was in the never-to-be-forgotten FA Cup second replay against Carlisle United. Shrewsbury were 2–1 down four minutes into injury time when Broadbent became their saviour with a vital equaliser. Shrewsbury were awarded a free-kick and the diminutive winger, Trevor Meredith, swung over a cross which Broadbent met perfectly with his head to set up 30 minutes of extra-time.

'It was, indeed, a rarity for Broadbent to score with a header but he did and Shrewsbury, after a tension-packed period of overtime, went on to win 4–3. I, and I'm sure all those jubilant Shrewsbury fans still in the ground, could hardly believe what had unfolded in a dramatic, fluctuating game containing so many twists and turns. But the important thing was that Broadbent had played a significant part in extending the Cup fairy tale by earning the little side from Division Three a trip to mighty Chelsea, of Division One.

'Fifteen thousand of us from Shropshire were among the 51,000 fans at Stamford Bridge, 15,000 praying for a miracle. Those prayers were so nearly answered as Shrewsbury gave Chelsea the fright of their lives, taking the game to them and finally going down 3–2, with the Pensioners amazingly forced to run the ball into the corners to waste time in the final 10 minutes.

'It was the big stage and the perfect setting for Broadbent to rise to the occasion, which he did by producing a masterclass of inside-forward play which often left a fledgling Peter Osgood – later of England fame – chasing shadows. It was crowned by another Broadbent goal to emphasise that, despite his all-too-short stay at Gay Meadow, he will always be remembered there as something of a genius.'

Malcolm Cookson first saw Broadbent during Peter's courting days. 'My dad was a friend of Shirley's dad. The family lived in Manlove Street, Penn Fields, and we lived off Merridale Street West. I often used to see Peter walking round to Shirley's house and that was great because he was my favourite player.

'Peter was the best footballer I've ever seen. He was so good it looked as though he was trying to rub it in but he wasn't. He wasn't that kind of player but he had so many tricks. I've seen him run off without the ball, just leave it there and the man marking him would go with him. I've never seen a better ball player than Peter. Johnny Haynes was good but never as good as Peter. My other favourite player from those days was Bill Slater and he had that same quality Peter had – he made everything look effortless. It was all about being in the right place at the right time, reading the game. They both could do that.'

Robert Davies, who now lives in Billericay, used to travel from Broseley in Shropshire to watch Wolves. 'I seem to recall one match when he had the ball at his feet and made as if to go to the left and the whole of the opposition defence went left. Then he made as if to go right and they all went to the right. That was Peter. There were some truly great players in that Wolves team but he was my favourite. I'm not saying he was the best but he was different, the way he moved was different. You just never knew what he would do next. When he scored his hat-trick against Portsmouth from centre-forward, there was a headline in a paper "Broadbent broadside sinks Pompey". It's always stuck in my mind.'

Muriel Bates, who is treasurer of the Wolves Official Supporters Club, of which her husband, Albert, is chairman, has no doubts about Broadbent's standing, 'He was a fabulous footballer. I'd put him in the George Best class, a one-off. We'll never see another like Best and we'll never see another like Peter. He was just a special player.

'In many ways he was before his time. He could see three moves ahead because he read the game brilliantly. If he got the ball with his back to goal he could turn and know exactly where everybody was and find them. He also used to send some lovely passes ahead of the wingers for them to run on to.

'I just reckon I was lucky to have seen that great Wolves team. A lot of them got into the England team but we always felt they should pick all of them. They were good enough and I always felt that if Peter had been with a London club he'd have won far more caps.'

Paul Goddard, who now lives in Cheam, Surrey, told me 'Peter is my favourite Wolves player, even to the extent of having a large signed photo in the loo. I have several happy memories of watching him in the late 50s. The game was slower then but his ability to control midfield and spray passes to Deeley, Mannion, Horne and the rest will always be with me. The physical presence of Flowers and Clamp helped Peter to become one of the best schemers, as they were then called, in the English game, and a player we all adored. My memories also include playing with a tennis ball at the back of the old South Bank at Molineux, all of us trying to drag the ball like Peter. I also seem to remember a local barber was offering to do a Peter Broadbent hairstyle, which was basically just having the hair straight and combed back. Happy days!'

Keiron Boyce, as a youngster, lived in the Finchfield area of Wolverhampton not far from Wolves' Castlecroft training ground, and he and his school pals would often go there during half-term and holidays to watch their idols training. 'They would arrive in a minibus and do their training,' said Keiron, 'but once Stan Cullis and Joe Gardiner had gone into the office under the stand, several of the players would stay and have a kick around with us. Peter would show us how to kick the ball properly and how to trap it. He'd sign autographs as well. Malcolm Finlayson would let us have shots at him – they were all pretty good. Peter was one of the quieter ones. Eddie Clamp was one of the characters and sometimes if he'd arrive late Stan Cullis would tell him he had to walk back to Molineux. I think we saw him hitch a lift on a milk float once.'

When Wolves fell on hard times in the 1980s, the Castlecroft ground was sold and is now used by the RFU for their schools and youth rugby squads. 'It was a lovely ground,' Keiron recalled. 'I played there once for Staffs Schools and it was a very good playing surface.' His final words on Broadbent, 'Peter was a really gifted player, probably one of the best I've seen in my lifetime.'

Michael Nokes, a Wolves fan from Redditch, remembers, 'My father first took me to Molineux in 1955 to watch the Wolves play. In the 50s Wolves had a great side with a wonderful magical playmaker, the incomparable Peter Broadbent. Peter was my football idol, as he was to so many Wolves supporters. Most of the skilful, ball-playing inside-forwards those days seemed to be small men, 5ft 4in–5ft 7in, but Peter was the exception. He was, I recall, about 5ft 10in. That was quite tall in those days for an inside-forward, but for a taller man he was just as nimble on his feet as the smaller guys.

'Peter had great ball control and also performed "nutmegs" on defenders, along with back heels and body swerves. With his deft touch and his feints he seemed to glide past defenders, who, at times, looked bewildered as to how to get close enough to stop him. Like so many players of his generation he was a great sportsman. I don't recall him ever being spoken to by a referee, let alone being booked or sent off. I feel so privileged to have watched Peter play so many times. He was absolutely top drawer, the very best.'

Ian 'Sludge' Lees, that hilarious Black Country comedian, was happy to be part of the cabaret when a special tribute dinner was staged for Broadbent at the Hayward Suite, Molineux, in 2006, and holds the player in high regard, 'The way he could dribble that ball, it was as though it was tied to his boots and he could jink and drop his shoulder. He was just special. The only one I've seen who came close to him for skill was Peter Knowles.'

Bob Pugh was one of the legion of fans who used to watch Wolves from a packed South Bank, after catching a trolley bus from Sedgley to Molineux. 'If you didn't get to the bus stop about 1 o'clock you did not stand a chance of getting to the ground in time, but it was worth the wait to see Wolves in those days. I thought Peter was absolutely fabulous. Alf Ramsey once said Martin Peters was 10 years ahead of his time and I think you could have said that about Peter in terms of technical ability. I think he should have played for England many more times. I used to love going to Molineux in those days, even though the first game I remember was when my uncle took me there and we lost to Bolton in the Cup. They always seemed to beat us around that time.'

Bob Blower was a schoolboy in the village of Bilbrook, a few miles outside Wolverhampton, where Broadbent and wife Shirley had their grocery shop. 'We were always going in there if Peter was serving,' said Bob. 'We'd club together to buy one of those Jubbly drinks and ask him for an autograph. He'd always sign. He'd rip some paper off one of the brown paper bags and sign it. He never seemed to get fed up of us and he once gave a pair of boots to a pal of mine, Adrian Nicklin. We'd never seen boots like them. We used to have the ones which you knocked the leather studs into – but these were Continental style, multi-studded, the studs moulded in. I also remember Billy Wright and Joy calling to see Peter and Shirley once. It brought the place to a standstill once the word got around.'

Alan Goldsbrough, who grew up in Wednesfield, and whose father later kept the much-missed New Hotel in Victoria Street, Wolverhampton, says 'Peter was a great player, arguably Wolves' best ever. When I was a lad and we'd play in the street you'd say "I'm Peter Broadbent today" in the hope you might be as good on the ball as he was, not that you ever could. I've waited outside the ground for about an hour for his autograph along with other youngsters and Peter would always sign. He always had time for us.'

John Pike, a Wolves fan for well over 50 years, who later covered the club for BBC Radio WM during Wolves' darkest days in the Fourth Division, saw Broadbent's Wolves debut in 1951. 'I can honestly say that immediately I saw him I saw something different. He was up against some very good players that day against Portsmouth – Jimmy Dickinson, an England international, and Jimmy Scoular, a Scottish international who was really hard. Yet Peter stood out and you could see why the management had brought him to Wolves. He looked good then and he went on to get even better.

'He was so different. He had so many tricks like that way he used to bring his left foot alongside the ball and flick it or do something wonderful with it – things like that. If, for some reason or other, he wasn't playing, you always felt it was a disappointment.'

Malcolm Jarman was another who saw Broadbent's League debut at Molineux. 'He looked quality even then. I thought "He's a good 'un" and so it proved. His ball control, his dribbling ability and his distribution made him one of the best inside-forwards I've ever seen. He was also a model citizen on and off the pitch.'

Now let some of his playing contemporaries give their verdict on Broadbent…

Ron Atkinson, the former boss of Villa and Manchester United, as well as several other clubs, was a groundstaff boy at Molineux, and admired Broadbent as soon as he saw him play. 'He was one of the greatest inside-forwards of the last 50 years. In a team that was often wrongly labelled a long-ball outfit, Peter was a supreme artist. He had the most incredible body swerve that could twist an opponent inside out and was underrated as a goalscorer.'

George Best, one of football's all-time greats, went on record as being a Broadbent admirer, 'There was something magical about Wolves in the 1950s. I remember them taking on the top foreign sides and beating them, and that was so different and glamorous. As far as individuals were concerned, the one player who sticks in my mind is Peter Broadbent. I remember him as an old-fashioned inside-forward, who was very skilful and always used to score lots of important goals.'

Jimmy Dunn, one of Wolves' most accomplished players in the years after World War Two, was a 1949 FA Cup winner who eventually made way for the young Broadbent early in 1952–53. Broadbent's time at Molineux did not overlap that of Dunn by much – they played together in the reserves but in the first team on only eight occasions – but enough for Dunn to have been impressed. 'He was a very clever player. You could see he was good and once he got into the team he never looked back.'

Norman Deeley played alongside Broadbent more than any other Wolves winger and the two had a great rapport on and off the field. 'He was my friend all through my career,' Deeley confirmed. 'It was great to play alongside him. He was such a very good player. I rated him better than Johnny Haynes. He could beat a man just by shrugging his shoulders. We all had our good points and bad points but Peter had a lot of good points. I'd put him on par with someone like Wilf Mannion. I think he should have had a proper run in the England team, but he didn't really.'

Peter Dolby was in the Shrewsbury side when Broadbent arrived at Gay Meadow and confessed 'We were in awe of him – well I certainly was – and could he play or could he play? He was just staggering. Just playing in the same team as him helped improve our game. It was because he was so likeable that he was made very welcome by all the players. He and Shirley would socialise with us after games and Peter was always down to earth. I used to take some mates of mine along for a drink after a game and he would talk to them, too. I could not get over just what a lovely fella he was.'

Ted Farmer is fulsome in praise of Broadbent. No player making his Football League debut in the top flight ever made a better goalscoring start than Farmer – 28 goals in 27 games. Injury brought a premature end to his career but he played many games alongside Broadbent and saw enough of him to state 'He was one of the greatest ball-playing footballers we've ever had in this country. He was class.

'Peter was not a small player but he was not particularly physical. He didn't need to be. I would not say he was really fast either. He had speed of thought and action. He could get the ball down and do things before any of the opposition had realised. He could out think people. He was the type of player who would glide over the ground. He was very deceptive and his shoulder movement was unbelievable. They used to say when Peter moved his shoulders, the fans in the South Bank moved with him. He also had that partnership with Norman Deeley. They were great together, they could interchange and knew exactly where the other one was. Peter was also a very nice bloke. He had no airs and graces.'

Malcolm Finlayson, goalkeeper in two Championship triumphs and the 1960 FA Cup Final, first played alongside Broadbent for the RAF. 'We were called up to play for the RAF against the FA at Stamford Bridge. Four years later I signed for Wolves from Millwall and we teamed up again. Peter had the great knack of making space for himself so that when he got the ball he had that extra bit of time to use it. He was an unassuming player who never had his name taken and was very elegant on the pitch, with a touch that was so sure. Unfortunately, Johnny Haynes was resident in Peter's position in the England team. Johnny was a great player, but the media always tended to favour southern players and Peter didn't get much of a look in. He could, and should, have won many more caps.'

Ron Flowers's career ran fairly close to Broadbent's. They were the youngest members of the 1953–54 Championship side and key men in the team who won three trophies in three seasons at the end of the 50s. Flowers won 49 caps and the only Wolves man to play more times for England was Billy Wright. Flowers's verdict, 'I always felt that when you were on top, Peter could turn it on. He didn't do it until we were on top and he was having to work harder rather than produce his tricks. When we were 1–0 or 2–0 up, then he would really go to town. He had a lot of talent. He could do his shuffles and his shimmies and they could not get near him. When he was on song he was very, very good – an entertainer.'

Gerry Harris, left-back in two Championship-winning years and in the 1960 FA Cup-winning side, remembers Broadbent as someone who was always relaxed before a game. 'He was a lovely gentle person, a smashin' chap. There was nothing loud about him and maybe he was too quiet on the pitch sometimes and should have shouted a bit more, but he was such a fabulous player. If we were under pressure he would drop back and you could give him the ball and know he would calm things down. He and Norman Deeley played so well together. They both had a lot of skill and Norman had a heart as big as a bucket. Norman wasn't exactly quick, but if you've got skill, like they both had, then you make time for yourself – you don't need to be quick.'

Harris also said the team spirit helped Wolves to be so successful. 'We all got on and Peter used to enjoy it when we had a night out. Two or three times a season after a home game I'd organise a trip for all of us to some of the pubs where I live, around Claverley and Six Ashes. We'd just unwind and enjoy ourselves.'

John Holsgrove, who joined Wolves shortly after Broadbent and moved to Shrewsbury, told me 'I can't imagine Peter without a smile on his face. I cannot speak too highly of him as a player or as a man. I met him when my wife and I were looking for a house after I joined Wolves and I found him to be a fantastic person, so friendly and bubbly. When I was a boy Wolves were my team because they were the best in the country. I liked the rest of the team as well, but Peter was the one I noticed. They don't make 'em like Peter Broadbent any more.'

Peter Knowles was a player many Wolves fans felt would emulate Broadbent, had he not given up the game at 24 because he could not reconcile playing football with his beliefs as a Jehovah's Witness. Knowles has the greatest admiration for Broadbent, 'I was 16 years of age when I first met Peter. I used to clean his boots and often, when I cleaned the first-team dressing room out, I would listen to Peter and the other first-team players talk about playing for England and the great floodlit matches at Wolves. As I got to know him I watched his kind of play very closely – his body swerve, his long passes, his touches on the ball. To me, he was like a ballet dancer on grass. He used to glide over the pitch. Yes, Peter was the man I modelled myself on. He was the only football player who could send the crowd the wrong way with his body swerve!

'He was a very quiet man. He did not brag or push himself and I don't know one player with a bad word for Peter. He was respected by everybody. He was one of the greatest players to wear the black and gold shirt. It was a pleasure to have met him and I know I was taught how to play football by one of the best – and that body swerve is something I'll never forget.'

Bobby Mason won Championship medals in 1958 and 1959, and played in every round of the successful 1960 Cup run, apart from the Final itself. He made himself a valuable member of the team and learned to fit in well with Broadbent. Mason said 'The thing I really remember about Peter as a player was that when he got to the 18-yard box you knew that he would beat that last man, or two, and square the ball across and you could time your runs accordingly. Ninety-nine times out of a hundred he would get that ball across. He had a special way of running – stylish, similar to the way Bobby Charlton ran. He also had that ability to find space.'

Bill Shorthouse, stalwart centre-half in the 1949 Cup Final team and 1953–54 Championship side, said Broadbent's speed of thought was one of his great assets. 'He had such a quick brain and reacted to any situation easily. Peter was as good as anybody in his day.'

Nigel Sims, the goalkeeper who was understudy to Bert Williams at Wolves but then moved to Villa, where he gained an FA Cup-winners' medal in 1957, describes Broadbent as a 'natural', adding 'They talk about width today but Peter knew how to use the whole width of the pitch and bring wingers into play and how to make space for himself. He would sometimes go out on the wing – in fact, he would turn up all over the place.'

George Showell, who first came to prominence as Billy Wright's trusted deputy and won a regular place at full-back in time to play in the 1960 Cup Final, says 'I regarded Peter very highly. He had everything, great ball skill and a good football brain. He and Shirley were big friends of ours. We had some lovely times and even went on holiday together.'

Bill Slater, Flowers and Broadbent are the only three Wolves men to have played in three Championship-winning sides and in an FA Cup-winning side. Slater joined Brentford as an amateur about six months after Broadbent had left for Wolves and remembers travelling home after making his Brentford debut. 'I was on the bus going back to my wife-to-be in Ealing. This chap next to me only wanted to talk about Peter Broadbent, non-stop for the half-hour journey. He didn't recognise me and I don't think he knew I'd been playing! Peter was very highly regarded at Brentford and I felt I knew a lot about him, second hand, when I arrived at Wolves.

'He was one of the few of us who overlapped from that early part of the 50s to the latter part and he was a big influence all through. He had lovely ball control and that sort of hip wiggle that could send players the wrong way.

Another thing about Peter was that he always seemed to be available. If you were in trouble he would be there to take a pass. He always seemed able to produce a bit of magic and though people said he was a playmaker he scored a lot of goals.'

Barry Stobart, a shock choice to play in the 1960 Cup Final, has no reservations, 'Peter was the best player I've seen when it came to ball control and running with the ball. His control was magic. No matter how the ball came to him, he could kill it dead and use it. He could show the opposition the ball then send them the wrong way.'

Eddie Stuart, the man who took over the captaincy of Wolves after Billy Wright's retirement, figured in three Championship sides with Broadbent, of whom he asserts 'He was one of the all time greats. If he'd been playing today, he would have been worth tens of millions of pounds. He was the complete inside-forward. His ball control was phenomenal. People may not have appreciated his running off the ball, as well. If a player is good at running off the ball and taking up positions, it makes the game so simple and Peter could do that. He was always creating space so it was always easy to find him. In addition to all that, he was so easy to get on with. I got to know him and Shirley and their family and they were such lovely people.'

Roy Swinbourne, the centre-forward in the 1953–54 Championship side, was a first-team regular when Broadbent arrived at Molineux and recalled he had been immediately impressed. 'His control of the ball and body swerves were something else. I always likened him to my football hero Wilf Mannion, the Middlesbrough and England inside-forward. Peter used to float between that great half-back line we had at Molineux and the forwards as the playmaker. As well as being a great player he was a lovely lad off the pitch. It was an absolute pleasure to play with him.' Swinbourne, too, remembered seeing him bamboozle Danny Blanchflower, one of the great players of his era. 'Danny ended up on his backside after Peter had just gone up to him with the ball, shrugged his shoulders and gone past him. He was something else, Peter.'

Bobby Thomson, the England full-back, was a teenager, over 10 years younger than Broadbent, when he made his debut in the Wolves side and has fond memories of him. 'I thought he was a superb player. He could pass, he could head the ball, he had that little feint which could make people go the wrong way, he had the lot. I think I was very fortunate to play in the same team as people like Peter and Ron Flowers. As a young player I always found Peter very helpful. He always had time for you. He was a gentleman.'

Johnny Walker was one of several good inside-forwards on Wolves' books when Broadbent arrived from Brentford in 1951. Walker starred in Wolves' run to the FA Cup semi-final that year, scoring five goals on the way, but that proved to be the high point of his Wolves stay as, in 1951–52, Jimmy Dunn and Jesse Pye gained preference before Broadbent started to force his way into the team. Walker recognised the talent of the newcomer, 'He was a natural. He loved the game, like all of us. We were just happy to be playing football and Peter was like that.'

Terry Wharton was a teenager when he made his debut alongside Broadbent. He told me 'Peter could not run particularly fast but he did not have to. His brain gave him two yards on anybody and his body swerve was magnificent. Peter Knowles could have become a second Peter Broadbent. He admired him as much as I did and tried to model himself on him.' Wharton is yet another who cannot speak too highly of Broadbent the man, 'He always accepted me and Alan Hinton even though we were just kids. I admired him because he was cool and calm. He dressed casual but was always so smart and immaculate. You just looked up to him. Peter and Ron Flowers were brilliant golfers as well. I'm sure it improved my golf, playing in foursomes with those two and Waggy at Oxley Park.'

Bert Williams, who won 24 caps as England's goalkeeper, retired just before the three epic seasons that saw Broadbent at his peak, but played alongside him many times and watched him many times. He has no doubts about his standing, 'I would put him in the same class as Len Shackleton, Raich Carter and Wilf Mannion, the great inside-forwards. His ball control was uncanny. Beckham was a good player but he had not got the same skill that Peter had. Johnny Haynes kept him out of the England team and he could use the ball really well, but Peter could use the ball and could take on three people and beat them.'

Dennis Wilshaw, who died in 2004, was part of that splendid 1953–54 Championship-winning forward line and once spoke to me about Broadbent, 'He was a star, a brilliant dribbler. His ball control was excellent. His transfer of the ball was excellent. He wasn't there as a goalscorer but I am surprised what a lot of goals he did get.'

Billy Wright, the Wolves and England skipper, once recalled a piece of Broadbent magic in Wolves' emphatic 6–1 defeat of Arsenal in 1959. 'With the ball at his feet, he actually invited Tommy Docherty to come in and tackle. Without moving the ball, he sold Tommy the dummy and a perfect dummy it was. Then he flighted over a centre, which resulted in one of the six goals we scored that day.'

Wright also explained how Broadbent's all-round game had improved over the years, 'When Peter first arrived at Molineux he had the art of controlling a football absolutely sewn up. Then, as now, he was one of the finest ball players in England. He discovered that Stan Cullis demanded more than mastery of the ball. He had to learn to adapt himself to the Wolves style. When he passed he would stop and watch what happened. He was told that a Wolves player never stops – especially if he's a forward. "After the pass," Cullis told him, "get up there into the goalmouth for the return. Keep in front of the play, not behind. Work harder. Chase harder." Peter found it hard at first but he was always a sensible lad. He did the very best to follow Mr Cullis's instructions and the more he tried to do so, the more valuable he became to Wolves.'

Bibliography

Banks, Gordon *Banksy, My Autobiography* Michael Joseph, 2002

Calley, Roy *Blackpool A Complete Record* Breedon Books, 1992

Collett, Mike *The Guinness Record of the FA Cup* Guinness Publishing, 1993

Cullis, Stan *All For The Wolves* Rupert Hart-Davis, 1960

Flowers, Ron *For Wolves and England* Stanley Paul, 1962

Gibbs, Nick *England The Football Facts* Facer Publishing, 1988

Goble, Ray with Andrew Ward *Manchester City A Complete Record* Breedon Books, 1993

Goodwin, Bob *Spurs A Complete Record* Breedon Books, 1993

Goodyear, David and Tony Matthews *Aston Villa A Complete Record* Breedon Books, 1988

Haynes, Johnny *It's All In The Game* Sportsman's Book Club, 1962

Hugman, Barry J. *Football League Players Records 1946–92* Tony Williams Publications, 1992

James, Brian *England v Scotland* Pelham Books, 1969

Joannou, Paul, Bill Swann and Steve Corke *Newcastle A Complete Record* Breedon Books, 1990

Jones, Mike *Breathe on 'Em, Salop* Yore Publications, 1995

Laschke, Ian *Rothmans Book of Football League Records* Macdonald and Jane's, 1960

Matthews, Tony *The Wolves Who's Who*, Britespot, 2001

Morrison, Ian and Alan Shury *Manchester United A Complete Record* Breedon Books, 1992

Oliver, Guy *The Guinness Book of World Soccer* Guinness Publishing, 1992

Ollier, Fred *Arsenal A Complete Record* Breedon Books, 1992

Payne, Mike *England The Complete Post War Record* Breedon Books, 1993

Turner, Dennis and Alex White *The Breedon Book of Football Managers* Breedon Books, 1993

Rigby, Ian and Mike Payne *Proud Preston* Carnegie Publishing, 1995

Warsop, Keith *British and Irish Special and Intermediate Internationals* SoccerData, 2002

Wright, Billy *One Hundred Caps and All That* Robert Hale, 1961